will the real israel please stand up?

by Leon Fine

PELMAS/MASSADA LTD

Edited by Pnina Kass
Cover design and illustrations by Aharon Shevo

All enquiries to:
Pelmas/Massada Ltd.,
11 Alouf Sadeh Street,
Givatayim

ISBN 965-10-0003-1
Cat. No. 003602

PRINTED IN ISRAEL
by Peli Printing Works Ltd.

Contents

A Note from the Author

Few subjects arouse such unusually emotional debate and seemingly irreconcilable contradictions as Israel and its people. Attempts to generalize are often erratic or misleading, perhaps because Israel the reality does not always conform to the preconceptions and notions of even well-meaning and unbiased observers, whoever they may be.

Guidebooks, texts and tributes have been written about different aspects of Israel by scholars, experts and professional writers. Very few have dealt with what this book is all about — the surprises, frustrations, disappointments and joys of an American-Jew who came as a tourist and stayed, after going through most of the experiences and situations described in the pages that follow.

I have emphasized certain subjects and written about them in a manner which may be most familiar to Americans, but they are equally valid to readers elsewhere in the English-speaking world.

There are no footnotes in this book regarding historical facts or totally subjective impressions. Contemporary information and descriptions are subject to the frequent, sudden and sometimes unusual changes that take place in the complex and dynamic society that is Israel.

If anything is unduly controversial or indulgent, I trust it will be relevant and thought-provoking. As far as I know, many delicate and sensitive subjects treated here have never before been made available in a candid and popular style for those who have a right to know what is really happening in Israel.

Tel Aviv, 1980   LEON FINE

Living in a metropolis is a hardship
(The Talmud)

Chapter One

FIRST IMPRESSIONS

CITY & PEOPLE

There is an unspoken rivalry between the major cities of Israel. Jerusalem is called boring and small-townish by some perhaps jealous of its history and importance. Jerusalemites know Tel Aviv is noisy, dirty and commercial. Living in what is more like the suburb of a large city in Europe or America, the Tel Avivian claims:

"Ours is the only *real* city in Israel."

"Our city is compared to Rio and Naples," boasts the Haifaite, "and our buses run on the Sabbath."

"But where can you *go* there?" rejoins the smug Tel Avivian.

"We are the country's heart and soul — the reunited capital of the new Israel" cries the proud inhabitants of the capital. "One *goes* to other places but *ascends* to Jerusalem."

"Hah!" sneers his rival, "as soon as sessions at the University and Knesset are over for the week, your students and politicians can't wait to *des*cend to Tel Aviv. Let's face it — *we* are the Beautiful People of Israel!"

Tel Aviv is the largest all-Jewish city in the world, though no one has ever claimed it is beautiful. It began 60 years ago as a new neighborhood for Jewish residents of Arab Jaffa, an ancient seaport and one of the oldest cities known to man. Opposite the shores where Jonah went on a voyage that ended in the belly of a whale, Zionist pioneers founded what was to be a peaceful European style suburb. With funds furnished by the Jewish National Fund the first houses of "Little Tel Aviv" were built on the sand dunes outside of Jaffa. Soon the new neighborhood outgrew Jaffa and when it became an independent town it was called Tel Aviv (The Hill of Spring). Today it is a brash, throbbing city of half a million and the hub of the crowded coastal area where every third Israeli lives.

In some places it is an aesthetic and architectural hodgepodge with carpentry shops, fruit and vegetable stores and shabby food-stands squeezed in between rows of functional office buildings, apartment houses and the inevitable dreary housing projects. Plaster and cement yield to the Mediterranean sun and many buildings have a drab, peeling look. As if to make up for it, there are dozens of little parks, playgrounds and surprisingly lovely old world houses, avant garde buildings and works of sculpture where one least expects them. Interspersed between the TV antennas, strange barrels and glass reflectors cover roof-tops. They are the Israeli invented method for heating running water through the rays of the sun.

Noise, litter and dust clutter the downtown and shopping areas where thoroughfares are filled with people and vehicles of every origin and vintage. Bicycles, pushcarts and Vespas slip past ancient diesel engined Checker taxicabs that once plied the streets of New York. Porters pedal and push goods laden carts and tricycles alongside of trucks and trailers. All compete with the Dan transportation cooperative buses which bully through the streets to crowded bus stops. The lines — if there are any — quickly disintegrate as passengers push their way in talking in a babble of tongues at the top of their voices.

Renaults, Fiats, Volkswagens and occasional American cars filled with the new middle class wait impatiently for traffic to move, passing the time listening to the radio, talking, making faces or remarks to other drivers and glancing at newspaper headlines, sometimes all at once. Nonchalant horse pulled carters ignore cars and buses or reply heatedly and curse in a variety of languages. Cyclists, motorcycles and purveyors of watermelons, corn on the cob, kerosene and a variety of snacks and goods weave through traffic and along the sidewalks calling out their wares and adding to the traffic jams.

The sight, smells and sounds are overwhelming. Sometimes it seems like a psychedelic wonderland of fascinating images and especially people. A burly, mustachioed truck driver reluctantly accepts a scolding and a traffic ticket from a petite and nonchalant policewoman while passersby circle around and tease him. A dozen itinerant laborers squat in the sun, awaiting the pick-up truck that is to take them to a field or orchard for a day's work. A bearded Hassidic rabbi tries to entice a bystander into a tiny *Shul* (synagogue) while school pupils urge him to contribute to some charitable cause. Soldiers, housewives, businessmen and vagrants mingle with the shoppers and tourists. Modish office girls and clerks walk through the crowds munching the local junk food, listening to pop songs on the ubiquitous transistor radios and talking in that melodious rising falling inflection that is Hebrew.

Milling pedestrians slow down and glare at the red "Do not Cross" sign, their common enemy. They look hesitantly at one another and then a few dash across. While some may chastize them, others follow and suddenly the whole waiting mass spills over into and around the stalled traffic while drivers brake and blow their horns in a cacophony of noise and frustration. Boys and old men scurry excitedly through the main street yelling "Yidiot! Yidiot!" over and over, at the crowds around them. Has Tel Aviv gone mad? No, they are only the newspaper vendors of the afternoon *Yediot Aharonot* (Latest News) which is out on the streets at 10 in the morning.

Here and there stands a uniquely designed museum, shop, attractive apartment house or stylish office building. Along the shabby and neglected sea front, the beaches are crowded in the summer. On every street a building is being torn down, renovated or built. Luxury hotels loom up surrounded by tourist shops and restaurants. In the midst of Little Tel Aviv near Jaffa, now the country's banking and commercial center, rises the highest skyscraper in the Middle East. Thirty-four stories up in the observatory of the Shalom Tower you can see the foothills of Lebanon in the north and the wall around the Old City of Jerusalem in the East.

Tel Aviv is the Orient and yet very much an outpost of Europe. There are dozens of movie theaters, two universities, a philharmonic and chamber orchestra, ensembles and choirs, jazz and pop groups, an opera company, planetarium, country clubs, all year round swimming pools, art galleries and boutiques. Here you can find cultural and social facilities any large city in America or Europe would be proud of, as well as most of their problems.

Almost anything can be bought or sold at the Flea Market in Jaffa and outdoor Carmel Shuk and, like their counterparts in Cairo or Damascus, they are always crowded. Barkers sing and shout out their wares, bargaining with shoppers around stalls containing everything from razor blades and underwear to fruits, vegetables and exotic foodstuffs. Street hawkers of *humus*, *felafel* and other delicacies of eastern cuisine are never far away, yet more newspapers and book stores are found in Tel Aviv, it seems, than in all of the surrounding countries together.

Tel Aviv is the city of the present, but Haifa is the symbol of the future. A funicular cable car subway (the Carmelit) runs underground through its three levels, connecting the port with the Hadar midtown and the residential Carmel heights. The lowest area is built around one of the most beautiful natural harbors in the Mediterranean and is the home of Israel's merchant marine and navy. Taverns and ship chandlers line the streets, and although Haifa is not known as a port city, a visiting sailor can find waterfront cabarets and bar girls who will gladly relieve him of his shore leave money.

It is also the site of the country's heavy industry (chemicals, petroleum, steel), the world Bahai headquarters and the internationally famous Technion scientific and engineering university complex. Haifa University and the newest suburbs spread out over the mountain top overlooking the sea. This is a city covered with parks and wooded areas, and the largest one, *Gan Ha'Em* (Mother's Park) is the butt of many jokes about what goes on there at night. It is the cleanest of Israel's cities and has fewer drab *shikunim* (housing projects) than most places. To its residents it is the most wonderful place in the world, and gazing down at the harbor and bay from Panorama Road on the Carmel, one is tempted to agree.

If Tel Aviv has bluster, Haifa strength, then Jerusalem is surely the city of majesty and memories. Almost every structure is built of the beige gold local Jerusalem stone and only a few high rise buildings spoil this image. In recent years, housing projects and urban sprawl have come to

11

Jerusalem also, but not on a large scale. One of the oldest and most important cities of the world, it was the capital of a mighty nation centuries before the birth of Paris, Rome or Athens.

Rising 2,500 feet above the Judean Hills is the city where Abraham offered his son Isaac to Jehovah, David loved and reigned, Solomon judged and built the Temple, Jesus preached and died and Mohammed is believed to have ascended to heaven. It is the capital of Israel and the home of its Parliament and most government ministries. It is also the site of three of the largest and most highly regarded institutions in the Middle East: Hebrew University, the Israel Museum and Hadassah Medical Center. It is above all, the city sacred to three religions.

For almost 20 years it was divided by barbed wire and minefields running along the Jordan-Israel armistice lines that arbitrarily cut through neighborhood streets and houses. Reunited under Israeli administration, Jerusalem is at once a charming small town and an international capital where Jews, Arabs and citizens of the world mix freely. Bearded priests and rabbis mingle in the streets with artists and students. Ultra-orthodox Jews from Mea Shearim, hippies, street hustlers and tough slum kids, Christian missionaries and nuns all walk by, each in their separate worlds and with their own thoughts, but acknowledging the existence of the others and their equal right to be there.

This mutual forbearance — if not brotherhood — is remarkable in view of the existing state of war between Israel and the Arabs. Israelis freely visit the Old City now incorporated into greater Jerusalem, especially the Western (Wailing) Wall and the reconstructed old Jewish Quarter. Others shop for bargains in Arab outdoor markets or frequent its cafes and restaurants. Former Jordanians stroll just as casually in the modern downtown of what was "Jewish"

Jerusalem. Some inhabitants can already speak both languages, and while mothers sit on benches and gossip, Arab and Jewish children play together in the city's parks and playgrounds. It is hard to believe that only a decade has passed; a decade that has proven that Jew and Arab can live together in the City of Peace.

The north of the country is covered by the fertile Galilee and the coastal plain. The southern half of Israel and its largest area is the *Negev* (dry lands), Israel's land bridge between Asia, Africa and Europe. This is no sand filled desolation like the Sahara but a sun scorched, rocky wilderness prairie resembling the badlands of western America. Temperatures are hot or boiling in the daytime and near freezing at night. Fantastically colored canyons and cliffs form strange apparitions and winding rock formations suddenly give way to sharp falls and wadis (dry ravines). In the midst of it all spilling over the horizon, lie a series of gaunt, moon shaped craters that predate even the most ancient of civilizations and almost every major geological formation and structure can be found here.

At the northern edge of the desert are the imposing remains of Massada overlooking the Dead Sea, with its salt marshes and mineral wealth. The desert's southern apex leads to the refugee filled Gaza Strip and to the west the Sinai Peninsula. Further onward is Eilat, and the copper mines of King Solomon, now an international tourist attraction and the Red Sea in the east.

Except for Beer'Sheva the regional capital of the Negev, and several development towns, there are few inhabited settlements here. An occasional Bedouin encampment or isolated kibbutz with its slim ring of green is quickly swallowed up in the silence and immensity of the desert. Great expense and effort must be poured into this area in order to exploit its vast potential and its strategic link with the Red

Sea gateway to Asia. Its importance will be even greater after Israel vacates the Sinai and returns it to Egypt. In the secrets of the Negev lie great challenges to Israel pioneering, to its security needs and to the future of the country.

THE WAY WE LIVE

For some Israelis the day starts as early as 5:30 or 6 am. Groceries are open and housewives are already shopping for morning rolls (only tourists eat bagels and lox in Israel) or beating rugs over the railings of their apartment balconies, each one at her own tempo. This is the Tel Aviv morning symphony with an orchestra of thousands and no one in town really needs an alarm clock. Thousands of radios blare out early morning news and calisthenics instructions and street vendors — vegetables, watermelons, eggs and of course the *Alte Zachen* men, some of whom now use megaphones to collect old clothes and junk, are already on their way. The first shift in the factories has begun and by 10 am thousands of offices and plants are slowing down for the *hafsakat boker* (morning break). Workers and clerks munch away at cheese and fish sandwiches and drink Turkish coffee or tea with lemon.

The work day ends early for many and by 2 or 3 pm government offices and institutions are closing their doors. Banks and stores close between 1 and 4 pm and reopen till early evening. During the hot afternoon hours Israelis who can do so are resting at home or indoors. The week is a long one and "weekend" means Friday afternoon and Saturday, the Sabbath. Except for a few industries, a two day weekend remains a luxury that Israel's economy cannot yet afford. Israelis work hard and play hard and they usually do it together with family, friends and neighbors. Not many prefer to be alone and there is too little of that precious leisure time to waste it.

Going to the beach is a national sport and for enthusiasts the season is the whole year long. By 11 am on Saturdays during the long summer, parking lots along the Mediterranean are filled up and radio announcements keep the country posted on up to the minute traffic developments. At 2 pm they return home for their afternoon rest and soon there is hardly anyone at the seashore but tourists or eccentrics. The hardy soul joining the crowd for the first time is in for a treat. After getting through the traffic jams and arriving at the beach, he must first find a bit of sand in the jumble of brightly colored tents, blankets and people. He can then observe or join in several forms of typically Israeli beach behavior.

Many of the younger set prefer *raketot*, the Israeli version of paddle ball. Picture a stretch of beach along the Mediterranean coast with sand and sea almost blocked from view by near endless couples — it is difficult to count them — vigorously pouncing and jumping about on the sand. They are playing an eyeball to eyeball kind of tennis with a noisy, black rubber ball, wooden raquets and no nets. The endless "pings" and "pongs" cannot be ignored and tourists may be somewhat nervous until they get used to it all.

Fancy kites, rubber dinghies, rafts and a variety of expensive, imported games are brought along for the little ones. They run around with great exuberance and noise and what parent will reprimand them or tread in their path? Fathers who are daring paratroopers, sharp tongued clerks or tough steelworkers trek back and forth obediently returning stray balls and toys and bringing a supply of ice cream, corn on the cob, cold drinks, candies and other snacks to their demanding offspring.

Young mothers, who only yesterday were absorbed by romance and finding a good man, now sit together on the sand looking at and talking about the little objects of their

15

adoration and having collective *naches* (untranslatable). It is one of the greatest of Israel's many miracles that these youngsters will somehow overcome this smothering parental love and grow up to be more or less adjusted, independent and even imperturbable human beings who will spoil and pamper their own children in exactly the same way.

On weekends and holidays, with it singles have another form of recreation called, *"Efo hamesiba ha'erev?"* (Where's the party tonight?) *Sabra* (Israeli born) girls wearing the latest bikinis mingle with the crowd, dodging lunging raketot players and the ubiquitous black balls, flirting and trading rumors and gossip. Dates are made, plans for the evening are lined up and all return to the city in another traffic jam. For the more sophisticated set, the game is played out at the luxury hotel swimming pools and country clubs. Others spend their weekends in less energetic pursuits, walking the dog or just taking it easy at home, while religious Jews spend their Sabbath as generations have before them in the more spiritual surroundings of synagogue and family.

MAN AND WOMAN, ISRAELI-STYLE

Outwardly Israeli women justify every fantasy about them. Whether alone, in pairs, or in trios, with arms linked, talking away in fast paced slang filled sabra Hebrew, they are the shapely epitome of the full beauty appreciated all over the Mediterranean. They have facial characteristics and personalities familiar in other countries and climes, from coffee colored Yemenite beauties to "gingi" (red heads) and nordic looking blondes, and sometimes you think you are in downtown Rome, Cairo, Paris or Stockholm. In their tight jeans and open at the top shirts they are at once feminine, sophisticated, confident, friendly and flirtatious — and completely male dominated!

Yes, in spite of the example of Golda Meir, Israel is

definitely still run by men as is no other country in the modern world. Equality of the sexes is grand illusion and if Women's Lib has come to town, only a brave small handful are interested. What women in Israel want — or have been quietly brainwashed into believing they want — are husbands and children and there is no doubt about it. They may reach the pinnacle of the professional and business world, become judges, professors or industrial tycoons, but if they do not have a husband and family, they are regarded by all and often by themselves as a failure. They demand equality with their men, but are tied to their families, ethnic affiliations and national traditions.

It is not surprising then, that the *Shadchan* (Marriage Broker) is still a respectable institution. Newspaper classified columns — even the English language *Jerusalem Post* — carry daily ads from matrimonial bureaus and "he" and "she" columns for "marriage" or "serious purposes only," from teenagers to mature spinsters, divorcees and the widowed. Breach of promise law suits, once a legally recognized practice in Victorian England and early America, still exist in Israel and the spurned party can collect money damages in Court if the facts are proven.

There is a lot of hand holding, hugging and kissing in public and many Israeli women are as liberated as elsewhere. On the other hand some ethnic groups impose strict restraints on their sisters and daughters. In a few Arab communities when a female has misbehaved according to the standards of her brothers or family, they may decide that the protection of her honor compels them to beat, kill or banish her and/or the man involved from home. Many of Israel's prostitutes, Jewish and Arab, entered the profession when they were thrown into the streets by their family after a romance that was not approved of.

17

Even in the discos and at the young set Friday night parties, beyond the sabra effervescence and energy, there is more inhibition and less wildness of the kind that goes on in the American scene. If there is any wife-swapping it is a well kept secret. Gay people are well hidden in the closet, since homosexual sex is still a criminal act, and while prosecutions are rare, there is very little public acceptance of Gay ways. More and more voices are being heard in protest of this lack of tolerance in private morality, but such things change slowly in Israel.

Perhaps it is a sign of the times that the great emphasis on marriage is not proving all that it should be. The country's largest marriage registrar is located at the side entrance of Tel Aviv's modern and impressive Rabbinate, but the imposing, main entrance leads to the divorce courtrooms that fill up most of the building and where the waiting period can be a year.

Israeli women have been taught that as soon as they are out of high school it is time to settle down and many are engaged or married by the time they are discharged from the army. At 25 they are considered old maids and at 30 a single or divorced girl is a loser. In the meantime, they may be sleeping around as much as they are in openly permissive countries, but they are trying to keep it from getting around. Competition is extremely keen, the pressure to find and keep a suitable mate is intense and the game goes on.

The Israeli man is, in reality, far removed from the image of the tough, virile warrior lover described by journalists and writers who actually should know better. There are Israeli women who feel that their men are in fact to blame for the unequal status of the sexes. For many sabras the approach to women is a combination of Latin macho plus Arab disdain for anything more than either a sexual or mother role. The standard explanation for the alleged wham-bam approach to sex has been expressed in a wry joke Israelis tell: "Why does the Israeli male reach a climax so quickly? Because he is in such a hurry to go and tell his friends . . ." Basically he can be as tender and considerate with his woman as anyone, but he is the inevitable product of his environment and has grown into the spoiled, tough, independent male image that he believes is expected.

Even modern and educated Israeli men are not happy when their wives or daughters go to work, especially at jobs where careerism might interfere with male predominance. Israelis of both sexes are clearly happy when women give birth to baby boys and the *Brit* (circumcision) celebration is a major occasion equal to weddings. The approach of a birth is always greeted by deadly serious joking like, 'I don't care if it's a boy or a girl, as long as there's a Brit." If it's a baby girl, everyone consoles the parents. Even graduation from law or medical school or becoming a Colonel in the army will arouse mixed feelings in a girl and her family, perhaps because statistics and experience have shown that academic and career success will only make it that much harder to find a husband.

In another one of Israel's never ending surprises, that same daredevil, free spirit who knows he holds the best cards, will very soon after he gets married become what may be the most docile and domesticated husband of the modern world. Again showing his remarkable ability to adapt quickly and well to new circumstances, the couldn't care less Israeli male soon becomes a thoughtful, devoted family man. Rude driver and tough paratrooper he may be, but once he becomes a husband he is no longer the man he was, or thought he was. He will do the dishes and take out the garbage (without being asked) and will meekly visit his mother-in-law every week without a word of protest and perhaps he is receiving no more than his just deserts.

NORMALI—LO NORMALI

That oft-heard and innocuous question: "What is the average Israeli like?" leads to a consideration of the extraordinary variety in the human landscape of Israel — blonde, olive and black Jews, pious, agnostic and atheist, westernized and Levantine. Attempts to stereotype usually fail miserably, and ethnic sociological anthropological terminology is too often misleading and inappropriate except for those subtle nuances and patterns in behavior and mentality that a veteran Israeli watcher discerns and which constitute the most important parts of the "Israeli personality".

One noticeable trait is the intense, almost compulsive desire to be with and like "other people". This is a manifestation of the cult of being *normali* — belonging to and being accepted by the peer group. In the frenzy of social activity that typifies the Israeli weekend — movies, theater going, parties, nightclubs and just plain visiting friends and family, one can feel and see this urge to meet and mingle, argue and discuss, hear and make oneself heard on every subject under the sun, often being *dafka* (contrary) just for the sheer pleasure of it.

On the national level is the longing to become a full member in good standing in the Family of Nations — accepted and not merely feared or hated by the Arabs who dispute Israel's very existence, the Communist and Third World who shun her and even the handful of friends and allies who so often behave hypocritically and impatiently with her.

The opposite of normali is *lo normali* (abnormal) i.e. aberrant and therefore unwanted and unaccepted. It is a surprising paradox that in Israel, a country which was populated by such unique means, the supreme value of the "average" Israeli, his way of life, goals and attitudes are an emulation of what he believes is desirable and acceptable in "normal" people and countries. This has led to a tendency that thwarts and frustrates the development of individuality, nonconformity, civil liberties and tolerance of dissension from the accepted mores that are deemed Jewish traits in the countries of the Free World that Israel so emulates and admires.

Every Saturday night after dinner, families assemble and the early evening promenade begins. Except during the brief cold and rainy winter, everyone walks around sockless in leather sandals. An occasional tie is seen but men and women tend to favor clothes that are comfortable and casual. Babies in carriages, kiddies in strollers and Israeli children in remarkable displays of energy and mischief lead the way, grandparents and visitors follow as families take to the sidewalk. Now and then they pause for steak sandwiches, humus, felafel, pizza, ice cream sundaes and a variety of nuts. Future sociologists will no doubt have profound and interesting theories about the continuous (there are snack breaks every two or three hours) and over eating habits of the Israelis.

There is lots of table hopping, constant buzzing of gossip and small talk and the pedestrian traffic spills over and around the sidewalk cafés into the streets. Laughter and loud greetings are exchanged, often in Arabic slang "Kif Halik!" (How're you doing?) "Ahalan" (Hi!) when someone recognizes a friend or acquaintance. The moving crowd is occasionally held up momentarily while families and clans in front of them exchange greetings. More sedate café patrons sip at drinks, staring at the passing parade. After an hour or two the whole thing comes to an end. Children are put to bed and youth and adults prepare for the evening get-together that may continue until the late hours of the night.

While going out on the town is popular, many prefer small parties or visiting friends and neighbors. This is an extremely mobile society with everyone travelling and visiting whenever they are not at work or something equally important. In Israel a man's home is rarely his castle and people just drop by uninvited or unannounced. When they do, even a surprised family greets them with a smile and "Shalom." Before coming, visitors might say to themselves, "Oh, are we going to them again?" and when they leave the hosts might think aloud: "Thank God they've finally gone." The need for being together with other people prevails and those who do not conform are considered either *snobim* or *lo normali*.

If it is hot, guests sit on the inevitable outdoor balcony and drink bottled soda water and fruit juices. Large quantities of food and snacks are laid out on the table and it is the rare guest who needs an invitation to eat. Strangers informally introduce themselves to each other and chat easily. Even if one is on his first visit it is not considered bad taste to wander around the flat freely or to ask the hosts how much they paid for it. Israelis do not usually engage in flattery, sincere or otherwise, but whatever the answer might be, a gracious visitor exclaims: "Why, your apartment surely cost a million more." After possibly adding, "How originally you've furnished it!" (almost always an exaggeration) the social graces are over and the main event begins.

Guests are arrayed in a semicircle or circle facing each other as though at a seance. When the light banter and gossip slows down, the group discussion begins and it encompasses almost every possible subject. Israelis can agree and suddenly disagree and toss quotations, theories and conclusions on each issue. They argue even insultingly, but few take offense. The talk fest has some talking and much harangue, bombast and exaggeration. It goes on with no respite, with everyone joining in the verbal free-for-all. American fashions, Israeli politics, Soviet intrigues and Arab provocations are all mentioned in passing, but without real passion. It is common to assert the most contrary, unique and amazing opinions and conjectures, just to be *davka*.

To a Gentile looking at a map of the world, Israel seems to be a tiny country. Moslem countries cover almost one third of it from Morocco on the Atlantic to Pakistan and Moslem Asia in the east, from Turkey in Europe to deepest Africa. In this vast Islamic sea filled with nearly a billion people and dozens of Arab countries 100 million strong, Israel is a mere speck of land — a patch of desert some ten miles wide at its most narrow point in its center.

For the Israelis global geography and population statistics are not upsetting. As far as they are concerned, Israel is the axis around which the rest of the world revolves and the important subjects are Israeli. Should Arab territories occupied in war be handed over to the PLO? Are the new milk containers better than glass bottles? Who has visited the new art gallery in Jaffa? Does that certain politician really have a mistress? Will the Prime Minister really retire? No other issue absorbs them more than peace and security.

Although there are few sacred cows and a sensational variety of opinions are expressed, in the end there is usually a general consensus of opinion about the important issues. Sabras of every background think and talk alike on major issues in spite of other differences between them and their greatest striving is to be "normali."

In its truest sense, the average Israeli is well adjusted. He may be somewhat neurotic, a little claustrophobic or hypochondriac, but in the language of the psychiatrist he is well oriented, well functioning and in no acute distress. He certainly does not suffer from paranoia; history has proven that even a paranoid can have real enemies.

Israelis tend to be more suspicious, nervous and impatient than other people but these characteristics were learned during centuries of pogroms, suffering and trying to get along without succeeding. They are gripers but what else can they do considering the heavy load they bear? What other people could endure such problems and keep their sanity, much less their good manners?

Here is a people facing daily threats of war and terrorism, stress and tension that sometimes are almost beyond human endurance. Even the weather, with its daily extremes and subtropical caprices is debilitating for many who come from the temperate zones of Europe. The constant wars and threats of war, the long work week, low salaries, high taxes, reserve duty callups, red tape and bureaucracy; what a steep price to pay for sharing that special experience that is life in Israel.

In few other nations will a new "voluntary" deduction from their pay check, unexpected reserve army callup order or other call for sacrifice be accepted without murmur except for that continually repeated rationalization *ein breira* (no alternative). Where else, and in spite of all adversity, will so many people keep saying and believing *yihiye tov* (everything will be alright)! When they are happy the whole world is Jewish and this is the essence of the Israelis. They may have little tranquility or prosperity but are masters in their own land. They are aware and informed, but cool; sincere and to the point yet sentimental; curious about what is going on in the rest of the world but above all concerned about what happens here; sick and tired of war, but not ready to give up their independence for what will be less than true and lasting peace.

Israelis — a most *normali* people in the most *abnormali* of conditions and circumstances are doing the best they can. They are indeed like everyone else, only more so.

The Land of Israel is called Life
(The Talmud)

Chapter Two

PAST AND PRESENT

HOW IT ALL BEGAN

I t is an innocent observer of the Israeli scene who sees only a picture album of history, tribulations and achievement. Kibbutz and resorts, sun, sea and desert, Israel is all of this, yet almost everyone is aware of another and greater dimension. Perhaps no other country arouses such a conflicting array of feelings and impressions and there are moments when every tourist silently mumbles, "Will the real Israel please stand up?"

One of the most sobering monuments in Israel is situated near the tomb of King David on Jerusalem's Mount Zion. Somewhat reluctantly, visitors enter the cave's inner chamber in total silence. Flickering candles cast their eerie light in the darkness. In a corner of an otherwise empty room stands a large urn. It contains the ashes of a few of

27

the six million Jewish victims of the Nazi death camps. A carved tablet bears only the names, Auschwitz... Buchenwald... Bergen-Belsen... Dachau...

These are the ghastly relics from the cruellest of disasters ever to befall the Jews — an empty cylinder of Zyklon B gas, instructions from a German factory explaining the proper use of their furnaces for the disposal of dead bodies, bars of soap made from human fat, lampshades from Jewish skin. There is a pile of small shoes and hats, the sole remnants of one million Jewish children and babies who were beaten, starved and gassed to death in a madness that defies belief.

Visitors move from one grotesque, real life exhibit to the next. It is the rare Jew or Gentile who passes through without a lump or dryness in his throat. Nobody speaks here and the only sounds are the shuffling footsteps and moans that cannot be suppressed. This is the "Chamber of the Holocaust", one of Israel's most startling memorials of the near destruction of the Jewish people.

There is another historical monument of struggle and death symbolic of a somewhat different mood of Israel today. It stands on a windy plateau called Massada, high in the Judean desert. Here, in the midst of sand and stone, an extraordinary chapter occurred in world history. It bears a profound meaning for every Jew and is the reason for what is sometimes called Israel's "Massada complex". It was the final chapter in a brave and desperate revolt against the Roman conquerors of the ancient homeland in the 1st century AD.

For two years and against overwhelming odds, several hundred Zealot families held out against the most powerful empire ever known to mankind and their mighty Roman Legions. Though Jerusalem and the Holy Temple were conquered and in ashes and the survivors of what had been a

Jewish Commonwealth slaughtered or enslaved, Massada continued to resist. When the siege could no longer be contained an incredible drama took place. In the words of Flavius Josephus the historian of that remarkable era, families kissed for the last time and..."lay down in close embrace".

"Then they were divided and as they lay in groups watching the enemy approach, ten of them were selected to end the lives of their loved ones. Then they offered their necks to the stroke of those who by lot executed that melancholy office and when these ten had without fear slain them all, they made the same rule of casting lots for themselves, that he whose lot it was should first kill the other nine and then should kill himself..." Thus ended what is known as the Jewish Wars and the struggle of a small nation to retain its national freedom and identity.

On that day the Jews began their long march into exile and dispersion among the nations of the world. When they regained their independence 2000 years later, this wind-swept plateau became both a symbol and warning. At the base of the rubble of the ancient fortress a small plaque carries the brief legend that is the unspoken pledge of every Israeli — "Massada shall not fall again". In Jewish history death and survival are themes emphasized to an over-whelming, some will say even morbid extent, but in this land and only here life, that most basic of human rights, cannot ever be taken for granted. The struggle for national survival — "le netzach" (For Eternity) is more than any other factor, Israel today.

After the fall of Massada, the Romans proclaimed the defeat of the Hebrews throughout their empire and engraved the legend "Judah is destroyed" on a com-memorative coin. Two millennia would pass, Nazi Brown Shirts would raise the chillingly similar cry of "Germany

Awake, Let Judah Perish" and the circle be completed, but the pageant of the Jews did not begin with Rome nor end with Auschwitz. More than twenty centuries before the Christian era an old man named Abraham entered into a Covenant with God and became the first Jew.

Since then Hebrews, Israelites and, as they became known in exile, Jews, have trodden through every age and epoch to become a unique and indelible part of history. They have been peasants, peddlers and prophets, merchants and generals, philosophers and martyrs. While dozens of other civilizations have risen and then fallen into obscurity, they have continued their march, against the rules of history and historians to remain a most unusual people, imbued with a remarkable vitality, creativeness and a will to live in their own, unique way.

They have never been more than a few million and the fourteen million Jews in the world today constitute less than one half of one percent of the human race. Had they not been decimated throughout the centuries by forced conversions, wars, pogroms and holocausts, they would have numbered more than a hundred million today. Gentiles pondering their "strangeness" with mixed feelings have not always been willing to admit the extent to which they have contributed to and affected mankind — the monotheism of Abraham, the Ten Commandments of Moses, the world's first democracy of the Judges and united tribes of ancient Israel.

From the people about whom some have said "how odd of God to choose the Jews", came Jesus of Nazareth and Saul of Tarsas, who as the Disciple Paul transposed a struggling cult into a religion that has shaped the character of western civilization and is the faith of nearly one billion people. In our own era a Jew named Karl Marx has become the prophet of a new faith that has swept an equal part of humanity. It was Sigmund Freud, a Jewish physician, who opened the minds of modern man to revelations about the human psyche, while a Jewish scientist Albert Einstein ushered in the nuclear age.

During much of this long passage through the ages, Jews had no country of their own. They knew wandering, slavery, freedom, glory, revelation, exile, disaster, and finally political independence. For all of its tangible attractions, the pull of the ancient homeland was an emotional, inexplicable, but undeniable force. It was born and developed out of this tumultuous past and nurtured in the struggles and triumphs of the infant State. Only for Jews has *"The"* Land (*Haaretz*) meant *our* country to generations of those who dreamt the impossible dream and this accumulated weight of the centuries has become an integral part of the psychological climate of Israel and its people. It is a part of the national consciousness and the Israelis will not forget it.

Almost every road and crossroad, every hill and valley bears a reminder of some event in this historical pageant. On a raised platform overlooking the main coastal highway near Herzlia rests a small dilapidated ship. It seems incongruous poised over the speeding cars. Only the Hebrew words *"yad lemaapil"* (Memorial to the Immigrant Runner) are etched on its sides. On this fragile vessel and others like it thousands of survivors of the Nazi death camps were smuggled into what was then Palestine. Somewhere along the nearby shore a human cargo would be discharged in the dead of night before it sailed back to a port in Europe to prepare for another journey. Some immigrant runners never reached the shore. Like the *Struma*, a cattle boat loaded with nearly a thousand refugees, they sank without survivors.

At the gates of Degania, the first *kibbutz* (communal farm) in the lush valley overlooking the Sea of Galilee stands a rusted Syrian tank. A small printed legend tells the story known by every Israeli child; how the leading tank of the invading Syrian army was stopped by a Molotov cocktail thrown by a kibbutz member to break the Arab advance in the War of Independence and save the valley from capture and destruction. Burnt out skeletons of armorplated trucks and buses lie on the sides of the winding road from Tel Aviv to Jerusalem. Long faded flower wreaths bear the names of soldiers who died in the battles to end the Arab stranglehold on Jewish Jerusalem.

Since the rebirth of Israel hundreds of millions of trees have been planted. Many are still only saplings in parks and small woods that are hopefully called "yaarot" (forests) Some are dedicated to the memory of important and famous friends of Israel but most were purchased by contributions from hundreds of thousands of anonymous Jews and Gentiles in almost every country. It has been said that this is a country where every tree and stone has a birth certificate. School children and ordinary citizens tramp these forests and countryside and know and love every corner of it as few people do in other countries.

There are no lush valleys here, no rain forests, mighty rivers or majestic mountains. What is called a mountain in Israel is only a hill. The Jordan River, so dear to Jew and Christian, is hardly a stream in most places. Harsh sun, rocky hills and the ever present sand and desert are its main features, but for Israelis there is no fairer land. What does it matter that the "National Park" in Ramat Gan would easily fit into a corner of New York's Central Park? Its grassy lawns and tiny artificial lake are the pride and joy of the local inhabitants. The King David "waterfall" overlooking the Dead Sea in the desert of Sodom is just a small brook but it is sweeter and more beautiful to Israelis than any Niagara.

There is a physical beauty in this land which even the eye of the uninvolved can behold. It is there in the haunting loneliness of the desert and the bold panorama overlooking Haifa harbor. It is in Jerusalem, the eternal city of gold, at twilight and in the verdant fields of the Galilee. But the true essence of Israel lies neither in city, countryside or landscape. It is to be found in the vividly colored human mosaic that is the Israeli people and their striving to build a nation.

RETURNING TRIBES

The most striking characteristic of Israel is the diversity inherent in its geography, landscape, climate, religions, and especially its inhabitants. No facet is more important, colorful or confusing than the Israelis themselves. In biblical times there were a dozen Hebrew tribes in the country. Today its immigrants and settlers come from a hundred lands and cultures and are sometimes referred to as though each belongs to a "returning tribe". German Jews are called "Yekkes" (jacket-wearers) and Yiddish speakers are "Vus Vus" (their usual reply to anything said to them in Hebrew and meaning "What? What?"). A Jew from Sofia is a "Bulgari" and the former Istambuler becomes a "Turki."

The Jewish settler from New York, Chicago or London suddenly discovers that he has become an "Anglo-Saxon" or as some Israeli would have it Anglo-Sexis! the loose Israeli term for native English speakers. This droll nickname delights most Americans here and would no doubt confuse their Jewish and Gentile friends back home. It is only the first of many surprises in store for one who makes that special journey that Zionists call *Aliya* (ascent or immigration) to Israel.

Continuous waves of mass and individual immigrants have been its lifeblood, and the relationship between the various groups constitutes one of the country's most vital and complex issues. Even the seemingly simple question, "Who is a Jew?" has been enough to confound sociologists, theologists and jurists and is the cause of a national crisis every few years.

Terms of reference and definitions regarding Israel's ethnic groups are equally bewildering to one not aware of the special context in which they are used. Jews from North and Latin America and Western Europe, for instance, are considered "Westerners," but an educated Czech Jew is also so regarded. If he happened to speak English, he might even consider himself an Anglo-Saxon.

Arab-speaking Jews from North Africa are linguistically and culturally distinguished from *Sephardim*, the descendants of the Spanish and Portuguese Jews, as those from Yemen, Iran, India and Bukhara are distinctive from Sephardim, North Africans and each other. In Israel they all are known as "Orientals" (*Mizrachim*) or Sephardim. That each group is ethnically distinctive from the other, as a Canadian Jew is from a Hungarian Jew and the latter from a Belgian Jew is disregarded. The Jews of the "West" are Europeans or *Ashkenazim*, while the others — who now constitute some 60% of the Jewish population of Israel — have officially become *Bnei Edot Hamizrach* (the "Children of the Eastern Communities").

"West" in this context has come to imply European or advanced, and "east" is often a near-synonym for backwardness. There is an absurdity in describing Jews as Easterners and Westerners, when Eastern Morocco or Tunisia are actually more westerly geographically and politically than the so-called Western Poland or Hungary. A sophisticated, Jewish intellectual from Casablanca is fated to be a son of the East, while a proletarian Jewish plumber or butcher from a village in Poland becomes a Westerner.

Only a few decades ago this terminology was carried to tragic extremes in Europe. In the first years of the Third Reich, would-be Germans "of the Mosaic persuasion", like their Aryan neighbors, were castigating the "primitive, Oriental hordes of the east." They were referring to the Ost-Juden, the millions of poor and lowly born Jews of Poland and Russia. A few years later the Nazis would find a single "final solution" for all Jews, east and west, and it would be carried out, without exception, on Ashkenazi and Sephardi alike.

Americans living in Israel encounter these strange word games in especially startling fashion. An Israeli suddenly refers to "*you* people" while talking about race riots or crime in the streets of the USA. "*Your* President" will mean President Carter even to an American Jew who has lived in Israel for 30 years. A French speaking Syrian Jew, who might never have been in France, is suddenly called upon by acquaintances and fellow workers to explain French hostility to Israel. All of this and more is a bittersweet part of the phenomenon of the rebirth of the State of Israel.

Imagine the confusion of the Rumanian Jew, fortunate enough to flee that country and its anti-Semitism, when Israelis belonging to other "tribes" suddenly congratulate him for "the independent stand *you* have taken" in not breaking off diplomatic relations with Israel as other communist countries did after the Yom Kippur War. The official nationality of a Jew in Soviet Ukraine or Georgia is Jewish. When he comes to the land of the Jews he becomes a "Russi" and often he cannot even speak proper Russian.

These contradictions are inherent in the basic raison d'être of the State of Israel. The Zionist movement was based on two doctrines, the first and most important of which was *Kibbutz Galuyot* (Ingathering of the Exiles) as described in Deuteronomy and repeated by the Prophets

Isaiah, Jeremiah and Ezekiel... "He will assemble the dispersed of Israel... from the four corners of the earth"... "and I will bring them back into the land of Israel." This aim has been accomplished in part through the near miraculous return of a million Jews to the ancient homeland and the recreation of an independent Jewish nation, although the refusal of the great majority of Free World Jews to settle in Israel has caused distress and frustration to Israel and Zionist idealists. It is the second and related theme of *Mizug Galuyot* (Merging of the Exiles) that has given rise to the puzzling terminology mentioned and to the problems arising from that terminology. The merging of Jews who have returned to the ancient land has in fact produced some of the most challenging problems of this new old country.

Jews were in exile in Babylon even before the Christian era, but only after the Roman conquest of ancient Judah were they dispersed to every corner on the face of the earth. In the course of the centuries, their cultural and behavioral patterns were influenced by the peoples and societies in which they lived. Every Jewish community developed as part of and yet separate from those they lived among. Then suddenly, Israel is reborn and the exiles are transported on the wings of necessity or idealism to their new lives. Having been Jews in a hundred different lands, they return to the ancient homeland only to discover that they are really Persians, Greeks and Anglo-Saxons. Not even the pluralistic melting pot of America was ever the focus of so confusing and intense a social and ethnic cauldron as Israel.

This is surely the strangest irony in a land of many. The Jewish State exists because the Jews never denied their Jewishness and the Gentiles never really accepted them. For centuries life among the *goyim* (Gentiles) was a cheerless lot. At worst the Jews suffered hell on earth; at best, they were a tolerated minority. Having no other choice, they adjusted to their lives in the Diaspora and partially or completely emulated and assimilated with their neighbors. Surely the average English Jew today is not unlike his Christian English counterpart, at least outwardly. His point of view, method of expression and very image is "English." The Iraqi Jew, no less, resembles an Iraqi. He usually looks, thinks and acts more like an Arab from Baghdad than, for example, like a Parisian who is Jewish.

In Israel the process of merging such Jews has to a great extent been traumatic for all concerned. Even after learning to communicate with each other in their differently accented Hebrew, the various groups often cannot find any real common language. Cultural, educational and behavioral traits and nuances accumulated through the centuries remain a divisive force, often for an entire generation. The Englishman immigrating to Israel may soon wonder if his neighbors are truly his brethren. The Iraqi settler suspects that his frustrations and problems are due to Ashkenazi European scheming. The native born Sabra often reacts with what is a marked indifference and feeling of superiority to all the greenhorns.

This, then, is the ironic climax of the long, tortuous history of the Jews. Denied their own land for 20 centuries, they wandered everywhere, irritating, influencing and enriching the nations of the world. They gave of their personality and genius to a multitude of lands and civilizations. Today they again have a land of their own where they are, so to speak, "the Gentiles," and yet they remain divided into different tribes and communities. The hope expressed in the Book of Samuel that "...we may also be like all the nations" has not yet been fulfilled and a new generation of settlers is still engaged in that painful and unique aspect of Jewish nation building called the Merging of the Exiles.

ASHKENAZI — SEPHARDI

When and where did it begin? When did Jews first become Sephardim and Ashkenazim, Easterners and Westerners? There are a few Israeli villages like Pekiin, where Jews have lived without interruption since biblical days. After the Roman conquest of Judah, the vast majority of those not slaughtered, converted or enslaved, were dispersed to different parts of the ancient world. Later they were banished from those lands and forced again to move on in the search for a new place of refuge. During every century and from every country of their dispersion, individual Jews and families continued to drift back to their conquered and devastated land.

Until they were expelled from Spain in 1492 by order of the Inquisition, there were no Sephardim or Ashkenazim. Sephardi, which is Spaniard in Hebrew, became the name for the banished Spanish Jews. Most of them settled in the nearby countries of the Balkan and Mediterranean and developed a language of their own called Ladino, a mixture of Spanish and Hebrew written in Hebrew characters. Ashkenazi, meaning German in Hebrew, originally referred to Jews who settled in that country and thereafter in Eastern Europe and the Americas. Today, even after the destruction of six million Jews in Europe during the Holocaust, they still comprise the great majority — perhaps three quarters of world Jewry. Thus was born the division of the Jews into two different cultural communities.

It was Sephardic Judaism that dominated Jewish culture for 1000 years before the modern era. While Ashkenazis were living in squalor in shtetls and ghettoes, Ladino speaking Jews were scientists, philosophers and advisors of royalty. If there is a Mayflower generation in Israel, it is the Sephardim who were living in Palestine long before the waves of Ashkenazi immigration in the late 19th and the early 20th centuries.

In those relatively peaceful days, Ladino speaking Jews were the leaders and comprised the great majority of the Yishuv (Jewish community) in Turkish ruled Palestine. Dressing like Arabs and speaking their language as well, they no doubt looked with some dismay upon the singing, dancing, Yiddish speaking, Zionist halutzim (pioneers) from Poland and Russia. Few in either group realized that within several decades pioneers would outnumber Sephardim, set the tone and take over the leadership of the new homeland in Palestine.

Some Sephardic Jews actually came to Palestine directly from Spain. The great medieval poet, Yehuda Halevi, set out for Palestine even before the expulsion from Spain, singing "My heart is in the East though I am in the West" and as early as the 13th Century there was again a Jewish settlement in Jerusalem. Sephardim absorbed Arabized Jews from Yemen, Iraq and North Africa who had formed small settlements in the Holy Land. All were integrated within the Sephardic community, the only Jewish one recognized by the Turkish Sultans. During four centuries of Ottoman rule from 1517 to 1917 the Turks regarded the Sephardic Chief Rabbi as the leader of all the Jews in Palestine and he was accorded the title Rishon Le Zion (First in Zion), the name by which he is still known.

Ashkenazim also returned to Palestine during the long period of exile, but most came after the 16th century. Nearly all spent their time in religious study and prayer in one of the four holy cities (Jerusalem, Safad, Tiberias and Hebron) where the last famous centers of Jewish learning had flourished. Here were the uprooted stones and pillars

39

of their synagogues, destroyed by the Crusaders and the graves of their rabbi teachers. These Jews devoted themselves to the rigid and austere life of Orthodox Judaism, sustaining themselves by petty trade and charity from abroad. They had little in common with the dynamic and not very religious pioneering Ashkenazim who would come later in the wake of the Zionist movement.

Most Sephardic Jews in Palestine were content to patiently await the coming of the Messiah who would herald a new Israel. Ashkenazi Zionists believed that pioneering in the Holy Land would hasten his arrival and the return of the Divine Presence (*Ha Shechina*) as well as their own redemption. From Herzl, the Viennese journalist who became the father of modern Zionism, through Ben Yehuda, who inspired the revival of the ancient Hebrew language, Jabotinsky the godfather of the Israeli army, Weizmann, Israel's first President, Ben Gurion, Meir and Begin, European-Ashkenazis provided the impetus and leadership in the struggle to re-establish the Jewish homeland in Palestine.

In Palestine they became the first Jewish shepherds, farmers and fishermen since the days of Arab rule. Their villages and kibbutzim (communal farms) were the first all Jewish settlements since the days of the 2nd Jewish Commonwealth. By 1900 they had done much to reclaim the barren and neglected soil. They built schools and hospitals, established industries, theaters, newspapers and organized underground resistance forces and political movements that later became the army and political establishment of Israel. By the time the tragic survivors of European Jewry made their way to the Yishuv, it was predominantly Ashkenazi with the Oriental Sephardic populace absorbed within it.

Every President, Prime Minister and Chief of Staff was to be an Ashkenazi and they would dominate the political, economic and social world of Israel. Then came the war between new born Israel and the Arabs in 1948 and the demographic face and character of Israel underwent a sudden and complete change. Hundreds of thousands of Palestinian Arabs fled to neighboring Arab lands while the same number and more Jews were fleeing in the reverse direction to seek refuge in the Jewish homeland. Often they were forced to abandon everything they had and arrived destitute in their only place of refuge in the entire world.

THE OTHER EXODUS

The story of Iraqi Jewry is typical of what occurred all over the Middle East during the Jewish-Arab wars of 1947-8. A well-to-do community of one hundred and twenty thousand, that predated Arab settlement by a thousand years, was forced to leave with nothing but their bare lives. First they were systematically forced out of government schools and positions. Zionism became a capital crime and the teaching of Hebrew forbidden. Kidnapping, rape, murder and confiscation of property were commonplace, but world opinion remained indifferent. The personal and community wealth they left behind was immense and easily exceeded that of the Arab residents who were leaving and fleeing Palestine, creating in effect an exchange of populations.

The ancient Babylonian exile dramatically ended in "Operation Ezra and Nehemia" when nearly all of Iraq's Jews were rescued and brought to Israel. Fifty thousand left Egypt in a modern day exodus to the Land of the Children of Israel. Yemenite Jews walked and rode through the desert to assembly points, where they were flown to Israel in an air shuttle operation called "Magic Carpet". For the God fearing and proud Yemenites it was a Biblical prophecy come true, for they were verily taken on "eagles' wings" to the Promised Land.

In the years during and immediately after the War of Independence, more than three-quarters of a million Jews from Arab and Moslem countries arrived in Israel. Some came from underdeveloped and primitive lands and were unprepared to compete successfully in the rugged, technological, European oriented society that was being formed. Many lacked employable skills and education or suffered from serious illnesses and required medical treatment and rehabilitation. Those with little means and no vocation could only take the simplest jobs and whatever housing remained available. Israel was bursting at the seams with mass immigration, and these were the harsh days of austerity and rationing, but no Jew was turned away.

Families were taken off the plane and moved into neighborhoods and villages abandoned by Arabs, like *Katamon* (in Jerusalem), *Wadi Salib* (Haifa) and *Hatikva* (Tel Aviv-Jaffa). The overcrowding and physical conditions soon turned these neighborhoods into the slums of the large cities. Others were brought directly to brand new settlements in the Negev and near the borders. These so-called "development" towns established by the government were soon inhabited almost entirely by new immigrant families from Middle Eastern countries. Thirty years later, only the name "Development Town" suggests vitality or confidence and many are near the verge of social and communal collapse.

They remain inhabited by a relatively small working population with large numbers of welfare cases and crime. A feeling of bitterness pervades what is today openly and more accurately called the "Second Israel". While cities and kibbutzim enjoy a pleasant way of life and relative economic well-being, development areas have come to mean struggling working class immigrant families, marginal workers and unemployed. *Kiryat Shmoneh, Beit She'an, Shderoth* and *Ofakim* are the real, although not geographical, frontiers of Israel. Veteran towns like *Petach Tikva, Rishon le Zion* and *Rehovot*, which were once farming villages are today Israel's suburbs, while the outlying areas removed from metropolitan centers, with their immigrant Oriental population lag far behind.

There are several traits that are common to the non-Ashkenazi immigrant such as the male-dominated household. Large and close-knit families were the rule in the countries of origin and life styles were extroverted, interdependent, and centered around the *hamoula* (clan or greater family), grandparents, cousins and all. In Israel this traditional family structure received a severe jolt as newcomers were encouraged to emulate the modernity and individuality of the veteran community. Now, the Oriental family is smaller and more independent of the hamoula and the husband-father is no longer the absolute or even dominant figure. Having yielded to the Israeli i.e. Ashkenazi way of life, they might justifiably be confused or bitter that the country's leaders deplore the growing disrespect of the young for their elders and plead for an increase in the Jewish birth rate.

The ethnic personality of the Oriental Sephardic immigrants is often described as "levantine" and "primitive" and they have been urged to practice European ways. Today, the country's rabbis, secular leaders and intellectuals alike condemn the emphasis on materialism and lack of spiritual values prevalent among Israelis of both European and Oriental origin.

This ethno-cultural merging of the exiles and attempts to pressure cook the established, mostly European Ashkenazi community with the new, mostly Oriental Sephardic community has created mutual recrimination as well as confusion. Some veteran settlers see the values and idealism they implanted in the society being dissipated and the pioneering efforts of decades being eroded by standards and mores they deem *"primitivi"*, a term heard constantly in almost every possible context. Having fled the degradation and poverty they experienced in the Arab countries, the newly arrived Children of the Eastern communities have been no less frustrated by the often insoluble problems of adjustment in western Israel.

The slums in the cities and towns of Israel are still inhabited mainly by Oriental-Sephardim. Their older generation in particular has suffered the pains of adjustment to the new circumstances. Unable to adapt successfully to the new way of life, they remained in self-imposed ghettos where they tried to continue in the old ways, but even their own children rebelled and westernized, turning against parental authority. Alleged discrimination by the established Ashkenazi community became the explanation for all of their troubles.

"Protektzia" or *"Vitamin P"* as it is also referred to, the presumed favoritism by and for European Ashkenazis, became the rationalization of two generations of distraught Oriental Sephardics, while *primitivi* was and still is the standard reply of indignant and complacent veterans and pioneers. In this tragi-comic social condition, there is even an Israeli translation of the American WASP acronym: White, Ashkenazi Sabra (with) Protektzia. These attitudes still find popular expression and are a symptom of what is both Israel's most extraordinary achievement and serious failure.

Stereotype characterizations have superimposed themselves on real life tribal traits, as European Ashkenazi became synonymous with pragmatic and rational, while Oriental Sephardic came to mean emotional, exuberant and of course primitivi. Snobbery exists even within inter-tribal relationships and not merely between the two main ethnic groups, although it is slowly being replaced by a common emphasis on material values and careerism.

A *"Yekke"* might still look with disdain upon a *"Polisher"* while the latter feels somewhat superior to a *"Rumaneska"*. Even an affluent Iranian immigrant lacks the social standing of the blue blood Sephardi families, but may believe he enjoys a status superior to a *Mograbi* (North African Jew). An Iraqi can only defensively point out that he is not from Kurdistan; *"Al tihiyeh Kurdi"* (Don't be a Kurdi!) were once fighting words and an expression of the local folklore that Kurdish Jews were the most primitive of all. Today it is *"Al tihiyeh Gruzini"* and it is the Jews of Soviet Georgia who are the lowest on the ethnic status ladder.

Attempts to mix new immigrants from different countries within the same town and apartment building soon after arrival were not very successful. Schools, youth movements and especially the Israeli army have proven to be the most decisive factors in the struggle for tolerance and unity. Objective observers agree that there is very little official discrimination, but that it does exist on a subconscious level. Ethnic prejudices of individuals and groups is the sad relic of tribal fears and taboos of centuries in exile and it has impeded the process of integration. Israelis of every background live and work together, but many frankly prefer to be with their own kind. Marriages between children of Oriental Sephardim and European Ashkenazis while no longer unusual, are still the exception rather than the rule.

There are Israelis who defend this pluralism and insist the country should ultimately aspire to be a western, multi-ethnic society like the USA, rather than a nation of identical looking and acting Israelis. A less cheerful scenario has Israel becoming a Jewish Lebanon rather than a Switzerland or America of the Middle East. The conventional explanation is that it is only a "question of time" before the social problems of Israel disappear through complete integration of all the immigrants. Politicians and optimists believe Israel will then comprise the best of east and west; pessimists suspect it has already become the worst.

Very few deny that there are ethnic problems and most concede the existence of two Israels; one mainly European Ashkenazi and advantaged and the other almost entirely Oriental Sephardic and deprived. Almost every openminded visitor knows there are thousands of poor and culturally deprived families in Israel and that economic and social disparities parallel ethnic affiliations. In the last few decades the gap between the haves and have nots has been passed on to a new generation rather than disappear and "time" is no longer deemed the magic remedy.

Although Ashkenazis constitute nearly eighty percent of world Jewry, more than half of the Jews in Israel are Oriental-Sephardic and with their higher birth rate they are continually increasing their numerical majority. While their economic and social positions have substantially improved and the number of slum poor families has greatly diminished, they still lag behind European Ashkenazis. In politics, national leadership is nearly totally dominated by the latter. Oriental-Sephardics have never numbered more than two dozen of the 120 Knesset members and only a few have been ministers in the Cabinet.

Younger, native born Israelis are less impressed with tribal considerations than their elders and the urge to improve standard of living and life style is a more compelling motivation. They have less time and energy for concern with ethnic prejudices, although subconscious jealousies remain. Fortunately these prejudices (subconscious or otherwise) have not prevented Israelis from standing together to face common struggles at a time of need. The Six Day and Yom Kippur Wars proved that they can fight side to side with equal courage and strength. This unity in the nation's hour of trial and the common selflessness, and courage of all the ethnic communities has engendered a mutual respect but has not substantially changed existing patterns.

There is a purposeful and powerful trend towards westernization and particularly the adulation of America; this trend continues in seeming contradiction to the rapid levantization of Israel. *Savlanut* (patience), indifference and "wait and see" remain the mood of citizens of every background who have made it, while struggle and bitterness are the lot of families living on the fringe of society. More than anything else, it is the way Israel regards and resolves these issues that will determine its character in the generations to come.

THE RUSSIANS ARE COMING

The biggest tribes still in the Diaspora are the six million Jews of America who don't want to live in Israel and the two and a half million Russian Jews who can't. For years Soviet authorities absolutely prohibited dissidents of any religion or ethnic group to leave its borders. In the last decade, due to brave and stubborn efforts and growing support from western sympathizers, some one hundred thousand Jews have been let out from behind the iron curtain in order to "join relatives" in Israel, but not all arrive even for a visit. Even in the beginning, there were some who left at the first opportunity and moved on elsewhere in the western world.

Today, most of the ostensible "Zionists" from Russia never even make it to Israel, but immigrate to Western countries. Those who do come are greeted with mixed feelings by Israelis because of their high drop-out rates. On the one hand, there is an awareness of the discrimination and oppression that has been their lot, the product of Russification and anti-Semitic policies that pre-dated Stalin. Every visitor to the USSR knows why its Jews are called the "Jews of Silence".

Though their Soviet ID cards may say they are "Ivris" a cruel and systematic reign of terror has smothered Jewish cultural and religious life. Synagogues and Hebrew schools are stifled and secret agents of the dreaded security services in their midst have done their work well. Russian Jews are afraid to speak to foreigners except with their eyes. Hitlerite caricatures, virulent anti-Semitic books and articles, arrests and criminal trials for "Hooliganism" and "Parisitism" are the lot of those who dare apply for permission to go to Israel. Many are active in and even leaders of the liberal protest movement while others, "the Prisoners of Zion'" are guilty only of the openly expressed desire to be in Zion. Some spend years in the labor camps of Siberia solely because of a love for a faraway land they know only by word of mouth, through the Zionist underground in the Soviet Union.

At first Israelis were thrilled when the first trickle of "Zids" became a stream. "The Russians are coming" were good tidings and they were eagerly and sincerely welcomed by most of the population. After all, they were the largest potential immigration for a nation hungry for reinforcements against a sea of Arab enemies. As time passed, it became clear that the expectation was greater than the fulfillment. Israel of the seventies was not what these newcomers had hoped for, nor were they what the country had awaited.

Once again, the culture shock took its toll and for many it was overwhelming. The Jews of Silence had been plunged straight from a strict, doctrinaire communist society into rugged, individualistic, western oriented, levantine-flavored Israel and the encounter was disappointing for both. The anonymous national joke says it only too well . . ."There's good news and bad news today. The good news — Jews in Russia have received permission to leave! The bad news — they're coming to Israel!"

On balance, the Russians have adjusted to their new lives in Israel as well as the other tribes before them. Considering how little formal Hebrew and Jewish education they had, often none at all, their adjustment has been very successful. Some, particularly the Georgian Jews, have greater problems and cause more local resentment. The Georgians tend to be extremely clannish and their customs are quite different than those prevailing in the country. Today, nearly half of the Sick Fund physicians in Israel are newcomers from Russia. *"Russit"* is heard on every bus and in every factory and the Russian influence is felt everywhere. As they too adapt to their new country, the nation is hoping for greater immigration from the Soviet Union.

BLACK AND WHITE

A mong the score of ethnic groups, two of the smallest are of particular interest to Americans. Though it is true that some Sephardi-Orientals are as dark skinned as the peoples they lived among for hundreds of years, it is the "Black Jews" from Ethiopia and the "Black Hebrews" from America who have elicited the comment — "That's interesting, they don't look Jewish". This is a new and surprising twist to an already complicated and confusing national issue.

Falashas (meaning strangers in Ethiopian) or as they call themselves *Beta Yisrael* (the House of Israel), trace their origins to the biblically recorded union between King Solomon and the Queen of Sheba, but their actual history is unknown. Sephardi Chief Rabbi Yosef has ruled that they are none other than the lost tribe of Dan that disappeared from Jewish history nearly three thousand years ago. His Ashkenazi counterpart and erstwhile rival Rabbi Goren and the divided Rabbinate have not even agreed that they are Jewish, but a government committee recognizes their eligibility for citizenship under the "Law of Return". Falashas in Israel and their supporters charge that Israel has been indifferent to rescuing *Beta Yisrael* because of underlying racial attitudes.

For thousands of years they lived in the isolated highlands of Ethiopia, unheard of by other exiled tribes of ancient Israel. Just a few centuries ago they numbered half a million and ruled a part of Ethiopia. Under the rule of the self-proclaimed Lion of Judah, Emperor Haile Selassie, Israel was considered a friendly nation and full and correct relations were maintained between the two countries. Since his downfall there has been no Israeli presence in Ethiopia.

Today there are only a few thousand Falasha survivors of the centuries of forced conversions, persecutions and abject poverty that has been the lot of this and other small and isolated Jewish settlements in Africa. Scattered among hundreds of tiny mountain villages where no roads or communications exist, they are trapped in a country gripped by continuous war and rebellion.

Since Israel's independence only a few hundred have made their way to Israel, ironically through the same route that brought the Queen of Sheba through the Red Sea to Eilat. In spite of the controversy surrounding them they are well liked and have been absorbed successfully into the society.

The "Black Hebrews" of America have existed since early in the 20th century when there were "Jewish" congregations in Harlem and other Black ghettos. They first became known in Israel in 1969 when a large group arrived from Liberia where they first unsuccessfully migrated and then left in what are still regarded as mysterious circumstances. Confused passport control officers at Lod Airport permitted them entry as tourists and they and those that later arrived directly from America were invited to settle in Dimona, a successful town in the Negev. Soon they numbered more than a thousand and Israel was confronted with yet another puzzling new aspect of the "Who is a Jew" question.

After a year or two the initial goodwill disappeared. This was inevitable in the wake of public statements made at press conferences called by Black Hebrew leaders, who declared to the world and a startled Israel, that Negroes and not Jews, were the true descendants of the original Israelites who they claimed, were dark skinned people like themselves. They also proclaimed themselves to be the vanguard of millions of Black Americans who were actually Hebrews like themselves and would now be returning to what was their homeland.

No historical evidence was offered in support of their theories and Rabbinical authorities ruled that the Black Hebrews were neither Hebrews nor Jewish according to their self-described religious beliefs and practices. Nevertheless, it was decided that those who would undergo formal conversion to Judaism could become naturalized citizens and remain permanently. The problem deepened when the Black Hebrews refused to go along with this ruling, insisting that they were entitled to unconditional entry and automatic citizenship like Jewish immigrants. Soon they were making even more militant anti-Israel and anti-Semitic declarations and threats.

Ten years after their initial arrival, they number several thousand and are still concentrated in Dimona and nearby

51

towns, where they live in near isolation from their Israeli neighbors. Very few have received official acceptance of their demands for citizenship and their initial visas have long since expired, not to be renewed. Black "tourists" who are not clearly intending a temporary stay are not welcome to enter the country. The Government and most Israelis would frankly prefer that the Black Hebrews leave but they have resisted every effort to bring this about. Aware of its already tenuous position in the third world and sensitive to political and international implications, Israel has not deported any except those convicted of criminal acts. To avoid attempts to return them to the USA many have formally renounced their American citizenship and destroyed their passports and become stateless persons.

The Israelis who are their neighbors concede that they are good-natured and clean living. They don't smoke or drink and many are vegetarians. Most complaints leveled against them are limited to the noise and nuisances arising out of their congested living conditions; almost all live commune style in crowded apartments. The majority are employed in handicrafts or in nearby factories. They seem to radiate an inner peace and self-confidence but critics have charged that they are a brainwashed and naive cult exploited by a small group of self-declared messiahs.

Israeli free thinkers feel the country is sufficiently strong and mature and can also absorb these settlers and that anyone mad enough to want to be Jewish and live in Israel should be allowed to do so. Others regard them as a dangerous menace to the nation. Black Hebrews already living in Israel are permitted to stay but they are not recognized as Jews within the meaning of the Law of Return and their friends and relatives in America are not allowed to join them. Their presence in the country adds still another hue to the coat of many colors that is modern Israel.

THE "LOST" TRIBE

There is one Jewish tribe in the Diaspora whose existence Israelis would prefer to totally ignore. They are neither oppressed like Russian Jewry nor bewildering like Black Hebrews, but they arouse unusual controversy and passionate debate. They are the former Israelis, *yordim*, those who have "descended" or gone down from Zion, plural: *yordim*, as Zionist ideologists would have it. *Nefolot Nemushot* (wormy creatures) was former premier Yitzhak Rabin's blunt, Sabra definition and many indignant and patriotic Israelis would add "deserters, losers and good riddance".

It is nearly as difficult to decide who is a *yored* as who is a Jew. Only a few of overseas Israelis admit they intend to stay abroad permanently even though some have been away from Israel 10 and 20 years, often without returning even for a visit. They continue to consider themselves Israeli — even though they have since acquired some new citizenship. They always insist they are just "studying" ..."trying to save money to come back" ..."recharging batteries" ...The reasons, motives and rationalizations are as many and different as there are *yordim* and even that is not clear.

Many Israelis leave the country, sometimes for the very first time, without any plans one way or the other except to travel around a little, see what the rest of the world looks like, and forget their problems for a few weeks. For tiny, locked in Israel surrounded by implacable enemies, more than a share of claustrophobia is understandable and the instinct to "get away for a while", to *chutz-laaretz* (literally, outside the land) is natural. The vast majority come back after their trip or holiday, feeling more than ever that Israel is the only place they can really call home. Perhaps as many as half a million Jews who were born or lived in Israel or Palestine before it are now permanent or semi-permanent residents of a score of other countries in Europe, South Africa, Australia, Canada and especially the *"Goldene Medina"* — America.

There are some fifteen to twenty million aliens living in the USA, who at different stages and with varied degrees of success have tried or are trying to become American citizens. Among the refugees and adventurers from the old world who have arrived at Kennedy Airport as alleged tourists, businessmen, students or otherwise, to become American residents, are some three hundred and fifty thousand Israelis. More discreetly and often with guilt feelings, they too are in full pursuit of that compelling but elusive symbol of a bright tomorrow, the "Green Card". In fact, the small plastic certificate confirming that a foreign national has officially become a permanent alien resident is blue, but this is usually just the first of the illusions and surprises awaiting the Israeli émigré.

Only a lucky few actually receive Green Cards from the Visa Consul of the American Embassy in Israel to officially enter the US as approved immigrants, and become naturalized citizens five years later (only three years, if they have married an American citizen). This is possible only for those who qualify under the increasingly stringent immigration laws of the INS (Immigration and Nationality Service), which awes every foreigner in the USA.

After decades of liberal, open door immigration policies, the largest and most popular immigrant country in modern history has been slowly and surely closing the door of welcome to the tired and weary of the world. Except for special cases, such as Cuban and Vietnamese refugees and a few Soviet Jews, the new policy is clearly geared to limited and selective admission of needed or desirable experts, specialists, immediate family members and unusual hardship cases.

An Israeli with an American spouse, parent, brother, sister or child receives alien residence status without too much delay or difficulty after the American sponsor files a petition on their behalf. Those who want a Green Card but who have no such American relative need sufficient money, skill, luck or bluff to get it the hard way. If they are licensed and trained in the handful of professions or occupations where there is underemployment in the USA, they may get through if the US Department of Labor approves a petition filed by the prospective American employer, based on a job offer to the requested alien.

Foreigners who can afford it and are so inclined, sometimes have no choice but to take the plunge and invest substantial capital — sometimes everything they own — in some new or existing business in order to apply for an "Investor's Visa" which is tantamount to a Green Card. Today the regulations are strictly enforced and putting up a mom and pop felafel stand or opening a candy store in Brooklyn or LA will no longer do it. Most foreigners cannot or do not wish to become investors and have to come over without the magic card. If they have an academic background, they can apply for entry as a student, exchange student, postgraduate or for specialized training.

Another way is to become a *shaliach* (emissary), one of Israel's most popular and possibly unnecessary occupations. Many ministries as well as private companies, institutions and organizations maintain offices in America and the chance to work overseas is an attractive proposal and more than a few try to prolong these assignments for a while. Merchant seamen, El Al personnel, fund raisers and even diplomatic employees have been known to enter the States as proud Israelis and when the urge overcame them, to quietly make the changeover to yored. It has been suggested, not entirely in jest, that Israel could balance its budget and create an instant mass immigration by recalling all of its shlichim.

The unfortunate Israeli emigrant who cannot fit into any of these categories usually has no alternative but to stay home or become a "tourist". Alone and in family groups, they try to convince sceptical officials of the American Embassy they are really "only going on a vacation trip", or to "cousin Harry's wedding". Often they go over on a guided tour with other genuine tourists and return as soon as they take a quick look at New York, the White House, Grand Canyon and Disneyland, but now and then there is an empty seat or two on the plane going back. Those who seem to have permanent roots, family ties and jobs in Israel receive a "Visitors" visa, but for many the visit will last for years.

America is an unusually open society where individual liberties, even of unauthorized aliens, are matched by few countries. Because of this and due to the presence of millions of other illegals, wandering around the country, INS now follows a strict policy regarding both tourist applications and entry procedures. Visa Consuls carry out the spirit and letter of the law which states that applicants for *any* visa are presumed to actually be intending immigration unless they establish entitlement to same to the satisfaction of the Consul.

Therefore, requests for the latter must be accompanied by evidence substantiating the purpose of the visit and intention to depart after a brief stay. Even when a tourist visa is granted for business reasons or pleasure tourism, one may be stopped at the port of entry if he is listed in the "Lookout" book, the computerized registry of convicted or suspected felons maintained by the American police authorities. INS operates a similar system, which screens out entering "tourists" who are deemed undesirable because of overstay or accepting employment during previous visits, etc.

Once the new arrival has entered the country and reaches New York, Miami and points west, a friend who has been through it all before, refers him to an immigration lawyer who knows just how to handle his case, and some are already Hebrew speaking! Frequently some way is found to "adjust status" as it is called officially, for the person who has entered America on a non-immigrant visa. A petition is filed to grant them a Green Card and this makes it even harder for the Israeli "tourists" who apply after him.

Often it will take a year or two until one receives the magic card without which he is deemed an illegal alien and forbidden to work or bring over wife and children. Other visitors renew their tourist visas as long and as often as their Israeli ingenuity allows, in a game of cat and mouse with INS that can last the rest of their lives.

Younger Israelis fly over to join friends or to see if all the wonderful tales of big cars, beautiful and sexy women, considerate and generous men and easy money are really true. Sometimes they end up with an American wife or husband whose family can alleviate their adjustment pains — and there are Israelis who arrive on America's shores for this very purpose. Those with real ability, fortitude and a little help from their friends do it on their own. Maybe the girls are not all that sexy and the money harder to come by but they rely on that well known Israeli trait *le histader* (getting along).

Some make a living as taxi drivers and waitresses, typically "Israeli" jobs in New York, and other cities in the States, even though many were doing better in their own country. A few slip into the local underworld and "Ugly

Israelis" and Hebrew-speaking gangsters pop up in Amsterdam, London and New York and elsewhere with embarrassing frequency. These emigrants may get the big cars, shiny appliances and "villas" they want but there is rarely a pot of gold at the end of the rainbow.

Not very many really feel they are or can ever become Americans and all are afraid that their children will. Rarely is there any "merging" with their Gentile neighbors and they share a mutually distrustful and lukewarm relationship with American Jewry. Like many English speaking immigrants in Israel, the émigrés become part of a small colony abroad on the fringe of a new society. Other greenhorns feel better with their own countrymen and so do the former Israelis. There is a "Tel Aviv" or "Sabra" cafe or restaurant in nearly every American city where they can eat humus, read Israeli newspapers and magazines and gossip with friends and acquaintances about how they are making out on the job and their progress in the quest for a Green Card.

For many this is a chance to unwind and talk about that most inevitable but unreal subject — going home, this year, next year, some day, the apartment, the children ...By then the children no longer speak Hebrew or want to leave their new friends and new lives. The apartment money they were saving is gone, spent on a mortgage and house that is hard to sell and an unexpected pregnancy or long awaited pay raise can make it that much more difficult to return. The "next year in Jerusalem" promises are a farce, even among their yordim friends and they stay another year or two or more in the new Promised Land, an enigma to themselves and the country they have abandoned.

Like millions who have preceded them, old ways and ties are forgotten and new ones made and this is what happens to yordim. Each day that passes makes it more difficult to pick up and return and the days turn into months and then years. Some insist angrily or ambivalently that they are content or even happy. Often this is a mechanical response that hides an inner and deep malaise closely related to their leaving Israel. Sometimes they are blatantly hostile to their native country and eagerly tell you how bad it was and how glad they are they left, though these are a minority.

Almost all keep in touch with friends and relatives back home and there is a dialogue of a sort between them. The mutual pretense is that they have never really left Israel or stopped being Israelis, despite the fact that their passports may have expired and in effect, they have completely severed their ties with Israel. Some are not pretending when they insist they are coming back while others are never sure what they want. They may have acquired everything they thought America could give them but somehow it is not enough. Israel was too small, too provincial, too limiting professionally and socially, but America is too big, too cold, too competitive, too different. Only inertia, fate or the fear of making still another big move in their lives keep them where they are.

For years Israel was unaware of or disregarded the growing dimensions of the *yerida* problem and comments like: "After every wave of immigration there are returnees", soon became "they aren't important". Indifference and scorn turned to fury — "traitors!", "worms!" when each new approach or solution failed to bring about their prompt return. During the Six Day and Yom Kippur Wars there was a small revival with renewed concern for Israel and some spontaneously flew back to rejoin reserve army units while others dropped everything to devote themselves to fund raising and pro-Israel demonstrations in the hour of need. Individuals and families have gone back sooner than expected, sometimes for no apparent reason except a sudden realization that it was now or never.

This mass emigration to America is in effect a mutual loss, both in sheer numbers and for ideological and psychological reasons. Intentionally or not, Israel's émigrés make a mockery of Zionist slogans and efforts to encourage large-scale Anglo-Saxon *aliya*. Former Israelis living in the US have become a relatively affluent, educated and westernized group of the kind that Israel wants so much. Sometimes there are glimmerings of a change in tactics within the Jewish Agency and the Zionist officialdom where policies are made. Instead of insulting or trying to frighten yordim, the hand of friendship and understanding is extended, to be withdrawn when it meets hesitation or procrastination.

No simple or single resolution to this very complex situation has been devised and most likely there is none. What is probably needed is less politicians, PR men and their glowing promises and enticements. Yordim are not waiting for bigger and better material benefits to convince them to take the fateful step. Their returning to the Israeli financial economic scene with the sudden reduction in real income and purchasing power would be difficult, but who understands this better than the ex-Israeli. The factors that would bring them home would also compel American Jews to consider settling in Israel.

More than anything they need to feel wanted and to see changes or the beginning of a change in the unattractive facets of Israeli life that induced them to leave.

What both Israeli emigrants and potential new settlers want, is some candid self-examination in the national mirror and acknowledgement that something serious has happened with the great Zionist dream. It can no longer be denied that most of the ills and evils of other western societies and not all of their achievements have come to Israel. It seems to the questioning émigré or potential immigrant that ideals, self-sacrifice and simplicity of the pioneering veterans has almost slipped away entirely, and has been replaced by a new morality and a new Zionism. That Zion is becoming a shoddy imitation of life in the affluent west rather than a return to the wellsprings of the ancestral east.

Whatever happens in Israel cannot change human nature and there will always be those who must see if the grass is greener on the other side, especially when it is America that beckons with its alluring lights. Still, what Israel is and where it is going is the most vital question for many in the Diaspora, who would want, each in his or her way, to come to the country and make it more like that beautiful, but now faded vision of yesterday.

If Zion remains smug and is content to await the Messiah, he may not come in time to gather up the Children of Israel who have seen the Promised Land and left it behind. He may decide not to come at all. It is becoming increasingly obvious that life in the cities and villages of Israel is not what it should be. All is not well between Jew and Arab, religious and secular, Ashkenazi and Sephardi; there is too much pushing, impatience, egotism, careerism and crass materialism. These are the real challenges for the prodigal sons and daughters, for the lost Hebrew Jewish tribes who have yet to come and for the sake of the House of Israel itself.

ISRAELI ARABS

The development of the Zionist movement and the westernization of Israel has widened the gap in understanding between Jew and Arab and added to an Israeli lack of interest bordering on contempt for Arab history, culture and values. Even today, the common expression *avoda aravit*

("Arab labor") is street talk for shoddy or cheap work. The sabra slang *"al tihiyeh aravi"* ("don't be an Arab") speaks for itself. There is a somewhat greater awareness now than previously that Israel is physically part of the Middle East and must necessarily relate to and establish a modus vivendi with the Arabs. In the meantime, it continues to identify with Europe to a degree that cannot be attributed entirely to the need to compensate for Arab hostility. From political alliances and Common Market aspirations to the educational emphasis on European languages, culture and history, Israel remains true to its western orientation.

Now that it is involved in the peace making process, it has been forced to become more directly and intensely concerned with its Arab neighbors. Unfortunately there is still no special interest in a large Israeli tribe neither Oriental Sephardic nor European Ashkenazi, composed of 600,000 Arabs, citizens and residents of Israel since its founding. Due to their natural increase — the highest in the world — and the government reunion of families programs, the Israeli Arabs have quadrupled their numbers since 1948.

They are in fact the largest ethnic group in the country and it is the preservation of their communal separateness from the Jews that has brought about their affluence and benign and sometimes even harmonious relations with the Israelis. Interaction may exist in daily contact between neighbors and at work in cities such as Haifa, and towns like Acre, Jaffa and Tiberias, but it is self-protection rather than rejection of their Arab pride and identity — as with many of the Jewish "tribes" — that enables them to live side by side in peace in spite of political cold wars and incitement from beyond the borders.

Arabs conduct their own school system and syllabus in Arabic supported by the Ministry of Education and there are engineers, physicians and teachers who were born and raised in Israeli Arab villages. Many are employed by the government but some academicians do not find suitable jobs or outlets for their nationalist energies and have dropped out to join the Soviet oriented, Arab led Rakah Communist party, which is represented in Israel's Knesset.

Some Israelis regard their Arabs as a ticking time bomb and potential fifth column and would prefer less tolerance and a tougher approach to Arabs not absolutely loyal to the state. Optimists see them as the natural bridge to the Arab world. There is no evidence that the Arabs themselves would prefer an independent PLO-run Arab country with all the uncertainties and upheavals that would imply, except for a small and vocal minority who have so declared. In spite of much protesting and near incitement, very few have ever been charged with security offences.

The government is partially at fault for the growing radicalization in the streets of Nazareth and the villages of the "Triangle" between Galilee and the West Bank where the bulk of Israel's Arabs live. For understandable security reasons, they have not been allowed the complete autonomy that would be natural in times of peace. On the other hand, Israel has not and cannot effectuate a cultural merger with half a million people for whom Israelization would mean a denial of their own language, folkways, religion and culture, as well as historical ties to the neighbor-enemies of their country.

The result has been a carrot-and-stick approach; manifestations of loyalty and cooperation have brought about great prosperity and relatively great individual freedom which the recipients are not prepared to give up so quickly. Open demonstrations of enmity or incitement dangerous to state security are met with a tough law and order reaction and a withdrawal of the carrot. There are moral, philosophical and other aspects of the way a civilized nation must treat its minorities. By such criteria Israel has behaved decently and usually fairly, if not nobly towards its Arab citizens, particularly in comparison with the lot of the Jews who are living in Arab countries.

Although they speak a single language with several dialects and share most historical and cultural traditions, the Arabs of Israel are also a heterogeneous community. Jerusalem, Haifa, Acre and Nazareth have mixed Jewish and Arab populations, but most Arabs live in their own towns and villages. These somewhat resemble Jewish settlements in Israel but are clearly not as prosperous or as modern. The outdoor *shuk* (market), winding streets and alleys, picturesque minarets and stone houses with large, painted blue eyes to ward off the evil influence are clear signs of the Levant.

Arab villagers are more patient and courteous than their Jewish counterparts. Their streets contain less traffic and frantic activity, and fewer "busy" people rushing about as in the Jewish towns. Children seem content playing alone and cafés are filled with men drinking endless little cups of Turkish coffee, talking politics and playing the middle eastern *shesh besh* (backgammon). Women dress modestly and are not seen as often. Unlike the emancipated, working Jewess of Israel, the place of most Arab women is still either in the market place or at home.

Even compared to the Oriental Sephardim, Arab social and family life is strict and patriarchal authority firm. The family clan (*hamula*) is the most important factor in Arab society, as is the immediate family in the European Ashkenazi culture, with Oriental Sephardim somewhere in the middle. There is no dating among the young, If a young Arab is fortunate, his father will come to terms with the father of the girl of his choice and a substantial dowry will be paid to the bride's father. If it is not a love match, well then, *Allah hu akbar* — "Allah is great" and the couple will accept their destiny.

If an Arab's honor has been "insulted," often for reasons incomprehensible to western logic, a blood feud may follow, ending in maiming or death, and enmity between entire hamulas and villages that may exist for years. Then leaders of the family clans involved enter into elaborate and prolonged negotiations through intermediaries until they have arranged a *"sulcha"* (reconciliation) agreement between them. This usually results in a ceremonious celebration and payment of compensation to the family of the "insulted" or the banishment from the village of the guilty.

Arab villagers seldom move far from their parents' home and growing families or a young couple often simply add a room or annex to the family house or apartment. Occasionally a group of young men visit the nearest Jewish town or city where swimming pools, movie theaters and discotheques offer diversions. They speak Hebrew fluently and closely resemble the Jewish Israelis with whom they work and live among. Arab Jewish romances are rare and intermarriages virtually forbidden by both communities. Even personal friendships between them seldom extend beyond the framework of neighbors or comrades at work.

Most Arabs still live in small, farming villages where the *fellahin* (tillers of the soil) follow the ancient ways of their fathers. The *Mukh'tar* (village headman) is the main decision maker. He is usually the head of the largest or most powerful clan in the village, though young, educated Israelized Arabs have made inroads on their once total authority. Contact with neighboring Jewish settlements and government aid have improved their standard of living, and many once impoverished villages have roads, schools and community centers, although others remain backward and neglected.

65

The flight of Arab religious and political leadership during the War of Independence left its mark. The tendency of villagers to resist change and their reluctance to pay local taxes limits the degree of development in their communities. As a result of these circumstances, local democracy lags behind the Israelis and local councils are often mere rubber stamps for the Mukh'tar and the largest hamula. Though women are entitled to vote or run for office, it is not encouraged. Girls learn in separate classes and schools and few are able to go on to secondary or higher education.

The nomadic *Bedouins* (inhabitants of the desert in Arabic) form still a different ethnic sub-group. They are scattered about in the Sinai and Negev and their black goatskin tents are found on the outskirts of almost every city. Bedouins have traditionally spurned farming and the village life of the *fellahin*. Like gypsies, they continually move on in search of better wells and grazing land for their camels, goats and sheep. They are disdainful of foreign influence and rulers and their renowned hospitality to guests and visitors is an exception to their inherently introspective and independent ways.

The tribal Sheik is mayor, judge and sheriff and there are no political parties or local councils here. Substantial and often revolutionary improvements in schooling, medical care and in living standards have been made with government assistance and encouragement. Some tribes are well off, with jeeps and station wagons outside their tents and portable television sets and refrigerators within. Others still live the harsh and lonely life of their forefathers.

For years the government has been engaged in a not so successful effort to relocate them into permanent homes and communities; this program includes land appropriations which cause tension and ill feeling. Israel claims that

Bedouin tribes deliberately usurp and graze their flocks on lands not belonging to them, for political reasons and to obtain financial compensation they are not entitled to. In so doing, they have caused health hazards as well as severe damage to agriculture. Their leaders concede that Israel has raised their standard of living but accuse it of continuing anti-Bedouin policies which date back to pre-independence times and other rulers.

The approximately 100,000 Arab Christians are even more sectarian and separatist than the Jews and Moslems, belonging to dozens of denominations, some of which exist only in Israel. They are descendants and a reminder of the historical presence of Christianity which was born and nurtured in the Holy Land. Almost every Christian sect, order and creed exists here, and a few have custody of some corner of one of the Christian Holy Places. Israel's Arab Christians live in the mixed cities and in large Arab towns. Generally, they are better educated and more affluent than the Moslems and somewhat better integrated within the Jewish State. Like Moslems and Jews they enjoy autonomy in matters of religion, education and personal status and like the latter, they are a minority in the Moslem Middle East.

Another interesting non-Jewish tribe is the Druze of Haifa's Mount Carmel, Galilee and Golan Heights. With their high white hats and baggy trousers, they do not quite look like nor are they actually even considered to be Arabs. Centuries ago they broke away from Islam and have since practiced a mysterious monotheistic religion of their own. Their most venerated Saint is the Prophet Shu'eib whom they claim was Jethro, the father-in-law of Moses. The site of his tomb is their major religious shrine.

Druze tribes are scattered about the Middle East, many living in Syria. In Israel they enjoy the status of an autonomous religious community. They have shown their loyalty to the Jewish State by sending their sons to serve in the army and Border Police, special combat units known for their courage. As a non-conformist and secret sect, they have suffered oppression and persecution in Arab and Moslem countries. In spite of official favoritism they do not quite feel accepted or trusted by Israelis and younger Druze are sometimes as vocal as Moslem Arabs about what they claim is government discrimination against them.

Karaites and Samaritans each practice an ancient religion resembling Judaism but neither are regarded as Jews. Karaism, from the Hebrew *qara* to study scripture, was founded in the 7th century in Persia by opponents of Rabbanism. The Karaites, numbering about 1,000, believe in Scripture — the Jewish Bible, but do not accept the written liturgy and Commentaries of the Rabbinical tradition, the Talmud and Mishna. They have their own synagogues and minister-readers rather than rabbis.

Samaritans are named after the province of Samaria on the west bank of the Jordan river, where they still live. They reject not only the Talmud and Mishna, but all of the Old Testament except the Torah — the Five Books of Moses and Joshua. Today there are only several hundred left, descendants of an ancient nation.

Israel is also the spiritual center of the Bahai faith which originally developed out of Babism, one of the sectarian deviations of the Shi'ite branch of Islam. The approximately 2 million followers of Bahai throughout the world believe in the unity of all religions and in universal peace and education and have their major shrine and religious headquarters in Haifa. The remains of the Bab martyr founder were smuggled out of Persia a hundred years ago and his tomb in Israel is the center of their main shrine.

As in previous centuries, the Holy Land is the destination

and sometimes home of dozens of other religions, cults, communes and sects of every background and description. They are picturesque, quaint and even weird, and their presence here is part of the human mosaic of Israel.

Why do Jews answer every question with another question?
Why not?

Chapter Three

THE ESTABLISHMENT CULTURE

HOLIDAYS AND JEWISH HAPPENINGS

Deep rooted religious and historical differences as well as present day realities have preserved the age old cultural traditions of Jews and Arabs. National and religious holidays and even the calendar of each are different. Jews count from the beginning of Creation and the year 1980 of the Christian Era is equivalent to 5741 in the Jewish year. The Islamic calendar commences with the Hijrah flight of the Prophet Mohammed from Mecca to Medina in Saudi Arabia in 622 CE. The Christian day of rest on Sunday is just another work and school day for Moslems and Jews; for the latter it is the first day of the week after their own Sabbath. Moslems have their day of rest on Fridays.

The ten days from *Rosh HaShana* (literally, head of the year) through *Yom Kippur* (Day of Atonement), are the *Yamim Noraim* "Days of Awe" for Jews everywhere. This is the season of repentance and the time according to ancient tradition when God's judgment of every man and woman is decided for the coming year. On the fast of Yom Kippur the entire country suddenly slows down and for a single day comes to a strange and complete halt. The usual pandemonium and excitement give way to a totally quiet and pensive Israel.

No Jewish school, shop, office, factory, restaurant or café in the entire country is open. There are no newspapers, television or radio programs. No cars are seen in the streets except for a rare police patrol or ambulance. Even secular and agnostic Jews participate in sundown to sundown fasting and many go to Synagogue. In the afternoon, families slowly walk around the silent streets in a kind of communion, before they go home to await the sunset that brings the end of the prayer and fasting that has lasted 24 hours.

Succoth (Feast of Tabernacles) marks the autumn harvest and *Simchat Torah* (Rejoicing of the Law) celebrates the completion of the annual reading of the Torah. *Hannukah* (Feast of Lights) commemorating the victory of the ancient Maccabean warriors against Greek oppressors, is an especially happy time for children. On *Tu Bishvat* (Arbor Day) classes go out to plant cypress, pine or what the Arabs call the "Jewish" tree — the eucalyptus — and there is singing and dancing in schools and kindergartens. Each *Pesach* (Passover) families sit down together to eat unleavened bread *matzot* and ceremoniously read the story of the exodus of the Jews from bondage in Egypt. Children ask and elders tell of the miraculous escape and victory of the ancient Hebrews, a particularly pertinent story for Israelis.

Shavuoth (Pentecost) celebrates the first harvest, as well as the giving of the Law to Moses on Mt. Sinai. Israel's Halloween and New Year's eve comes at *Purim*, commemorating the saving of the ancient Persian Jews from destruction by order of the wicked Haman. It is the occasion for a brief, almost pagan atmosphere and mischievous children parade around in Halloween-like masquerades, while adults hold relatively uninhibited parties until the morning hours. For Israelis who ordinarily never drink liquor or have office parties, Purim has become the time of the year for making whoopee.

The highlight of the year comes on *Yom Ha'atzmaut* (Independence Day). It is preceded by Martyrs' Day in memory of the victims of Nazism and Memorial Day for the dead of five wars with the Arabs. There is hardly a home without a black framed picture of a family loved one. In the evening, sirens mark the end of the 24 hours of mourning and the beginning of merry-making that will take place in every town and city. Entertainment platforms and centers come alive and crowds sing and dance in the streets until after midnight.

Until recently, the holiday was climaxed ·by an army parade and mass public celebrations. The giant parade in 1968 celebrated the 20th year of independence and the victory of the Six Day War a year earlier. The largest ever held, it was seen by nearly half-a-million spectators. Hundreds of thousands of others watched on blurry television sets that inaugurated the coming of that blessing to Israel. During the 30th year of independence in 1978, there were special events in Israel and in major Jewish population centers of the free world, but no military parades.

Other happenings in Israel have turned into semi-official holidays. The *Maimuna* festival of North African Jews has spread to Israel with European Jews also joining in mass picnics and celebrations. *Tel Hai* day commemorates the last battle and death of the legendary warrior Yosef Trumpeldor whose final words were " . . . how good it is to die for one's own country". *Yom Hastudentim* (Students Day) is the once a year time for Israel's hard pressed college men and women to let their hair down and indulge in the pranks and fun that are an everyday thing on the campuses of America.

The annual March to Jerusalem has grown from a casual event to a national and international craze and tent cities spring up overnight to house an army of marchers. Institutions and companies train their best people for months in pursuit of the prestigious first prize. Teenagers and old timers join in the final ascent to the flower covered, crowded streets of the capital. Large contingents of visitors from abroad always join in, along with housewives, students, entire families, African trainees, diplomats and just plain hiking enthusiasts in Israel's annual carnival of walking fun.

There are *Maccabia* "Jewish Olympic" games, book fairs, a *Zimriya* song festival and concert hall festivals for children, Hassidic and Sephardic song festivals and a Druze *"Fantazia"* celebration in honor of Jethro. A Film Festival, kibbutz run Dance Festival, International Piano and Harp contests and even a Bach festival are annual events and hardly a day goes by without some other congress, festival or international convention somewhere in Israel. The main thing is to renew old traditions, initiate new happenings and to do things as well or better than they are done in other countries.

SCHOOLS, TEACHERS

For the People of the Book, education and culture have been of critical importance in the Jewish renaissance as well as vital forces for national unity. Bold solutions were necessary to cope with enormous problems especially those resulting from the large scale immigration from Middle Eastern countries following the War of Independence. Within two years school attendance increased nearly eight-fold from 100,000 to 800,000! While Israel was struggling for its economic life and very existence, it was required to find teachers and build schools for more than a half million new pupils, almost none of whom spoke Hebrew.

For years shacks and tents served as classrooms and schools and even today school buildings and equipment are hardly up to American standards. At best they are very simple, at worst depressingly inadequate. Wooden desks and benches remind the visitor of pictures of country schools in rural America. A crash program designed to solve the shortage of trained teachers in a short time was only partially successful. Poor salaries and difficult working conditions discouraged qualified men from entering what was already a woman's profession. Classes are still crowded, almost all of the teachers are female and sometimes two shifts have been necessary. Today most afternoon sessions have been eliminated but schools and classes are still larger than desirable.

In addition to these burdens, Israeli teachers are faced with classes made up of pupils from totally different cultural backgrounds. Few immigrant youngsters arrived with schooling that was on the level of Israeli children. Their faltering Hebrew and the inability of parents to help also inhibited progress and only a few years after independence, Israel already had an educational gap between the veterans and immigrant communities. An especially long school day was necessary but Israeli schools usually operate only till noon or 1 pm. Those who could not adjust became problem pupils and school dropouts. Today special programs and scholarship assistance for Oriental-Sephardi immigrants enable more to stay in school, but the gap is there.

In the land of the People of the Book (until 1978), a child who reached the age of fifteen had no legal right to education at State expense, nor was he even obliged to be in school. For thirty years, enrollment in the last three years of high school required payment of substantial tuition fees and tens of thousands of able kids were forced to give up what is taken for granted in most countries.

Now, free and compulsory secondary school education is provided for tenth graders (high school sophmores) and qualified pupils, with free education in junior and senior years as well. The catch is, that the school system is still based on the European model of turning out an intellectual elite, rather than the American style, open, mass education for all. What Israel needs so badly is to bring the disadvantaged Oriental children back to school, but most secondary school graduates and the great majority of college students are Ashkenazis, and this pattern is changing very slowly. A long school day and compulsory tuition free schooling are worth whatever sacrifices are required. More than most nations, Israel must rely on its young and success or failure in the years to come will depend on today's students.

The educational system in the country also reflects the singular connection of religion and state. Government schools give extensive courses in Bible but this is not sufficient for adherents of the religious political parties. They operate a parallel system of government supported religious schools where Torah, Talmud and Orthodox values are emphasized, albeit at the expense of secular subjects and there is even a "religious" (Bar Ilan) University. This is not enough for the extremist Orthodox, who have their own system of schools with an ultra-Orthodox orientation which the government reluctantly supports.

Christian churches, missionaries and others operate schools and are recognized by the Ministry of Education. The Baptist community of the US operates a school, and the American Zionist Organization maintains a boarding school as well as their impressive ZOA House cultural center in Tel Aviv. Another English language "American" school is located in the prosperous suburb of Kfar Shmaryahu, catering to children of the diplomatic and business colony and affluent or social climbing Israelis. Not to be outdone, each of the three major kibbutz movements conducts *batei hinuch* (houses of education) where the emphasis is on a maximum of pioneering socialist values and minimum of religion.

Israeli children are rarely too young to be in school. Government run kindergartens accept four year olds and private *ganim* (nurseries) in every neighborhood are filled with children of only two-and-a-half and three. For the children of working mothers there are creches that accept one and two year olds. In these institutions, they have their first supervised social contact with children their age and the world outside their homes. Years before they would be enrolled in any educational framework anywhere else, toddlers in Israel are learning about national holidays and heroes and already addressing teachers and adults by their first names. At nineteen some will become jet pilots and at thirty, colonels and university professors.

The most famous institutions of higher learning and among the most highly regarded anywhere are Jerusalem's Hebrew University and Israel's MIT, the Technion in Haifa. There are smaller government municipal and private colleges, teachers' seminaries and schools in other parts of the country. Scientific and research institutes are headed by the prestigious Weizmann Institute, Negev Institute, Nuclear Physics Center and National Physics Laboratory. The achievements of the scientific community of Israel have been stunning. Although businessmen, lawyers and kibbutzniks are prominent in the political leadership, Israel almost always chooses a scholar or intellectual to be its President.

While Jewish students in the States and Europe have often been in the forefront of college rebellions, their Israeli counterparts are suspiciously well behaved. There is no youth counter culture, little experimentation with drugs or radical politics and hardly any sexual revolution. There is no ferment or real action of any kind on the Israeli campus; in fact there is hardly any campus since most of the limited space available is. filled with classrooms and laboratories. The students of Israel in fact, are totally absorbed by that relatively prosaic pursuit called studying.

They are older and more mature than their western counterparts, and while eighteen year old freshmen in America are busy with fraternities, sports or parading around in ROTC or national guard units, Israelis their age are fighting real wars. Most college men and women are really just that. They are at least twenty-one and usually older; many are in their 30's and 40's and have completed three years in the army. Some are married or fathers and holding a job by the time they enroll in University.

There are no fraternities, university athletics and little of the year round, good natured nonsense and ritual that is such an integral part of the American campus. Intense studies, examinations and responsibilities of family and work leave Israeli students with no time for frivolity, even if they were so inclined. Students as such do not constitute a separate social class and studying is less a way of life than in other countries. They are simply clerks, workers and soldiers who happen to be students, a necessary and difficult means to a specific end for the career minded Israelis. For a few female students *chupalogy* (marriage altar) is the real main course and finding an *academai* (academic) for a husband is the major goal.

These factors explain the unusual lack of tension on the Israeli campus. Youthful individuality and rebellion has been tempered by army service and the immense demands of adult life in Israel. It does not mean they are satisfied with the establishment or the world they live in. They complain and occasionally demonstrate against a variety of ills from the high cost of tuition or the poor food in the student cafeteria to the hypocrisy of the political leadership and its inability to solve the problems of the country. Nevertheless, there are no riots or violent protests. If there were, the fact that almost all students are trained soldiers with access to weapons would produce disorders that would make those in other countries seem tame in comparison. These tough corporals and captains are often *studentim.*

Evening high schools designed for working adults as well as public and private institutions compete to broaden the horizon of all Israelis. A veritable flood of courses and schools offer instant knowledge and training in almost every possible occupation and subject. The army does more than its share and teaches recruits basic schooling and civilian trades as well as making them efficient soldiers. There are libraries all over the country, but most are small. The two million volume National Library in Jerusalem is equal to the best anywhere and almost every home has its bookshelf or private library.

Israelis write as much as they read and the country ranks second in the world after the Soviet Union in number of titles published annually in proportion to the population. The daily press is no less politically and linguistically heterogeneous than the population and Israel boasts a dozen daily newspapers. There are hundreds of magazines, pamphlets and newsletters and though there is no commercial Underground press, one can read This World (nudes and politics) and Good Will (politics and gossip), as well as topical, professional and scholarly journals of every leaning and in almost every language.

CULTURE, LIGHT & HEAVY

The most popular book in the country is easily the Old Testament. This is the Jewish family tree and the "Roots" of much of Israel's history. Interest in the Bible is widespread and affects every level of the population. Courses in its religious, cultural and national aspects are obligatory and are major subjects every year from first grade through high school. Study circles in every community meet weekly to study and debate Biblical subjects.

Ben Gurion's unorthodox theory about the actual number of Israelites in the Exodus from Egypt caused serious repercussions in the Labor-Religious parties' political coalition. Local, national and international Bible contests evoke intense interest and are even held in prisons and army camps, with spectators following the competition with Scripture in hand. TV and radio accounts of these events are no less exciting to the entire nation than international championship ball games.

Popular interest in the Bible is connected to other national crazes such as hiking, walking and especially archaeology, which is a centuries old tradition in the Holy Land. Possibly it is inspired by the hope of proving some Biblical theory or religious belief or disproving those of other religions. Today, professionals and amateurs from every walk of life join major expeditions and excavations. Action reports and publications are issued from the scene of the digs as though from a battlefield and findings cause great national excitement.

The best known Israeli archaeologists are former army Chief of Staff and deputy Prime Minister Yigael Yadin and former minister Moshe Dayan, who is a weekend enthusiast and owner of a large personal collection. The interest of old soldiers in the Old Testament and archaeology may be more than a sentimental coincidence. Ancient battles and campaigns are recorded in the Holy Book and they have been fought again in modern times. The "Burma" road that broke the Arab siege of Jerusalem in 1948 was discovered in a biblical reference and there have been other such examples.

Some of the world's greatest archaeological finds have been uncovered in Israel in the modern era. The parchments found by a Bedouin inside a cave in the Judean Desert now known as the Dead Sea Scrolls, contain complete manuscripts of the Book of Isaiah dating back to the pre-Christian era. Almost every new dig uncovers further confirmation of biblical stories, references and legends and is a major event in Israel.

Israelis also love going to the movies and there are hundreds of theaters in the country while portable projectors and screens bring films to isolated settlements and military outposts. Most come from England, France and America but they are also imported from Japan, Sweden, Poland and even the Arab countries. The latter, purchased indirectly in Europe are popular with Israel's Arabs and Oriental immigrants who delight in the melodramatic Arab style romantic-musical-comedies. A small but growing Israeli cinema industry offers its products to eager audiences and the locally made films about the rescue at Entebbe Airport and "Lemon Popsicle" Israel's "Grease" broke all records here and were equally popular abroad. Moshe Dayan's handsome son Asaf, not to be outdone by his famous father or writer sister Yael, is a sought after movie star and Israeli actors Theodore Bikel, Dahlia Lavi and Chaim Topol appear in international films.

Tickets are sold in advance for three separate performances and scalping for the most popular shows is a frequent occurrence in big city cinemas. Although the government television station has been stealing away some audiences, good foreign and local pictures are as successful as ever. Films are preceded by short commercials like those on American TV but Israelis are a hostile captive audience and clap their hands and stamp in rhythmic impatience. Just when they can stand no more invitations to buy soaps, chocolates and washing machines the feature goes on. These commercials are a convenient background for the arguments that invariably break out in different parts of the theater where people are sitting in the wrong seats or the same seats have been sold twice. Folding chairs are brought out, tempers cool and the show finally goes on.

In some movie houses the sound track is accompanied by empty soda bottles rolling down the aisles, crackling sounds of sunflower seeds and the tears of infants brought by parents who cannot afford or do not believe in baby sitters. Films are subtitled in Hebrew and either French or English and there is no dubbing. This is why there are some not so quietly whispered explanations here and there, for those who do not understand those languages. Americans who find they cannot hear the dialogue even in English but who know Hebrew, may end up reading the subtitles of Hollywood movies.

Some theaters screen art films and cater to a more subdued audience, while others feature extravaganzas or westerns. One Tel Aviv cinema specializes in classical-romantic films from Germany and Austria for the same delighted audience of Yekkes each week. Others screen home grown schmaltz, called *Borekas* or "Bulgarian westerns" and romantic-comedy films made especially for Israelis. Once a week the silver screen goes up in army camps, border outposts, moshav community centers and in kibbutz dining halls.

Theater going is also popular and more Israelis attend

proportionately than in any other country. At least a dozen repertory and independent theaters and dance companies perform classical, contemporary, ethnic and Israeli works. Like the movies, they travel to rural and outlying areas and sometimes appear abroad. The range of theater encompasses everything from Shakespeare to Kabuki and Virginia Woolf, all in Hebrew. There is theater in Yiddish, English, Arabic and a dozen other languages and there is scarcely a settlement or institution without its troupe. Pop music and Israeli style vaudeville round out the light entertainment scene.

Mighty Samson and King David were the athlete heroes of Biblical Israel and symbolize the tradition of sport that has been renewed in the new Israel. The almost year long summer, proximity to the sea and the stress on physical courage have made sports consciousness natural. Twenty years ago few Israelis dreamed that the Maccabi basketball team from Tel Aviv, led by American immigrants and including a Black Jewish super-star, would be champions of Europe or that the national soccer team would be a three time, gold medalist of the Asian games. Today sports fans demand Olympic victories.

Contrary to popular belief, most Israelis are not in very good physical condition. Relatively few play or work out on a regular basis and most eat, smoke, work and worry too much. Those who indulge do so naturally, in athletic organizations that are affiliated with political parties, and are entirely amateur or semi-pro. While a Democratic Party Baseball League, Republican Party Golf Association or Women's Lib Boxing Club is unlikely, it is suggestive of the nature of athletics in Israel. The largest sports club is the Labor party controlled *Hapoel* and their teams in the cities and cooperative settlements are especially fond of basketball and soccer. *Maccabi* was founded by a rival political movement and neither would consider a sports coalition or merger.

The *Herut* (Freedom) party sponsors *Betar* (The Trumpeldor Alliance) whose enthusiasts indulge in the usual team games as well as the manly art of boxing and weight-lifting. *Elitsur*, the Religious party sports club, does not compete on the Sabbath and emphasizes non-violent sports such as rowing, sailing and gymnastics. There is skiing on Mount Hermon in the Golan Heights, ice skating on a unique (synthetic) surface, fencing, gliding, scuba diving, lane and lawn bowling and even cricket players can indulge in their game in Israel. Sheshbesh, chess and cards are popular with the older set. Practically the only games not played are those exotic new world eccentricities, football and baseball.

How good and pleasant it is
that brethren dwell together
(Psalms)

Chapter Four

ONLY IN ISRAEL

THE KIBBUTZ

For serious students of Israelology, as far removed as Scandinavia, Africa and Japan, the *kibbutz* (communal village — from the Hebrew word "group") is its unique and perhaps most admired attraction. The first such settlement Degania (Cornflower), was founded on the banks of the Jordan River seventy years ago by young Jews who fled Czarist Russia. They rejected both the communist revolution and its glowing slogans, and the life of prayer and religious study of Orthodox Jewry. Seeking a new way to combine the best in Zionism and socialism, they came to Palestine with high hopes, energy and zeal.

In the *yishuv* (Jewish community) of those days, there were neither capitalists nor exploited revolutionary masses. The Promised Land was only a dismal backwater — "forbidding isolation" was Mark Twain's description following his visit to the Holy Land in the late 19th century — a mere subprovince in the giant Turkish empire, the few Jewish settlements already started were floundering in the face of ruin or obscurity. The only land available for cultivation was filled with malarial swamps and rocky time wasted soil.

A communal farm, the *kibbutz*, became the answer. This new settlement and its new way of life would replace the individual and the family as the basic social unit. It would be the heart of the renewed Jewish society where happiness and justice for all would prevail. The community would be a collective man and not just a collective of men and a living example of the "Religion of Labor" Zionist philosophy. It would emphasize a return to physical labor and nature to achieve national renaissance through a merging of the spirit of nature in the Land of Israel, with the spirit inherent in the People of Israel. It would play a key role in shaping the development of the renascent Jewish community in Palestine.

This was the background and inspiration for the first and only permanent, large-scale utopia in modern times. Settlers lived, worked, shared, suffered and triumphed together in enlarged family groups. Their kibbutz was a completely voluntary collective, as contrasted with the Kolkhoz agricultural commune of Soviet Russia and soon attracted the best of the young Jewish pioneers. It became responsible for the labor, services and needs of all its members. All property and profits belonged to it. "From each according to his ability and to each according to his need," the credo of an assimilated anti-Zionist Jew named Karl Marx became the working slogan of the first modern really "communist" community and formed the basis of the hundreds founded after it.

Through one for all and all for one cooperation, the *kibbutzniks* became one of the crucial instruments of national rebirth. They cleared stones, drained swamps and irrigated deserts. From the fragile watchtowers, tents and donkey-pulled plows of the first days, the *kibbutzim* slowly but surely worked the grudging soil and became affluent, modern farming communities. Out of their way of life grew a growing strength and moral force that carried a great share of the Zionist enterprise that culminated in the creation of the State of Israel. It inspired much of the self-sacrifice, stubbornness, puritanism, egalitarianism and national pride that characterize the people of Israel.

Today the 250 odd kibbutzim retain much of their basic original framework. Most settlers are second and third generation descendants of the Ashkenazi-European founders. They are still small agricultural villages of 50 to 200 families who live in utilitarian rooms or efficiency apartments and take their meals together in the communal dining hall. The kibbutz supplies every need of its members from toothbrush to housing to organized picnics and theater outings.

On a majority of kibbutzim, infants leave their parents' care and custody after nursing and grow up with boys and girls their age in the dormitory-style children's house. Each year they graduate from house to house until as a group, they join and serve in the army together. At eighteen each receives his and her own room and are admitted to formal membership on the kibbutz. Until then they eat, sleep and learn the lessons of life in the children's houses under the supervision of trained counselor-teachers.

Every kibbutz is run by elected committees and the major problems of the community and its members are discussed and resolved at the weekly "Town Hall" meetings. Except for one Communist Party kibbutz and a dozen settlements affiliated with the Religious and Herut parties, they are part of the Labor movement and its political parties and constitute a key part of their power base.

New collectives are founded each year and endure hard

days, while veteran settlements like the rest of Israel have grown prosperous. Once spartan rooms are furnished with modern furniture, TV sets, hi fi's and refrigerators and members of established kibbutzim now enjoy holiday trips to Europe. Other changes in the traditional way of life are significant as younger people unabashedly spend allowances on formerly frowned upon city sins like pop records and cigarettes. Smoking is no longer forbidden though some of the puritan influence remains and liquor, lipstick, modish clothes and sexual permissiveness are unusual.

The total devotion to kibbutz and nation building brought surprising notions about sexual activities and this influence is still felt. As the Orthodox Jews are wed to the Sabbath Bride or Queen, kibbutz founders expended their energy and zeal on Mother-Israel Earth. A whole generation of young men and women sublimated libidal and romantic urges in favor of the soil. Sex and procreation was approached in a matter-of-fact "let's get it over with" manner and back-to-work thing that is still entrenched in the national psyche of the country.

The most startling difference is that the once socialist kibbutz has gone capitalistic. Simple workshops of a few years ago have grown into successful plants and industries. Now the problem is finding enough workers to man the factories. With no other way to solve chronic manpower shortages, they rely more and more on salaried and day laborers from nearby Arab villages and Jewish development towns. Caught in the constant spiral of industrial expansion, the movement has strayed from the heritage of an egalitarian farming community. The image of the pioneering farmer kibbutznik is rapidly becoming only a sentimental memory. Today many kibbutzim are semi-industrial employers and their children are sent to the Technion and Weizmann Institute to learn industrial science, and management.

Although they have small fields, tough soil and inadequate water supplies, kibbutzim have produced bountiful yields that have broken records everywhere. Only three percent of Israel's Jewish population produce one third of its agricultural products and export to dozens of countries, in one of Israel's greatest success stories. A surprising number of military and political leaders of Israel including the late Ben Gurion, and Eshkol, Allon, Ben Aharon and Yaari live on kibbutzim. Approximately twenty percent of the army pilots and combat officers are sons of the movement. Even so, they have lost much of the romanticism and moral leadership of 30 and 50 years ago.

In those days of fire and glory before the State was born, there were monumental tasks to be done in absorbing new immigrants and providing elite military units and the kibbutzim did their share and more. Like the stately homes and castles of Britain's aristocracy, once proud kibbutzim are now open to the paying public. Some have profitable guest houses, catering to tourists, while others have made a business out of music and dance festivals, museums and other local attractions.

Some kibbutzniks drop out, lured by career possibilities in the cities or in search of privacy, individual needs and aspirations they cannot fulfil at home. New immigrants are usually not interested in replacing them except for adherents of kibbutz youth organizations in Europe and the Americas. Once proud and self-confident kibbutzim are compelled to seek new blood through advertisements in the daily newspapers showing pictures of laughing, happy children and parents and asking the reader to ..."Think it over. Perhaps the kibbutz is the place for you. If you are healthy and able to work, if you feel qualified to fit into the social and cultural environment of a kibbutz, here is your chance" ...

The average kibbutznik is indeed a healthy, resourceful and decent person and their youth are highly regarded leaders in the academic, business and military world or Zionist emissaries and diplomats. Even after compulsory military service, many volunteer for an extra year in the army or in some new or struggling kibbutz. Embarrassingly few go out to help the immigrants in the nearby development towns who serve as their hired hands or in the city slums where there is so much pioneering to be done.

The kibbutzim keep busy these days with their own settlements and the acquisition of greater affluence and material comforts. After half a century of nation building, their unspoken slogan has become, "What's good for the nation is good for the kibbutz." Despite the erosion of their position they remain a source of pride to all Israel and an important link with the land in a rapidly urbanizing country. For visitors a look at these communal settlements is still a highlight of their trip. To a steady flow of officials and trainees from the developing countries, the kibbutz is Israel's most intriguing accomplishment.

THE MOSHAV

While the kibbutz is more startling and unusual and has attracted attention all over the world, there is another, equally successful and popular cooperative village in Israel — the *moshav* (literally — seat, or domicile). Moshe Dayan spent most of his early years at *Nahalal* after the biblical settlement of the same name, the first moshav established in Israel, and Chief of Staff Raful Eitan has always been a *moshavnik*. No less than the kibbutz it has played an important role in nation building over and beyond its numbers.

Each moshav is composed of a few dozen and sometimes scores of families engaging in agriculture, light industry and regional services. It is also based on the principle of physical labor and mutual help for the common good. The Collective Moshav (*moshav shitufi*) is most similar to the kibbutz. This is a farming commune where all land, capital, tools, labor as well as homes are common property of the community. The main difference is the complete freedom allowed each family to live as a separate unit and to pursue its individual life style.

There are no communal dining rooms, laundry, infirmary or children's dormitories here. Every family lives together in its own house and controls its own budget as it sees fit. Each works its own plot but does so with the help of its neighbors. Here too, all income is divided on the socialist principle of share and share alike and prosperity and failure are communal concerns. The committees and town meetings make for a cracker barrel democracy and decide matters of mutual concern such as work assignments, marketing, education and culture. While the family lives together in its own home and has greater freedom of choice, the moshav is very much a commune.

Founded in 1921, Nahalal was a breakaway from both kibbutz and the moshav shitufi which would soon follow. The latter resembles a small farming village, with neighborly cooperation between the families. Each owns and works its own plot and retains all earnings for itself. Supplies and equipment are purchased jointly, but only because this is more efficient and productive and not for ideological reasons. The committee management of the kibbutz and moshav shitufi exist here as well, but plays a small role. Only in times of distress does the one for all — all for one motto become meaningful. Here it is the homesteader and not the settlement who determines the success and way of life of each family.

The Industrial Moshav (*moshav ta'asiati*) was created in the last decade by and for those not interested in agriculture or for whom no land or water was available. It has attracted second and third generation *moshavniks* and immigrants who want to live in a collective away from the city, where they can develop workshops and industries based on science and sophisticated manufacturing. These villages also retain the committee administration and other attributes of the moshav, but not the farming atmosphere.

The newest and least known is the Regional Center (*moshav ezori*) and was set up by the government and moshav movement to provide central community services such as schools, police, fire and ambulance for the nearby moshavim. They facilitate joint production and export facilities for settlements in the area but retain the small village atmosphere and way of life of the other moshavim and the kibbutz.

Unlike the kibbutz the moshav has proved popular with Sephardi-Oriental immigrants and their villages are among the most prosperous and successful in the country. It has also proven attractive to developing countries of the third world who admire but are not ready for the bold changes of the kibbutz. Model moshavim have been established in Africa, Asia and Latin America. In contrast to the kibbutz, there are waiting lines for the few moshavim in Israel that are willing to accept new members.

ZAHAL — THE ISRAEL DEFENSE FORCES

There is an Israeli institution that retains the unbounded affection and respect of the people the kibbutz enjoyed just yesterday. Like the kibbutz movement it has been a crucial factor in the social and educational sense and in the merging of the exiles. The unexpected developments of the Yom Kippur War both tarnished and yet confirmed its image. It is the Israeli Army — *Tsava Hagana*

Le-Yisrael, abbreviated to *Tsahal* (or *Zahal*), in English the Israel Defense Forces (IDF) — and it is like no other army in the world.

This is the first Jewish army since 135 CE, when Bar Kochba led the final rebellion against the Roman conquerors of ancient Judah that ended with the capture of Massada. No less than home and job, it occupies a major part of the life of every Israeli family. Male and female citizens and permanent residents are drafted for active military service at 18 and after discharge remain eligible for *miluim* (reserve duty). In effect, every civilian remains a part-time soldier for 30 years and some fathers serve with their sons. The Israeli male not so jokingly claims to be a professional soldier who is permitted to enjoy some civilian life.

Only at 40 or 50 years of age can he expect to be transferred to a second line combat unit often referred to as *Ha'kash* (Old Men's Army) or to *Haga* (Civil Defense Corps), till old age prevents him from serving. For many this final transfer from combat duty is a sad and even traumatic occasion.

Teenage girls are drafted for two years, as in no other army, even in peace time; boys serve for three years. After basic military training they usually perform clerical, communications and other non-combative duties, such as teaching and nursing, that release men for fighting units. Although there are some women who see action in frontline combat units, the female paratrooper Jewish Amazon Wonder Woman is largely a fantasy invented by and for males by writers of cheap fiction and PR men. The real woman soldier is not very much like these cheap and often vulgar descriptions, and is an accepted, popular and important part of Zahal.

Every reserve army unit has a liaison office in the large cities and its emergency store of weapons and equipment. Reservists report to their units intermittently and serve in active duty for periods totalling up to two or three months annually. Practice mobilization, lectures, courses and intensive combat exercises help maintain a high standard of fighting ability. When necessary, essential units can be assembled and made battle-ready within 24 or 48 hours after call-up. These civilian soldiers also share in the family celebrations and personal problems of their buddies as in no other army and this deep, personal involvement of Israel soldiers in each other's lives is another essential element of the IDF.

Paramilitary training begins early, in the secondary schools and youth movements where *Gadna* (Youth Battalions) teaches them what war is about and how to use firearms. Gifted and motivated pupils are encouraged to undergo specialized training for future careers as pilots, naval or army officers in the military boarding schools operated by the Ministry of Defense. Others join *Nahal* (Pioneering Fighting Youth) where would-be kibbutzniks and moshavniks enlist together for a pioneering life combined with army service. After basic training they receive agricultural instruction at an established settlement and then are off to a dangerous or isolated border area to start a new outpost. This is continued by other Nahal units after them and eventually becomes a civilian community. Dozens of thriving present day kibbutzim and moshavim were started as Nahal outposts or in the programs combining military training and religious study.

The unusual valor and ability of the Israeli army has proven startling to many. Although cynical observers suggest that it is due to the relative incompetence of Arab armies and their disunity, most experts acknowledge that pound for pound the Israeli soldier is one of the best anywhere. Collectively in squad, regiment, division and army, they have more than once raised military prowess to new heights. The phenomenal exploits of soldiers like Meir Har Zion have become legendary in their lifetime. Commanders and generals such as Rabin, Sharon, Gur and Eitan are given high marks for their military brilliance and daring.

Ancient Israel also had its share of battles and warriors but during forty generations of wandering and persecution in the Diaspora, Jews were forced to depend on others for their defense and very lives. When they fought, often against Jews in other armies, it was for the nations where they lived and to whom they owed their allegiance. The memory of the Holocaust and the horrifying picture of unarmed, helpless Jews being led to death like sheep to the slaughter was a major catalyst in the emergence of the modern Jewish army.

The forerunner of Zahal was *Hashomer* (The Watchmen); made up of farmers and townsmen who patrolled on horseback to guard their young and isolated settlements in the decades before statehood. From this humble beginning came the Jewish Legion that fought with the Allies in World War I. Its successor was the *Hagana* (Defense) underground supported by the Jewish Agency and labor parties. The *Palmach* (Strike Force) was manned by members of kibbutzim and city adherents of the Zionist Socialist movement. *Irgun* (Organization) was an equally brave and dedicated partisan army led by Menachem Begin that had broken away from Hagana and its defensive posture and policy of non-violence and limited retaliation respectively, against British rule and Arab attacks.

Unlike Arab terrorists who are sometimes compared to it, Irgun did not indulge in kidnapping for ransom or murdering innocent and unarmed civilians. Military operations that backfired like Deir Yassin, the Arab village where non-combatant villagers were killed and the blowing up of the Mandatory offices in the King David Hotel are shrouded in mystery and controversy. They were rare exceptions to the battles of an outnumbered and outgunned few who fought fairly and bravely against advancing armies bent on the destruction of the entire Yishuv.

Atrocities, massacres and barbaric incidents were committed regularly by Arab armies and guerrillas against Israel's civilian population. In another of the ironies of modern history, Jews who were yesterday's ghetto fighters and escaped from what almost certainly would have been the completion of Hitler's Final Solution, are now called Nazis by their enemies. In today's Alice in Wonderland double talk, Arab men of action who boast of massacres such as Lod Airport, Ma'alot schoolhouse and the coastal road bus are "freedom fighters" to their admirers in a cynical world.

Lehi (Freedom Fighters of Israel), also known as the Stern Gang after Avraham Stern its founder, was a smaller and even more radical group of Hebrew soldiers. Originally part of the Irgun they insisted on continuing the rebellion against the Mandatory government during World War II, when other Jewish soldiers were engaged in battle against Axis armies.

In spite of different political orientation and military tactics, all of the underground fighters learned the lessons of war well. In 1947-48 they fought together and successfully defended the newborn State from the invading armies of Egypt, Syria, Jordan, Lebanon and Iraq.

Today the IDF is a unified force that is regarded as one of the best in the world. It is a "defense" army only in the sense that it is composed mainly of civilians who are mobilized when necessary, to defend their country. In a military sense it is an arrow rather than a shield, poised to strike out and destroy the enemy that threatens it. With so little territory available for retreat or defensive battle, it is oriented to fighting the aggressor on his land in blitzkrieg, all out campaigns or surprise strikes that will achieve quick, decisive and meaningful victory.

Key air and naval functions are manned by full time, professional soldiers and they maintain constant operational readiness. Zahal is built around a nucleus of career officers bolstered by draftees and reserve units. When fully mobilized it can field half a million trained soldiers. The country is divided into three autonomous military commands, approximately facing the borders of Egypt, Syria and Jordan where the major Arab armies are deployed. Every village and kibbutz along the border areas is armed and incorporated into the territorial defense system. Syrian army units and Palestinian terrorists in southern Lebanon opposite the formerly peaceful Galilee threaten to open still a new front against Israel.

Out of Zahal has come a small but sophisticated, military industrial complex that produces most of the equipment and weapons it needs. Each year it is less dependent on political winds of change and arms suppliers whose refusal to sell to Israel has made it more resourceful and self-sufficient.

Now *Uzi* sub-machine gun, *Galil* assault rifle and a full array of effective weapons from grenades to jet craft and rockets are eagerly sought after even by countries who once sold Israel arms and are now buyers of its high quality, battle tested products.

Since the Yom Kippur War there has been much harsh criticism of Zahal arms industry buildup and sales to countries such as South Africa, Nicaragua and Taiwan, the pampering of senior officers and the lack of discipline of soldiers. What was once a sacred cow is the open subject of public griping and complaints. In spite of it all, Israelis feel genuine affection for their army, its legends and heroes, and have popular museums that document its history and

99

achievements. Periodically a "Day" is dedicated to some army unit as municipalities and organizations vie with each other for the honor of "adopting" them. The IDF is the only national institution without the parties and politicians that have influenced such nonpolitical activities as education, sports, youth and labor movements.

Uniformed soldiers with compact *Uzis* slung over their shoulders are seen everywhere, yet their presence is taken for granted. High ranking officers enjoy no special status or privileges other than the esteem of the people and their absolute faith in times of war. There is no social caste of officers and to their friends and neighbors they remain Yankele and Shlomo. In another curious anomaly, the only colonels and generals who possibly threaten to take over the country are the retired senior officers. Now businessmen and technicians, some only in their thirties and forties, they have been swept up by industry and management eager to exploit their leadership and skills for civilian gain and profit.

This is an army that requisitions buses and trucks to bring soldiers to the front and then pays for the gas and any damage. It is an army where privates rarely salute officers and whose soldiers have an almost total disdain for military spick and span, but possess an overwhelming dedication and sense of duty in times of war. Zahal is middle-aged clerks and factory workers who compare family pictures and reminisce about old times as they ride together to report for reserve duty; where teenage tank commanders and pilots hitch rides home to kibbutz and town for the Sabbath, and girl-woman soldiers, singing in unison, march in perfect stride at army, navy and air force bases they serve in. It is the army that can mobilize overnight and disappear as quickly when the battle is won.

After the smashing victories of the Six Day War, there

was a state of euphoria and adulation of the IDF, with kits-
chy picture albums, books, records, exhibits and shows all
reaping the commercial rewards of those glorious days. The
chickens came home to roost when the Egyptian army cros-
sed the Suez Canal in the Yom Kippur War. Now the
superman image is gone forever, in spite of the astonishing
feat of throwing back the invading armies and striking deep
into the heart of Egypt. Unswerving trust in Zahal was
reconfirmed in the amazing raid on Entebbe Airport in
Uganda and the rescue of the skyjacked passengers in a
fantastic and brilliantly conceived and executed military
operation. Still, some things will never be what they were
in those days before the "Earthquake" of 1973, and many
now realize that this may be a positive development.

The seemingly boundless confidence of Israelis in Zahal is
in fact a major source of their strength. Faced with Arab
superiority in arms and numbers and their threats of endless new rounds, this confidence and the militant mood of
the country are unavoidable. Israelis are mindful of the lessons of history and the apparent danger if not inevitability
of conflict. Knowing these facts of life and conscious of the
consequences of defeat, they have developed an inner faith
in their strength and cause that is Israel's secret weapon. In
this cruel reality and the vicious circle of hot and cold wars
between Jew and Arab, it is this faith that makes life liv-
able.

HISTADRUT — A SPECIAL UNION

With such a long week and small pay check, it is
no wonder labor relations are not really very stable.
Industrial employees, academicians, and professionals are
ready to strike at the slightest grievance, but most problems
are usually solved thanks to that unusual union called the
Histadrut (Federation) of Israeli Labor. It is the largest union

101

in Israel and one of the most unique labor federations in the entire world. Membership exceeds the million mark and includes such "workers" as artists, lawyers, rabbis, nuns and cabinet ministers. It occupies a place in the country's life that has no parallel anywhere. Like the kibbutz, moshav and army, it is one of the most remarkable and original institutions of Israel.

The Histadrut was founded in 1919 by Jewish workers and farmers and has since grown into a state within a state and Israelis jokingly call its giant headquarters in Tel Aviv the Kremlin. Its Sick Fund medical and hospitalization services (*Kupat Holim*) cover the majority of the families in the country. It owns controlling shares in an international building industry (*Solel Boneh*) operating in Israel, Africa and Asia, a complex of factories and industries (*Koor*), the Co-op handling most of Israel s farm produce (*Tnuva*) and a supply agency for a variety of agricultural and industrial equipment (*Hamashbir Hamerkazi*). It is a partner in the national water development corporation (*Mekorot*) and shipping companies (*Zim*) and many other enterprises in Israel and abroad. It is the only labor union in the world that owns both a workers' bank (*Hapoalim*) and a capital investment company (*Ampal*).

There are few social or cultural activities in which the Histadrut is not active. It conducts classes in Hebrew conversation for new immigrants as well as seminars in philosophy and psychology for part-time intellectuals. It owns a publishing house (Am Oved), daily newspapers and supports *Hapoel* Israel's largest athletic club with branches in every sport and town. It is one of the most singular accomplishments of the Zionist movement.

Perhaps its proudest achievement is the Afro Asian Institute, which was established following requests for aid and assistance by developing nations in Africa. Since the early fifties it has conducted courses in Israeli methods of cooperatives and labor relations especially relevant to Third World and developing countries who want to learn from its experience. Lectures and material are in Spanish, French and English to accommodate the young officials, trainees and students from Africa, Asia and Latin America, often from nations who have broken or never had diplomatic relations with Israel. The Institute is only part of the technical assistance and aid given by Israel to the developing countries and may be the "light to the Gentiles" that was spoken of in the Bible.

Chapter Five

CHURCH AND STATE

THE STATUS QUO

Religious motifs are the first and most enduring links in the chain of history connecting the Jews with the Land of Israel. Belief in a national and spiritual redemption in Zion has been a fundamental aspect of Judaism since exile. It is towards Jerusalem that Jews turn when they pray three times a day: "May our eyes behold Thy return in mercy to Zion". On Passover and Yom Kippur, the prayers are climaxed by *Hashana Haba'ah b'Yerushalayim* — "Next Year in Jerusalem". Three weeks of mourning and fasting have marked the destruction of the Temple and the beginning of the Exile on every 9th day of the month of Av for 2,000 years.

The idealism and sacrifice of Jews who returned to Zion in every generation could not have been sustained had they come only to escape anti-Semitism or make the lost homeland a middle eastern Switzerland. It was the underlying consciousness and faith that their destiny lay here and in no other place that compelled their return to the ancient homeland.

From the biblical promise to the Patriarch Abraham "Unto thy seed will I give the land" until the present day, the life and culture of the Jewish people in their homeland have been inextricably bound up with religion. The Proclamation of Independence affirms "The State of Israel will be based on freedom, justice and peace as envisaged by the prophets of Israel. It will guarantee freedom of religion and conscience..." Political freedom has been won and there is a popular democracy in new Israel. Kibbutz and army are admired the world over and in a very substantial sense, there has been an awakening and vital renaissance of the Jewish people in their own country. However, real spiritual redemption and the flowering of religion have been dulled by the realities of Church and State.

There is no official or state religion in Israel. It is not even a theocracy in spite of what many believe, but only in Israel have "religious" political parties and "religious" politicians become so involved in non-religious activities and issues. In the land where once the Psalmist sang and the Prophets dreamed, religion is the domain of a government department — the Ministry of Religion. Religious leaders are engaged in the war on sin but are also battling against secularism, Reform Judaism and the separation of religion and state.

Religious "power" in Israel means religious political parties who hold key votes in the government coalition and a heavy price is paid for this alliance. It is within the power of a rabbi to blacklist a hotel that serves non-kosher food or conducts forums or entertainment on the Sabbath. A "religious" demonstration is an assembly of the Orthodox who protest the showing of films on the Sabbath or ceremoniously excommunicate Israeli physicians for performing post-mortem operations on bodies of deceased orthodox Jews, which they deem a religious sacrilege.

Relations between synagogue and state in Israel cannot possibly be understood except within the context of the history of religion in the Holy Land. The present status quo was established as long ago as the 7th century CE when Arab conquerors of Palestine made Islam the official religion. They granted protection and special, though still inferior, status to Christians and Jews whom they respected as "People of the Book" as opposed to heathens or unbelievers. For five centuries, the Turkish sultans who ruled after them and the British Mandate which followed the First World War also recognized these three religions by acknowledging the autonomy each had developed through the centuries.

This autonomy affected not only religious practices but was extended to all matters of so-called "personal status," such as determining the religion of their members, marriage, divorce and burial. Through their religious leaders and only through them, the "recognized" communities were granted religious freedom. This unique tradition was confirmed by the Congress of Berlin in 1878 which defined the rights and privileges of the autonomous religions. It was ratified by the UN decision which created a Jewish state but ruled that it do nothing to prejudice the religious rights "of the other communities in Palestine." It is this ruling that Israel's governments have defended to this very day.

Orthodox Judaism with its ritual and liturgy developed in the exilic period is not supposed to have officially preferred status in Israel apart from being, together with Islam and the traditional Christian sects, one of the three "recognized" religions. Both the Mandatory government and

Israel maintained the same delicate balance by refusing to grant such autonomy to other religions. Hence it is not so surprising that the Protestants, who arrived in the Middle East only after the status quo was in effect, do not have the government protected rights and privileges of the recognized Christian sects.

Protestants can worship freely and have their churches and Holy Places, but they do not have their own religious court. Reform rabbis are also denied the rights and privileges accorded to Orthodox Rabbis who regard them as an illegitimate aberration of the true faith, a sort of Jewish Protestantism. In spite of Orthodox hostility and official opposition stubborn Reform and Conservative leaders have succeeded in organizing more than a dozen congregations a school, settlement and youth movement and they have plans for more. If and when members of these congregations settle in Israel — and there have been very few so far — their claims for equality with traditional Orthodoxy may become more popular.

Freedom of religion in Israel in this sense is the freedom of traditional faiths to determine the spiritual life of persons registered as members of the various communities. Individual freedom of religious expression as known in the US is very much secondary, and is deemed violative of the centuries old rights of these communities. Israelis have reconciled themselves to this merging of religion and state more than the Jews in exile who are unaware of its historical background and who have grown up in a tradition of its firm separation.

Rabbinical Courts give legal sanction to judgments of rabbi judges, who possess exclusive jurisdiction in all matters pertaining to marriage, divorce and religious status of Jews, whether citizens or merely residents of Israel. Their rulings, even if offensive to the litigants, have the full power of law. A woman does not, for example, have equal rights before the law in matrimonial disputes with her husband. A widow without children must get *halitza* — which in essence is permission from her husband's eldest brother before being able to remarry — thus becoming a victim of humiliation at best and blackmail at worst. If she is declared to be a *moredet* (rebellious wife) according to the criteria of Rabbinic Law, she can be denied alimony payments.

There is a rabbinical ruling forbidding the marriage of a "Cohen" to a divorcée or widow. A few years ago this prevented none other than a leading Justice of the Israel Supreme Court from marrying the lady of his choice in his own country. He was the President of the International Organization of Jewish Lawyers and Jurists, but, as a Cohen, the Justice was deemed to be a descendant of the ancient priestly caste and forbidden by Orthodox religious law from marrying his fiancée. In spite of the furor and protest of the religious authorities, judge and divorcée were married abroad.

The Orthodox leadership is also engaged in a battle of nerves with Christian missionaries who claim that they are continually harassed and persecuted by official religious circles. The Rabbis contend that in other Middle Eastern countries missionaries are not allowed at all and that they exploit the poor and gullible Jewish immigrants and alienate children from their parents. The fact that missionary activity is carried on in church schools, youth clubs and slum neighborhoods lends some credence to these claims.

Under a recent law missionary activities that involve enticement of a person to change his religion by offering money or other material benefits can be deemed a criminal act. This legislation has been applauded by Orthodox Jews and deplored by civil rightists and Christian sects who allege that the law is really aimed against them. The statute does not mention any specific religion, nor does it prohibit missionary activity as such, only the use of financial payment to entice people to give up their religion for another. This law came into being in order to prevent the exploitation of the weak, but it also underlines the age old distrust that exists between the different religions in spite of the peaceful coexistence on the surface.

JEW & SUPER JEW

The conflict between the minority *dati'im* (religious) and majority *chilonim* (secular) Jews of Israel is accompanied by their apparent inability to enter into meaningful dialogue. The ultra-Orthodox will explain . . ."Anyone can see that Zionists are *epikorsim* (atheists) and responsible for the crime and moral decay in Israeli society. They let Jewish boys and girls learn together in the same classrooms and teach them such nonsense as biology and sports. Why, they even talk in the sacred Hebrew tongue which God intended for prayer only. This is surely too much for any reasonable Jew . . ."

These Super Jews are few in number and arouse the derision of many of Israel's non-religious citizens and embarrass some who are considered religious. A few refuse to pay taxes, report for military service or otherwise recognize the State and live in self-contained ghettos in Mea Shearim in Jerusalem and Bnai Brak, near Tel Aviv. Large printed notices warn the visitor " . . . O Daughter of Israel. The Torah obliges you to dress with modesty. We do not tolerate people passing through our streets immodestly dressed. Committee for the Preservation of Modesty . . ."

Long bearded and side curled men still wear the black caftan coat and large fur hats dating back to the Middle Ages. Boys and young men spend their days in Torah study and prayer as their fathers and grandfathers did in the Jewish *shtetls* (villages) of Russia and Poland for centuries before them. They maintain their own shops, schools, institutions and even their own separate ultra-Orthodox Rabbinical tribunals and have only superficial contact with the Israel that surrounds them.

The great majority of the Israelis are neither ultra-religious nor even Orthodox. They consist of secular and uncommitted Jews as well as the *masorti'im* (traditionalists), who respect the Sabbath and many religious traditions, but do not feel bound to follow all the Commandments of the Torah. All these "religious" Jews are distinguishable from the ultra-Orthodox in that they fully participate in all aspects of Israeli life. They live, work with, and share friendships with the approximately three quarters of the Israelis who are deemed secular. They may find some incompatibility between their own religious demands and orientation and the others but join with them in the shaping of the society in which all live.

This outward conflict is a product of irreconcilable attitudes towards the nature of Judaism. Each denomination worships the same God and Prophets of Israel but whereas the Orthodox believe in the divine revelation of the *Torah* (the Five Books of Moses), Reform and secular Jews only accept it in a rational and evolutionary context. In Israel a Jew may be agnostic or even atheist and none would deny that he is still a Jew but if he wishes to be "religious", Israeli fashion, he is required to be Orthodox. The Conservative school of Jewish belief is somewhere in the middle and tries to incorporate the best of both worlds. To be an Orthodox Jew still requires adherence to each of the 613 Commandments and *mitzvot* (obligatory good deeds) which were handed down to Moses on Mount Sinai or developed through the centuries by Orthodox Rabbinical sages. It is this rigid observance to a way of life which defies the

111

reason and instincts of most Jews today and alienates them from fundamentalist Judaism.

The Orthodox discrimination against the Reform and Conservative movements in Israel is especially ironic for western Jews who are members or sympathizers of these denominations. Christians and Moslems enjoy full religious autonomy and maintain their own Ecclesiastical Courts. Even the Druze were recently granted the status of an autonomous religious community. Protestant ministers, while not accorded all of the legal rights of "recognized" Christian clergymen can now perform valid marriage ceremonies in Israel for members of their faith.

Reform or Progressive Jewry as they are also known with nearly a thousand congregations in dozens of lands and more than one million members, is the invisible religion in the Holy Land. Together with Orthodoxy and Conservative Judaism it comprises the three branches of Jewry in the Americas and throughout the world. The Israeli economy, immigration authorities and fund raisers eagerly court them but they are rejected by the Rabbinate and Orthodox establishment. Correct relations are maintained with other faiths and even with the secular forces of Labor Zionism, but Orthodoxy in Israel will not grant equality to another form of Jewish religious expression.

A Reform Rabbi in Israel may pray or lead other Jews in prayer, but he is not regarded as a Rabbi in a legal sense. In fact he is virtually deprived of the right to practice his calling. He may not marry his congregants, join a religious tribunal or officiate at the funeral of any Jew in Israel. He is not permitted to serve as a Chaplain in Zahal because his ordination at world renowned, Progressive Jewish seminaries such as Hebrew Union College in America is not recognized by the Rabbinate.

There are Reform rabbis who have fought in combat units

in the army while ultra-Orthodox Jews refuse to serve a state some do not even recognize. Nonetheless the soldier rabbi and his congregants are denied the right to pray, men and women together in their fashion, at the Western Wall, the most sacred national monument of the Jewish people. For years Jordan forbade Israelis access to this last remnant of the ancient Temple until it was taken from the Arab Legion by Zahal in the Six Day War. Under Israeli administration, the Ministry of Religious Affairs soon assumed control of the Wall and erected barriers as in an Orthodox synagogue, to separate men and women.

These are some of the ironies of the world of religion in Israel. With so much energy devoted to politics and the rigidities of the status quo, it is no wonder Orthodox leaders have less time to deal with the ethical and spiritual issues affecting the non-Orthodox majority. The Ministry of Religious Affairs assists and encourages the several thousand Orthodox synagogues throughout the country. However with the only choice either Orthodox or nothing, most Israelis prefer nothing.

If religion means interest in the Bible, Jewish traditions and history then Israelis are unusually religious. Jewish holidays are celebrated by every segment of the population from Orthodox to kibbutzniks each in their own way and Israel's Bible champion is regarded as a national hero by all. Everyone admits there is something missing in a spiritual sense. Religious parties blame shortcomings on the straying from Orthodox values. On the other side, Christian missionaries offer a salvation which Jews have almost unanimously rejected in every century. Conservative and Reform Judaism believe they can provide the way. Only a few still preach that pioneering development of the Negev and frontier areas can restore the national mystique and fulfil the Biblical prophecies.

113

For many Israelis, Zionist pioneering (*chalutziut*) was once the true faith and it was the Religion of Labor that fired the hopes and efforts of the veteran settlers. This was the creed of the founding fathers who believed that Jews in exile were a half people and that only commitment to physical labor in Zion could bring about individual and national fullness and spiritual redemption. Professors and shopkeepers became farmers and common laborers and in so doing converted to the new religion that swept the early Jewish pioneers. Despite their disavowals, they were imbued with the religious spirit in its purest sense. Today the Religion of Labor is slowly dying out together with the aging idealists who brought it to Israel.

The gap between Jew, Moslem and Christian, Orthodox and Reform is a wide one but like the European-Ashkenazi and Oriental-Sephardic "separate pluralism", they have learned to live with each other. Intergroup social and personal relationships are superficial and separate religious schools, neighborhoods, political and youth movements only add to the estrangement. The clash of religious concepts has produced no substantial changes in the tenuous status quo and in the flow of prayers and aspirations, old ways continue, aided by political realities and a grudging tolerance or indifference towards dissenters.

The approximately 100,000 Arab Christians in the country are divided into dozens of sects and denominations. Their clergy and lay leadership, while not organized into religious parties like the Jews, seem no less absorbed by their own dogma and the traditional rivalry over custodianship of the Holy Places. The realities of religious life in the cradle of Christianity is disappointing to many visiting pilgrims.

Most of the country's half million Moslems do not show any unusual Islamic fervor. With some exceptions, mosques like churches and synagogues, are half empty except on holidays. Intense emotional feelings of Israeli Arabs are usually reserved for their other prophet, Yasser Arafat, the PLO and Palestine nationalism. Although Arab religious and political leaders in Israel invoke Islamic slogans, it is the increasing clamor for Palestinian Arab self-determination that arouses them. Religious leaders representing a billion Moslems in 34 countries make their stand clear in their frequently repeated call for *jihad* (holy war) against Israel.

Rabbis and priests, religious indifference and bullying notwithstanding, an almost miraculous, indefinable force in the Land of Israel lives on. It is beyond explanation and transcends rational description. It may be only an illusion but it is there. Torah imbued nomadic tribes with a sense of Jewish peoplehood and the development of rabbinic talmudism maintained them in a multitude of exiles, trials and tribulations. Now again in its homeland, Israel is still searching for spiritual peace of mind and the religious and ethical values that will be a guiding light to its future.

Safety lies in the counsel of multitudes.
(Proverbs)

Chapter Six

POLITICS, STRANGE AND OTHERWISE

ZIONISM & HISTORY

Israel's proclamation of Independence reads: "Eretz Israel (Land of Israel) was the birthplace of the Jewish people. Here their spiritual, religious and political identity was shaped. Here they first attained statehood, created cultural values of national and universal significance and gave to the world the eternal Book of Books. After being forcibly exiled from the land, the people kept faith with it throughout the dispersion and never ceased to pray and hope for the restoration in it of their political freedom" . . .

Israeli political parties and ideologies are inextricably bound up with Jewish history and the Zionist movement. Their policies are a reflection of the Mandatory rule and the three decades of independence. The yearning of the Jews to return to the homeland was a vital part of Judaism from ancient days when . . . "By the rivers of Babylon, there we sat and wept when we remembered Zion" . . ."How shall we sing the Lord's song in a foreign land? If I forget thee, O Jerusalem, let my right hand forget her cunning."

For 2000 years a central theme of Judaism was the loss of the Temple and the land that belonged to the Jewish People. Other nations were expelled from their lands by tragedy or fate to lose their sense of peoplehood as they entered exile and began new lives. For the Hebrews, and only for them, banishment was something different.

An extension and continuation of their unique identity, and a new type of exile was born — the Diaspora (dispersion). As their religion aspired to endow the individual man and woman with personal redemption through piety and good deeds, the precondition to national redemption and the coming of the universal Messianic age was a return to Israel. Anti-Semites cursed the Jews and chased them out of the countries of their dispersion, and this only served to strengthen their convictions and resolve to return to their own country.

The Wandering Jew became a haunted man who vainly tried to become a "whole" person like the Gentile. The few who attained wealth and position could become Court Jews and lackeys, protected by royal heads of state. The unusually talented could force a grudging acceptance from the Christians and Moslems they lived among. But for the masses, life could only be a struggle for survival. Even for those who accepted conversion, generations would pass before their Jewish origin was forgotten and they became "like the others", if at all.

Except for the few who came back in every century, the theme of return remained a religious and spiritual ideal until the 19th century. While Zion was still a dream, the immediate goal of Jews in exile was to avoid disaster or at best win acceptance by the Gentile world. For some of their best minds and pragmatic leaders, religious assimilation was a worthwhile price for admission to a better life.

Then, at the very height of the period of enlightenment in Europe, when ghetto walls were slowly but surely crumbling, the modern Zionist movement was born. Even with the dangers and humiliations of life in the dispersion receding, Jewish eyes began to turn to the East. This was not an overnight revolution, but revolution it was. The hopes and prayers of generations now became a living program for Jews who would work to make it happen. And in these last 100 years, a malarial backwater populated by 100,000 poverty stricken Jews and Arabs has become a modern, miniature superpower of close to four million inhabitants.

The saga of Zionism from religious Messianism to the actual renewal of Jewish nationhood was crystallized in the 19th century by several unusual personalities. Zion the stronghold in the ancient Jerusalem of King David, had long been the symbol of Jewish Jerusalem and Israel and Judah. Zionism's first modern prophet was a fiery German Jew named Moses Hess. While emancipated coreligionists were gratefully adjusting to the new liberal atmosphere or joining the budding communist, anarchist and socialist movements, Hess wrote *Rome and Jerusalem*, a startling political essay that was read and debated by Jews in every city and ghetto of Eastern Europe. His conclusion was that national independence in Palestine was a prerequisite for the physical and social wellbeing of the Jewish people.

Shocked by the massacres of Jews in the Odessa pogroms, a Russian Jew named Judah Pinsker wrote an equally brilliant pamphlet called *Autoemancipation* in which he openly declared what was only being whispered by Jews. Anti-Semitism or as he called it "Judeophobia", was a peril inherent in the Diaspora which only political and territorial independence could alleviate. Until then, Jews would remain a ghost people and unwelcome guests in the host nations of the world.

The third and greatest of the modern ideologists of Zionism and its leading statesman was Theodor Herzl, a handsome and naive journalist who had once considered converting to Christianity. After a lifetime of indifference to Jewish topics, the Dreyfus Affair in France and the virulent anti-Semitism it provoked made him a new man and he plunged himself into the study of Zionism to become its undisputed leader. His book *The Jewish State* became its gospel and his motto "If you will it, it is no dream" became the hope and byword for believers who would make miracles come true. In 1897 he convened the first World Zionist Congress " ...to create for the Jewish people a homeland in Palestine secured by public law". While affluent and assimilated Jews attacked him and Christians ignored him, the emerging *shtetl* and ghetto dwellers became his dedicated followers.

ZIONISM & ZIONISTS

From Herzl to Weizmann to Ben Gurion, a high sense of mission and purpose accompanied the Fathers of Zionism. The national renaissance in Palestine became the new way for Jewish salvation. It inspired belief that it could eliminate poverty, crime and injustice. It would create a new and noble Jew who would live by God's law and be a light unto the nations of the world and usher in the most glorious age in the long epic of the Jewish people. This idyllic and poetic aura was accompanied by a myopic disregard of the Arab population in Palestine and their own slowly nurturing nationalism. Only much later Zionists would discover Zion was not an "empty land waiting for its people" as the Jews were a "people waiting for their land". Arabs had been living there for centuries, but the grandeur and splendor of the Zionist ideal would cloud their vision and the Arabs would become an invisible people.

A multitude of ideologists and politicians sprang up and each knew exactly what the state would be like and how to bring it about. There were demands for immediate, full scale colonization from the impetuous, while the cautious urged restraint until securement of political rights and guarantees. Orthodox factions who for decades denounced and opposed Zionism now pressed for adaption of the Torah as the basis for its government. Socialists insisted that only communal development would lead to the new brotherhood on earth.

The "Territorialist" wanted Palestine but would temporarily agree to any country which would provide an immediate "overnight" refuge for Jews who needed to escape persecution that threatened their very lives, until Zion could be had. They even considered accepting an area in Argentina, or in Kenya (mistakenly referred to as Uganda) offered by the British, but for most only the ancient homeland would do. The "Political" Zionists counselled deferment of actual settlement until the kings, presidents and leaders of mighty nations could be convinced of the justice of their cause. Herzl himself spent most of his efforts in an unsuccessful attempt to win a "Charter" from the civilized world which he hoped would validate the claim of Zionism among the council of nations.

They were followed by the "Practical" or "Organic" Zionists whose prosaic goal was "dunam after dunam, goat after goat." These pragmatists correctly sensed that only large scale Jewish presence and Jewish pioneering in Palestine would bring about political victory and international acceptance. For them, *Aliya* would create the State in the making, even as Ahad Haam and other intellectuals were arguing for a cultural renaissance to be led by a Jewish elite. The latter, "Cultural" Zionists, warned against premature *Aliya* and insisted that redemption and restoration in Palestine must be preceded by a cultural awakening. It was this prolific rainbow of strategy and the men and women who would carry it out that brought the sun that began to shine on Zionism.

This was the heritage and mood of Zionism when the British captured Palestine from the Turks during the First World War. The die had been cast and the character of the future State and its politics already determined. The League of Nations conferred a Mandate on Britain making it responsible for the establishment of a Jewish National Home in Palestine. By another ironic twist, it was an assimilated British Jew, Sir Edwin Montagu, who convinced the British government to preface the expression "National Jewish Home" with the vague and less binding word "A" in the letter of intention known as the Balfour Declaration, rather than "THE National Jewish Home" they originally proposed.

This home would be realized through "Jewish immigration" and "close settlement" by Jews on the land. In accordance with their mandate, the British government recognized the World Zionist Organization and its executive arm the Jewish Agency, as official representatives of the Jewish community in Palestine. As different factions grew within this framework, they developed the institutions and symbols that would become a state within a state.

The *Magen* (Shield of) *David* found inscribed in ancient inscriptions discovered near the Western Wall had long been associated with Judaism. Now it was to be the national emblem of the new country. With the blue stripes on a white background reminiscent of the Jewish *talit* (prayer shawl), it was part of the flag of Zionism and the Jewish state. The haunting melody and inspiring words of *Hatikva* (The Hope) became the national anthem. The name given to Jacob after he had successfully wrestled with the angel — Is-ra-el — "He Who Will Prevail" was the name chosen for the old new Hebrew nation founded by the twelve sons of Jacob, whose progeny would become the twelve tribes of Israel.

The Zionist tradition of emotional and lengthy oratory and passionate party loyalty continued together with the inevitable committees, conferences and ideologies. Close behind, the feuds, splits, mergers and coalitions flourished as before. Only a mutual commitment to the goal of statehood by all the contesting groups maintained a fragile but vital unity against the common enemy. The trauma of the Holocaust was the final detonator for the explosive resurgence of long dormant Jewish emotion that was consummated in the miracle of miracles — Independence. On the very day the new state was born, a Jewish shadow government emerged, well prepared for its task.

Leaders of the Jewish Agency became ministers and their institutions and organizations, built up through the years, became ministries of the infant state. It has been truly said that Israel is more like a state within a government, than a government within a state. While military and underground groups were joining forces to form the army that was driving off invading Arab forces, a complex but effective de facto government and legislature was leading the political battle as though they had been preparing for two thousand years. With victory, the political unity disappeared in a flurry of party politics that has continued ever since. The first national elections brought no surprises and the power structure and fragmentation that had been built up through the decades became the official establishment.

Thirty years later, nothing substantial has changed, even though former opposition Herut is now the largest party and once powerful Labor, only a shadow of the power-house that provided a generation of leadership and accomplishment in nation building. Passionate and irrelevant speech making, forums and conventions still have their day and government coalitions carefully made after protracted negotiations are dashed over personality conflicts, petty issues and "affairs". Minor controversies quickly balloon into national crises and from time to time a politician renegades from party discipline, to be swept into a different party or become a one-man faction. New names and labels are born, old promises are broken and the business of politics goes on as usual.

THE SYSTEM

Israel's political system can be defined as a pluralistic, republican, parliamentary, democracy. It is pluralistic, due to the diversity and strength of non-governmental institutions which strongly influence the political life of the country. From the Histadrut to the rabbis to new immigrant societies and bus cooperatives, there are men and movements that serve as buffer between citizen and government, as well as forming powerful lobbies and pressure groups. It is a republic, since by every objective standard, its government and political leadership reflect the will of the people. This is true in spite of the anomalous proportional representation system of voting, which prevents a citizen from casting his ballot directly for the person of his choice.

In Israel one votes for a list of candidates to the *Knesset* (Assembly), submitted by the political party he favors. The candidates on each list, in order of appearance, enter office in proportional representation to the percentage of votes received by their party. Mapai for example, traditionally received some 35% of the vote and hence 35% of the 120 Knesset seats, giving it approximately 42 seats in the assembly. Under this system, an MK has no constituency and serves the electorate and country at large. There has been talk in recent years about a change to a direct elections system. In a typically Israeli compromise, the country would be divided into American style congressional districts which would become local constituencies for some, but not all the Knesset members. The party bosses would.still be able to put their men in office through a list to be voted in by proportional representation. The official debate has not subsided yet and elections are still conducted as before.

Israel is a parliamentary state since the legislative competence of the Knesset is absolutely supreme. Although there is a strong, capable and independent judiciary, it does not operate within the American balance of powers. As in England and the continental democracies, neither Judiciary nor Chief Executive may overrule laws of the Knesset. In the true test of democracy, all legislation, popular or otherwise, must face the ultimate challenge of compliance by the citizens of the country.

Israel is a democracy by all rational criteria. Almost every possible political party imaginable exists including an Arab anti-Zionist Stalinist Communist Party (*Rakah*). Only groups engaging in terrorist violence or open incitement against the state are outlawed. Freedom of speech and expression are limited by censorship imposed due to security considerations, but this does not inhibit citizens from grumbling, assembling or protesting. In the classic test of popular democracy any Israeli can stand on a soap box on Dizengoff Street, as well as in the Knesset and call the most respectable citizen a fool or scoundrel and sometimes it is no more than the truth.

Israeli Arabs openly tune in to inflammatory television programs from neighboring Arab countries. They show their opposition to Zionism and the government by voting for *Rakah* and participating in demonstrations, protected by laws they incite against and policemen they throw stones at. It would be naive to suggest they are as "free" as the Jews of Israel, but under the circumstances, there is no doubt they enjoy a great freedom of expression and dissent. One hardly need compare them with the few Jews still remaining in the Arab states, who dare not hint that they do not totally support Arab leaders and policies. In Syria and Iraq, men languish in prison merely because they are Jews, families live in constant fear for their lives and none can leave the country.

Almost every adult is involved directly or indirectly in *politika* and the heterogeneous and versatile Israelis are more than matched by their politics. Unlike the US where two traditional and somewhat similar political parties battle for power, Israel has about a dozen, distinctive, political factions, each representing different social, economic or religious attitudes. With no single party capable of achieving an absolute majority of the votes, coalitions and alignments, like the shifting sands of the middle eastern desert, are permanent elements of Israeli politics. Some national leaders are related by birth or marriage and in effect constitute a parallel Old Boy network that is an integral part of the Establishment.

The party in Israel is only the spearhead of comprehensive activities that involve the lives of their constituents in ways even Tammany Hall in its heyday did not dream of. Techniques have been developed in the art of politics that make big city power brokers in America seem feeble and unimaginative in comparison. Herut, Liberals, Mafdal and especially Labor, have built up networks of social, cultural, economic and agricultural institutions that compel the admiration and envy of foreign politicians.

Mapai (Israel Worker's Party) the largest faction in Labor, plays a major role in the giant Histadrut. Almost one hundred kibbutzim were founded by its adherents who are still politically aligned with and support it. If he so desired a loyal *Mapainik* or Laborite could spend most of his waking hours with the party. He could begin his day with a glass of orange juice that comes from a party owned citrus orchard while reading the party controlled morning newspaper. The school his children attend, the supermarket where his wife shops and Co-op, factory or insurance company where he works might be among those developed by the party or its labor union bastion, the Histadrut. Whether teacher, dentist or architect, there is a club or section of Labor where he can socialize in the evenings with his professional colleagues.

The background and activities of the Israeli parties should be observed within the context of the country's political system. Like every legislature the Knesset passes laws and serves as a forum for debates and criticism of the government. Its members are elected every four years by universal suffrage of all citizens, Jews and Arabs, over eighteen years of age. The government is formed by leaders of the majority party or by a coalition of parties that can command a vote of confidence — approval by a majority of the Knesset.

Cabinet ministries are then allocated to political leaders who head the party list of Knesset members and they collectively form the government until the next elections, unless it first loses the confidence of the Knesset. The Prime Minister and his Cabinet dominate the Israeli parliament, decide major policies and run the country subject only to legal restraints and a no confidence vote. The latter leads to frequent government crises, threats of resignation and political shifts, blocs and alignments that have taken place since Independence and there are few signs suggesting any change or a real move toward the two party system familiar elsewhere.

Presidents, Chaim Weizmann (1948-1952), Itzhak Ben Zvi (1952-1961), Zalman Shazar (1961-1971) and Ephraim Katzir (1971-1978) each had a surprising ability to win popular acceptance and to exert a symbolic if not real power, beyond the limitations of the office. The current President, Itzhak Navon, is the first Sephardi to become President of Israel. As an intellectual, native-born scion of a prominent family and husband of a young, former beauty queen, he is hardly a true representative of the immigrant, Oriental communities so under-represented in the leadership.

The Israeli judiciary stands on the other side of the Knesset. Together with the army, it is one of the few Israeli institutions that enjoys public trust and freedom from political influence. The independence of the Courts and professional caliber of the Judges has been a source of pride to every citizen. Judicial independence and integrity are assured by non-partisan appointment of qualified Judges to life terms rather than election for limited periods. This grants them immunity from the political influences and jeopardies which lurk close by to candidates for the judiciary who are compelled like politicians to run for office.

Except for a single case there has never been any charge of impropriety by an Israeli jurist. After one of the longest criminal trials in the country's history, a highly regarded member of the District Court was acquitted of bribery charges lodged against him by a lady lawyer. Some of the evidence indicated that the Judge had been adulterously involved with the complainant. Even in Israel however, this is no longer a criminal offense and more than a few Israelis would add, Thank God!

The great debate for and against a constitution followed soon after the founding of the State. Those who opposed pointed to highly democratic, but constitutionless Great Britain. The flowery and elaborate constitutions in backward and totalitarian states were shown as further proof of the irrelevance of a written constitution. It was claimed that the idealism and democratic traditions of the Jewish people and the Zionist movement together with legislative and judicial safeguards, would adequately protect fundamental liberties. Finally, it was argued that a written constitution while the State was young and growing, would only prove rigid and divisive.

Constitutional proponents replied that a comprehensive constitution would assure high moral authority and guarantee democracy in Israel. It alone could protect basic freedoms and rights of individuals and minorities against a government and bureaucracy that are baffling to the average citizen. In a newly developing country, whose citizens are of diverse backgrounds and many of whom have no tradition in self-government, a constitution could also play a vital unifying and educational role.

The underlying and dominant "constitutional" issue was cynical rather than philosophical or ideological; opposition parties were for it, while the government coalition opposed. Religious parties would support only a Torah-oriented constitution. The secular opposition envisioned an Israeli Magna Carta that would limit the role of the government and enhance their own chances of gaining power. Labor parties preferred to delay enactment of a written constitution until they could form a majority government alone.

The great debate in the Knesset finally ended, with a typically Israeli and somewhat ambiguous compromise. Israel would be a Constitutional state, but not just yet. "Basic" laws would be legislated on important subjects and incorpo-

129

rated into an eventually adopted Constitution. This compromise failed to ensure that Basic Laws would have special, constitutional status.

Hundreds of statutes have since been passed in the Knesset and pre-Independence legislation has systematically been amended and replaced by Israeli statutes, but only a handful of Basic Laws have been passed. Like a Yemenite army general, or Sephardic Prime Minister, a written Constitution remains a popular but nebulous goal of the Israelis.

Along with opposition parties, the State Controller has been a watch-dog of democracy in Israel. He is appointed by the President and is responsible only to the Knesset. The Controller and his staff of investigators and accountants, examine the legality, efficiency and ethics of government activities and enterprises. His comprehensive annual report has become a keenly awaited and highly respected document.

The Civil Service Commission has helped make modern government possible in Israel. It appoints, trains, disciplines and advises the more than 100,000 Israelis working for the State. In contrast to the flagrant nepotism and spoils system of some Western democracies, the Commission tries to maintain impartiality. Most appointments are made on the merit system and claims of protektzia by unsuccessful candidates are usually baseless. High level appointments are another matter and in such cases, a "candidate" for an available position may have already been selected by the ministry involved, with the Commission a knowing or innocent partner in the game by insisting the tender is open to all.

The procedures pertaining to government employ have not changed the character of the three ministries traditionally controlled by the religious parties in the government coalition (Welfare, Interior and Religion), where Orthodox personnel fill many and possibly a majority of key and lower echelon jobs. Another exception to the rule are government positions requiring security clearance. Here all appointments are made subject to the supervision of the wary and efficient intelligence services. Having a friend in the right place is no less important in Israel than in other countries, recalling Chaim Weizmann's alleged reply to the query of whether a Zionist was required to be crazy, "It's not required, but it helps!"

In the past decade or so, government employ in Israel has become synonymous with low pay and a slow work day. Except for top levels and some dedicated public servants, it does not always attract the best people. While a minority of those working in the ministries could do much better in the private sector, many petty clerks and officials stay because they have no other real alternative. Rudeness and red tape are ever present in encounters between citizen and government. Israelis sometimes justify this state of affairs by saying that it is worse in Arab countries, but this is unacceptable to those who believe Israel is or should be an efficient, Western democracy.

While the Middle East *bakshish* (bribery) is the rare exception, problems inherent in governments of developing countries have not escaped Israel. Too many matters involve government intervention, permits or forms and visits to officials and long lines are part of the system. Mutual annoyance, impatience, animosity or distrust are the unavoidable reaction of the citizens as well as the clerks and officials they must come into contact with so frequently. Services which could be provided more cheaply and efficiently by the private sector, like gas, electricity, telephone, mail and telegraph, are government owned or operated monopolies and add to the already giant bureaucracy.

131

The very existence of local authority in such a small country is a mixed blessing for most residents. In Israel, there are over 30 municipalities and two hundred local and regional councils, many if not most of which are superfluous. Jointly with the central government, they maintain such services as health, education, sanitation, parks, roads and water. Their functions and limitations are defined by law and they are assisted and supervised by the Ministry of Interior.

Local councils in Israel are characterized and dominated by partisan politics even more than on the national level. A major difference is that there is only one national government. Local government causes further inflation of already staggering public payrolls and budgets. Unfortunately it tends to attract the bottom of the political barrel. Small-time, would-be political hangers-on and glory seekers, who cannot make it in the more prestigious Knesset, ministries, Histadrut and economic enterprises, often are the defenders of the faith in the cities and towns.

There are no doubt many able and dedicated men in the city and town halls. Their efforts are frustrated by the rules of the game and by office holders who oppose consolidation and cut backs, that would compel many to look for a less cushy, more productive job. Inadequate financial means, unnecessary public building and spending, local-central government jealousies, ill-chosen and redundant personnel and apathetic or hostile local residents, are conducive only to mediocre government or worse.

A few councils are corrupt, nepotic or bankrupt, while others are barely able to prevent administrative or financial chaos. More than once the Ministry of Interior has been compelled to dismiss a mayor or local council and assume control until order can be restored. Cities like Jerusalem and towns such as Savyon and Kiryat Ono have municipalities on a par with progressive and modern cities of the US; others continue to drift along in the lethargic and labyrinth tradition of the Levant.

WHO'S WHO IN POLITICS

Until the elections of 1977 the most influential movement was the Labor movement, which was the predominant force in modern Zionism and a key factor in building the country. Labor-Zionism gave birth to the Kibbutz, Moshav, Cooperative and Histadrut and played the main role in the pre-independence immigration that smuggled tens of thousands of "illegal" refugees from the death camps into Palestine. It provided the leaders and soldiers of the Hagana army and its Palmach commando units. In the first three decades of statehood only *Mapainiks* — Ben Gurion, Sharett, Eshkol, Meir and Rabin were Prime Ministers and party stalwarts filled most important positions in the political, military and economic establishment.

From the beginning, Israel's Labor contained two basic trends; down to earth Zionist-Socialism with its inspiring "religion of Labor", under the leadership of pioneers like Gordon, Katzenelson, Brenner, and Ben Gurion, which led to the birth of Mapai. The other ideology of the left was traditional socialism and its champion, *Achdut Avoda* (Unity of Labor). Together they formed the largest and most powerful Jewish political party in Palestine until they split in 1948.

Achdut Avoda then moved further left to join the more militantly socialist, anti-clerical *Hashomer Hatzair* (The Young Watchman). The latter were backed by the largest and then revolutionary affiliation of kibbutzim, city workers and intellectuals in what might have been the New Left of that era. For years, Hashomer Hatzair was even somewhat less than

133

Zionist and supported the creation of a bi-national Jewish-Arab state in Palestine.

The new party became *Mapam* (Workers Party) and in the course of the years, it increasingly abandoned its previous loyalty to the tenets of Marxism and anti-Western policies of the Soviet Union. Eventually, Achdut Avoda broke away from its more radical partner and resumed its former role as an independent, socialist party of the Left. A few years later, it rejoined Mapai in a joint parliamentary bloc called *HaMa'arach* (The Alignment), at the same time that another split in Mapai led by David Ben Gurion was giving rise to *Rafi* (Israel Workers' List).

Rafi was born out of the struggle within Mapai, between Ben Gurion then in retirement in the Negev kibbutz of Sde Boker, and his chosen successor and later personal and political enemy, Levi Eshkol. The main issue leading to this breakup, was a security failure just before the Sinai Campaign, which led to the arrest of an Israeli spy ring in Egypt. The issue became known as the "Lavon Affair", after the prominent Mapai Defense Minister, whom Rafi-ites charged had improperly ordered the unsuccessful security operation.

Following a series of investigations, charges and counter-charges arising from the affair, Ben Gurion and his followers resigned from Mapai in protest at what they claimed was unjust condoning of Lavon's role in the failure. Rafi was initiated and formally headed by Ben Gurion, but its moving spirit were his young supporters, the Pragmatists (in Hebrew *Bitsuistim* — "those who get things done"), led by former Chief of Staff Moshe Dayan and Defense Ministry Director-General Shimon Peres. A smaller group of Mapainiks sided with Minister Lavon to form a now defunct adversary ideological faction in the party called *Min Hayesod* (From the Roots). Rafi has also disappeared and many of its adherents are now members of *Le'Am* (The People) and aligned with the Likud (Union) coalition.

In addition to the parties of the left, who can be compared vaguely to the Democratic Party of the USA, the usual junior partners in the coalition governments have been the "religious" parties. The latter were founded by Orthodox leaders to protect their interests against incursions and inequities of secular and socialist oriented Labor and the other parties. They have had their share of dogma, clashes and affairs leading to shifts, splits and 'alignments and it is their common resentment of secular policies and a common struggle for power that have been key factors in maintaining unity among the competing religious factions.

The ultra-Orthodox are usually supporters of *Agudat Yisrael* and they demand the strictest observance of the Torah in the administration of the State, through Orthodox Rabbinical supervision of religious, cultural and social life in Israel. Their major contribution to pioneering in the years before statehood was the erection of a network of *Yeshivot* (Rabbinical seminaries) and religious communities. Although they have always been represented in the Knesset and now support the Likud administration, they usually refrain from participating directly in any government coalition.

Poalei Agudat Yisrael (Workers of the Society of Israel) are slightly less religious fundamentalists. Both *Agudat* parties were founded after the First World War by rabbinical leaders of East and central Europe, but unlike *Agudat Yisrael*, the followers of *Poalei Agudat Yisrael* had no qualms about pioneering in Palestine. They too believe in salvation by the Messiah, but also that his coming might be hastened if they made efforts to prepare themselves in the Holy Land.

While most of the *Agudat Yisrael* did not take up arms to defend Israel, *Poalei Agudat Yisrael* joined in the struggle

135

against the British and Arabs. Following statehood both parties ran for the Knesset. They regard the Torah as the supreme law of Israel and the Jewish people but accept the primacy of the national government. Except for ultra-Orthodox extremists of the *Neturei Karta* (Guardians of the City) who refuse even to recognize the existence of Israel, the Orthodox parties have been its proud and loyal citizens.

The most nationalistic, though least Orthodox religious political movements, are united in *Mafdal* (National Religious Party). Founded in 1956, it represented a merger of the *Mizrachi* (East) and *HaPoel HaMizrachi* (Workers of the East) parties formed in the early 1900's as separate factions in the labor controlled World Zionist Organization. They also called for religious Zionism, based upon Orthodox Judaism and the Torah and played an active role in pioneering through religious kibbutzim, moshavim and institutions combining religious study with agriculture and trades.

Today's Mafdalniks are generally middle class, urban, Orthodox Jews who oppose the dominating role of the Histadrut and non-religious orientation of the government. Proving that politics make strange bedfellows, their party was the critical and loyal partner of secular Mapai for nearly 30 years. In exchange for a free hand and Mapai cooperation in matters of religious interest, they generally supported Labor policies in domestic and foreign affairs. In the course of the years this cooperation became a euphemistic example of the mutual abandonment of principles by politicians in exchange for power.

Mapai leaders filled the key Prime, Foreign and Finance ministries and this stability brought progress to Israel, but the price was a dear one. If today the non-Orthodox citizens of Israel — 80% of the Jewish population — cannot enjoy a film or ride a bus on the Sabbath, be married or divorced without Orthodox consent, they can blame the

Mapai-Religious coalition. It was this partnership that brought about Mapai support of religious schools, Orthodox religious tribunals and a long list of Orthodox demands on the non-Orthodox majority, including the creation of an Orthodox controlled Ministry of Religion.

Leftist, irreligious and even agnostic Mapai became the loyal ally of the religious parties, in implementation of Orthodox policies in education, welfare, religion and personal status. It is a role now being assumed to a great extent by Likud, which has replaced Labor as the senior partner with Mafdal still holding and exploiting its traditional balance of power position.

An entire generation of Israelis has grown up under practices and political gentlemen's agreements that constitute a near untouchable, religious status quo. Whatever happens hereafter, the entrenched position of organized religion in Israeli society will not be quickly or easily changed. Some claim that only the existence of the Arab-Jewish struggle has prevented a day of reckoning in Israel between Orthodox and secular.

The more extreme Agudat parties and moderate National Religious party form a type of Bible front, but internal maneuvering pressures and conflicts are always present. Elements of the ultra-Orthodox wing of Agudat Israel are sensitive to taunts and criticism of Neturei Karta. On the other side of the religious coalition, younger supporters of Mafdal, struggle with their conservative elders for liberal and progressive social programs. They frequently oppose the stricter policies of Orthodox leadership and empathize with the humanistic approach and social policies of other parties, if not with their secularism. Since the Yom Kippur War, younger Mafdalniks have also increasingly emphasized a strident nationalism, that is more akin to traditional Herut territorial aspirations than previous Mafdal policies.

137

To make the picture even more interesting and complicated, Israel has a third major, and now dominant, political bloc that is neither Orthodox nor socialist. It is composed of parties of the "right", even though some of their followers could be considered "religious" while others are "progressive". One branch is the Liberals, who like the American Republican, call for a strong, free enterprise economy, encouragement of capitalism and reforms in the social-economic system. Upon reaching office in the "Upheaval", they made good on some of their promises and many reforms in the economic and social welfare system are a result of their presence in the coalition government. Critics blame the menacing inflation on the same new policies.

Most of their programs were platforms of the General Zionists who merged with the Progressives to form the Liberal party. General Zionism also opposed a powerful Histadrut and government participation in the economic and everyday life of the country. It became the voice of the landlord, merchant and industrialist. In foreign affairs it was less critical of government policies and generally agreed with its Western orientation.

The Progressives were slightly to its left and found their support among the German speaking, professional and middle class immigrants from Central Europe. They were ethnically, linguistically and often politically alienated, from the relative radicalism of the Labor parties and their Russian and Yiddish speaking adherents. These parties also possessed a capable leadership and together usually polled about 10% of the vote, although in earlier years they almost doubled that. In 1961, they joined to form the Liberal party.

Herut is the other major party of the right and the movement is setting the tone in Israel today in what they call the "New Style" (*HaSignon HaHadash*). Since his arrival in Palestine during the Second World War, as a soldier in the Polish Army, Menachem Begin has led this party, formed from the merger of the Zionist Revisionists founded by Vladimir (Ze'ev) Jabotinsky and its closely related Irgun underground army. Both rejected the moderation of labor leaders in the Zionist institution and demanded aggressive policies against both Britain and the Arabs.

Until the last years of the Mandate, Hagana followed a policy of *havlaga* (restraint) towards both Arab nationalists and British authorities. Revisionists and Irgun refused to comply and when death sentences were carried out on captured Irgun men, they retaliated in kind and hanged captured British soldiers. When the British flogged Irgun men, English Tommies were captured and flogged. During the War of Independence, Irgun and Hagana fought together but even after the formation of Zahal, Herut continued its struggle for revisionism in the political arena.

Menachem Begin is one of the most unusual political personalities of Israel and one of the last of the giants in the struggle for statehood. His popular support surprisingly comes from the working suburbs and slums of the large cities where the Oriental-Sephardic immigrant population is concentrated. Other backers and most of the party leadership are Ashkenazi veterans of the Irgun underground and their sympathizers in the Yishuv. Like the Liberals, Herut also supports cutbacks in the role of the Histadrut and social welfarism and adoption of a modern Western economy.

From the day it arose until the Camp David peace talks with Egypt, its ideological and emotional raison d'être was "Revisionism" — "the territorial integrity of Israel within its historical boundaries," (i.e. on both sides of the Jordan River). A map of such an Israel was the emblem of the Party. Nevertheless, it is Begin and the Herut Party that commenced the first peace dialogue with an Arab nation.

Until the Upheaval, Herut was the largest and most vocal opposition party and the traditional nemesis of Labor. While Achdut Avoda and Mapai were merging to form their alignment, it joined with the Liberals to become *Gahal* (Herut-Liberal Bloc). Together they controlled some 25% of the electorate and in 1977 almost doubled it to become the largest party and lead the coalition government.

Herut has also been plagued with splintering and "affairs" which weakened it no less than Labor and the religious blocs. One such division occurred when the Begin led leadership was challenged by young and rising Shmuel Tamir. After his power ploy was defeated, he and two other party Knesset Members formed the Free Center party, but today the Tamir group is a part of the government coalition. Another unsuccessful rebellion was led by Ezer Weizman, who later returned to Herut, accepted Begin's leadership and became his deputy and likely heir. Additional fragmentation took place when a few members of the Liberal Party refused to approve the Gahal alliance with Herut. These dissenters formed a separate faction called the Independent Liberal Party. They paid a steep price for the independence after which they named themselves and were reduced to a single Knesset seat in 1977.

Arab Knesset representation has generally averaged 4-6% of the vote, even though Arabs form 15% of the population. Almost none have joined Zionist parties but most were willing to vote along with Mapai or Mapam. In the last few years, Arab voters have increasingly turned away from this alliance with the Jewish moderate left in favor of Rakah (New Communist List), or as it was first called, the Israeli Communist Party. Founded by Palestinian Jews in the 1920's, they opposed British and Zionist imperialism with equal ardor and were backed by Mapam. They encouraged demands for a bi-national Palestine and only when Soviet policy favored an independent Jewish state to compel the British departure from the Middle East, did the party suddenly become pro-Zionist.

The Palestine (and, after Independence, Israeli) Communist Party always drew its main strength from Arab villagers, plus a few Jewish intellectuals and workers. For two decades it obediently followed the anti-Western and anti-Israeli policies of its Soviet masters and like the Neturei Karta was a pariah among the masses of Israeli Jews. After Stalin's death the split that affected Communist parties in almost every other country also took place in Israel.

In Israel, Stalinism played a lesser role than the burning issue of Jewish versus Arab nationalism and the division reached its peak in the critical days before the Six Day War. Basic problems of class struggle and proletarian revolution were forgotten. While Israel's Arab Communists defended Russian arming and incitement of Arab countries, most Jewish Communists chose to stand with their non-Communist brothers. The Arab faction dropped out to form Rakah while the Jewish wing *Maki* (Israeli Communist Party) moved closer to the Zionist parties of the left. Rakah, now the leading power in the Arab street, openly voices the official Moscow line of "Zionism — a tool of imperialism," while the smaller Jewish Communist Party recognize Zionism as a national liberation movement and has joined *Sheli* (Peace Camp).

According to some observers, Sheli is the only real Zionist opposition party. It opposes both government, Labor run opposition and Rakah policies. Sheli bluntly supports the creation of an independent, PLO-controlled Arab Palestinian state in the West Bank and Gaza as the only practical and just way to bring peace and prosperity to Israel and the Middle East. Maverick Zionist leaders such as the publisher of "This World" Uri Avneri, former Director General of the

Labor Party Lova Eliav, military historian Meir Pa'il, Black Panther Saadia Marciano and scholar General Mati Peled lead this loose coalition of factions and dovish free thinkers, who claim to be the only "normal and practical Zionists". They have only two Knesset seats and are regarded as well-meaning but misguided and naive, by government and opposition parties alike. It is their belief that in the ultimate test, most of Israel will accept their views preferring peace now in this generation.

This was the political background of Israel with all its inflections and nuances until the Yom Kippur War and its aftermath when protest groups and movements began to sprout like mushrooms. Labor and its leaders were subjected to a torrent of criticism and accusations for its role in the mishaps that made the surprise Arab attack and its initial successes possible. Many Laborites dropped out to join the Democratic Movement for Change (*Dash*), the only new political movement to survive the national elections with widespread support. Although its leaders were familiar faces or disgruntled politicians from other parties, they had unusual success at the polls mostly at the expense of the Labor Party and became — just ahead of Mafdal — the third largest party. Just a few years after its meteoric appearance, Dash has split into factions and is a weakened and continuously diminishing phenomenon on the political scene.

The Likud was strengthened by public disappointment in and rejection of the Labor Party and the series of scandals that exposed some of its leaders. Retired General Arik Sharon plunged into politics, sparked unification efforts of the parties of the right and expanded Gahal into a real alternative to a Labor dominated government. With election results in, Menachem Begin finally achieved his long awaited goal of Prime Minister. Labor stalwart Moshe Dayan deserted his party to take over and leave the Foreign Ministry and the Religious parties and Dash joined the coalition. This is the political map of Israel at the beginning of the eighties, but nobody can say what the political scene will bring tomorrow.

HEROES, VILLAINS AND OTHER TYPES

A multitude of fringe movements and one man factions still come and go. The proportional representation system of voting makes such democracy possible and they have often been a refreshing light in the smoke filled rooms of Israeli politics. In the past, there have been parties such as The "Fighters", "WIZO" and The "Yemenites". The newest party is called *"Hatehiya"* (The Rebirth) and they are hard-line believers in Jewish sovereignty and unlimited Israeli settlement in the West Bank and Gaza. For many years the national gadfly has been Uri Avneri, representing *Haolam Hazeh* (This World). Avneri's party name is the same as the weekly magazine he owns and edits and its breezy gossip and tell-it-the-way-it-is exposés have made it the darling of the young and off-beat. He is a brilliant journalist and his political analyses are eagerly read by friend and foe alike. Avneri has been accused of being self-centered and demagogic but he is a healthy irritant to veteran politicians and political nonsense.

Abie Nathan is neither Knesset member nor party leader. An Indian born, former El Al pilot, for many years he was only another café proprietor in the Dizengoff district of Tel Aviv. A patron of the theater and the avant-garde and friend of artists and actors, Abie achieved instant fame when he "flew for peace" to Egypt. At the very height of the crisis before the Six Day War, he managed to land his small, unarmed civilian plane "Shalom I", at Port Said Airport and demanded to see President Nasser to talk peace.

Released by puzzled Egyptians, he flew back to Israel where it had been reported earlier that he had crashed, and was received with acclamation by his followers.

Israeli authorities thought otherwise and he was jailed briefly following conviction for illegal contact with the enemy, but they had misread the beginning of the protest movements Abie symbolized. Undismayed, he organized meetings and marches after the war in support of his peace efforts, was a leading figure in the fund-raising and flights for starving Biafrans and other international humanitarian causes.

His "Voice of Peace" pirate radio station is popular with Israelis and Arabs alike. Saint, sinner or fool, he has captured the hearts of many young Israelis bored or fed up with the official leadership.

The leading villain of Israel politics is Meir Wilner, the Jewish leader of Rakah. He and his Arab associate Tewfik Toubi are the official representatives of Palestinian nationalism in Israel and their appearance in the Knesset always heralds a noisy session. The election of Jewish Black Panther leader Charlie Biton as part of Rakah's Knesset list has diverted some of the attention from Wilner and Toubi and their pro-Soviet demagoguery.

Shulamit Aloni, a former radio personality was a member of the "Young Leadership" group of Mapai, anxious to inherit party control from an old guard that never retired. She is one of the few prominent women in the male dominated Establishment — Ben Gurion allegedly insisted that Golda Meir was the best man in Israeli politics. Aloni once caused a furore merely by wearing a mini-skirt in the august chambers of the Knesset, especially upsetting the elderly and religious politicians with whom she often does battle.

The grandest figure in modern Jewish history is easily the

ate David Ben Gurion and no living Israeli can be compared to him in deeds and stature. The architect of the Jewish army, leader of the Histadrut, Labor movement and Prime Minister, he was the major figure in Zionism and the State of Israel until his death in 1973. Against the counsel of others, he insisted on proclaiming the creation of the new nation on the very day the British gave up their mandate in Palestine. While approaching his 90th year, he passed away in the Negev kibbutz where he spent his active and still stormy years in retirement.

Until her death, the leading lady of Israeli politics for three decades was Golda Meir. "Golda" as everyone called her, was Israel's uncrowned queen. She was respected if not loved by all, as an inspirational if tough pragmatist. Once a school teacher in Milwaukee where she lived until settling in Palestine and then Foreign Minister, Prime Minister and Secretary-General of the Labor Party, she was the symbolic voice of Israel, at home and abroad until she passed away.

Only slightly mellowed with age, illness and the coming of high office, underground leader Menachem Begin is Israel's most impressive figure. His appearance at a Herut election rally is enough to raise the roaring chant "Begin! Begin! Begin!" from the throats of his young and passionate admirers. His personal and political generation-long feud with Ben Gurion and Labor ended dramatically before the outbreak of the Six Day War, when he played a leading role in creating the wartime emergency coalition government. By cutting off partisan debate and insisting on the appointment of Laborite Dayan as Defense Minister, he helped bring the Opposition into the government. Thus Begin became a part of the establishment he fought with such élan for so long, even if it took ten more years and five electoral defeats before he became Prime Minister.

Even critics and enemies concede that Begin has provided Israel with the firm leadership it had looked for since the days of Ben Gurion. While he has many opponents on the left and right who attack his policies and political philosophy, no one denies his ability and integrity. By far Israel's most important and articulate voice he is a master of the art of politics and at the best of his oratorical heights, a near Biblical figure. He is the most vivid symbol of the dramatic changes in concepts and policies that have taken place since the Upheaval.

There was a time when a young, brilliant Oxford graduate named Abba Eban seemed the brightest star in the Israeli political constellation. He was the polished spokesman of young Israel, as Ambassador in Washington, the UN and finally Foreign Minister. He is a prolific author, professional lecturer, linguist and Hebrew orator — his grandiose and Anglo-Saxon accented Hebrew is the frequent subject of Sabra jokes — but he has lost the Kissinger-like halo of yesterday. Having never developed a power base or grass roots popularity at home, Eban is more famous and respected abroad than in the country he has represented with such flair and style.

Housing Minister David Levy has worked his way up from development town stalwart, to his present position as one of the main power brokers in the Herut party. Along with Begin, he is the man who has brought in the votes from the Oriental blue collar neighborhoods. Caustic references to his lack of formal schooling and intellectual abilities have not stopped him from passing Establishment rivals. Unlike other leaders from the Oriental communities, Levy has stayed close to his roots and the life style of his North African origin. He is now one of the country's most popular politicians and a key figure in the Likud.

In addition to Labor's Itzhak Rabin and Shimon Peres his

successor as titular party head, the leading contenders for tomorrow's national leadership are Moshe Dayan and Ezer Weizman. Once a farmer and Minister of Agriculture, Dayan's reputation was won when he led the nation to its stunning victory in the Suez Campaign, as Commander in Chief of the Israeli Army. Dayan lost his eye leading a Palmach unit attached to the British Army in Syria during the Second World War. He is the head of the best known family in Israel and has a charisma few Israeli politicians can match. His unsmiling, stoic sense of duty has made him the prototype of the modern Hebrew warrior-patriot.

His escalation came during the dark hours before the Six Day War when grandfatherly Eshkol seemed shaken by the calamitous events. Israelis of every party and persuasion looked beyond him to Moshe Dayan, the one Israeli who could rally the spirit of the people behind him. In spite of the opposition of the Labor leadership, he was drafted as Minister of Defense in the emergency coalition to lead the nation in battle.

After the Yom Kippur War, he was charged as a major culprit in the blunders that made Arab war gains possible and for several years lost his position of prominence in Labor to Peres, Rabin and Allon. With Begin's victory, he was again called back from the political wilderness and named Foreign Minister. A lone wolf, disliked or mistrusted by party men and opposition as well as by a large sector of the public, he is up at the top again and in his 60's as ambitious as ever.

Ezer Weizman is Dayan's former brother-in-law; his wife Ruchama and Dayan's first wife Ruth are sisters. He is also a nephew of Israel's first President, the former head of the Israeli Air Force and the newest and shiniest star on the national level. His Sabra bluntness and pixie humor has endeared him to many in Israel and abroad and he is a favorite of Begin, Sadat and Carter. Once considered a hawk, he is the unnamed leader of the moderate forces in the Likud government. With the grey eminence of the Liberal Party Deputy Premier Simcha Erlich, he stands opposed to the militant camp headed by Begin and the flamboyant, brilliant military strategist and politically unpredictable Sharon.

LOOKING FOR PEACE

In five Arab Israel wars the Jewish nation and its citizens have been saved from likely destruction by the threatening Arab armies poised on its borders, and now there are cease-fire lines that make Arab cries for a fifth round less frightening to the Israelis. Soviet supplied rockets and bombers are no longer stockpiled in the Sinai peninsula and Egyptian divisions cannot march up to the very gates of the cities of Israel's heavily populated coastal plain. Until the Six Day War the Jordan Legion was poised at Israel's narrow and vulnerable waist just north of Tel Aviv, where a surprise attack could cut it in half in hours and Syrian artillery in concealed concrete underground bunkers in the Golan foothills could with impunity shell the helpless kibbutzim and towns in the valleys below.

The Yom Kippur War proved that time is not on the side of peace and that captured territories do not provide real security against new wars. In spite of military gains, Israel has come no closer to peace with the Palestinian Arabs than before. Islamic religious leaders still call for Holy Wars on Zionism and Arab statesmen speak of its political necessity and inevitability. Except for the Sadat-led moderate camp, their position is: no peace talks; no recognition; complete Israeli retreat to the armistice lines of May, 1967 and the return of all Arab refugees to Israel.

The two major issues are Arab refugees and the borders

of Israel, but the underlying theme is Arab refusal to accept Israel's existence. Historical truths in the Middle East rebut claims that imperialistic Israeli expansionism and aggression have thwarted Arab nationalism and the right to an Arab Palestine. Most of the territories — Golan, Gaza, Sinai and especially the formerly Jordanian occupied West Bank and East Jerusalem — were included in the Land of Canaan promised to the Patriarch Abraham and his seed. Though a succession of conquerors was to occupy it, only the Hebrews ever claimed it as a national homeland. Their physical and spiritual links with it became an integral part of the consciousness of western civilization, and only through their presence in and identification with Israel did it enter the chronicles of history as a unique geographical and historical entity.

The word Hebrew (in the Hebrew language *Ivri*) means "from the other side", and describes the nomadic Hebrew tribes from the other side of the Euphrates who established their national home in what was ancient Judah and Israel. Until they became a small province in the Roman Empire, they enjoyed over a thousand years of uninterrupted national sovereignty. Following the period of tribal rule and government by Judges, a Jewish monarchy was formed under King Saul. His successor, King David, famous for his boyhood defeat of Goliath and adventures with Batsheva, consolidated the kingdom and around 1000 BCE made Jerusalem capital of the Hebrew nation. His son, the wise and many wived King Solomon, built the First Temple and converted the city into the spiritual and religious center of a Hebrew commonwealth.

After Solomon's death, the country was divided into the separate kingdoms of Judah and Israel under the reign of a succession of monarchs. Though later conquered by the Babylonians, the Jews, as they were now called, returned from their first exile to rebuild the destroyed Temple and begin the 400 year period of the Second Commonwealth. When the mighty Roman Legions destroyed Jerusalem and its Jewish inhabitants, the survivors began their long march into the Diaspora, while Palestine, its new name, became part of a battlefield ranging over continents and kingdoms in the vast Byzantine Empire.

Finally the Persians became new masters of ancient Israel until they in turn were conquered by the Arabs in the 7th century CE. The latter ruled for 450 years, but, except during periods of the Crusades, it was only a small part of the Islamic Arab empire, stretching from Arabia to North Africa and Spain. The West Bank and Gaza were never part of any sovereign state. On the contrary, they were specifically included in the Palestine Mandate, intended to be an internationally recognized trust for Jewish as well as Arab inhabitants of what is today divided between Israel, Jordan, Gaza and the West Bank.

Arab claims to national sovereignty in Palestine as a separate nation were raised for the first time in the 20th century. Jordan was born only a few decades ago when the British broke off the eastern part of historic Judah and presented their ally, Abdullah Sherrif, with a kingdom. In 1948 the Jordan Legion seized and then annexed Judea and Samaria, including the Old City of Jerusalem, but only two countries in the entire world, England and Pakistan, recognized the annexation. This area west of the Jordan River was clearly within the ancient Israel that the British Government was mandated to reconstitute the Jewish homeland.

Unfertile Arab land was sold for double and triple its value and no Arabs were forcibly dispossessed. It was the growing prosperity and development that Jewish pioneering brought that attracted more Arabs from nearby Syria and Transjordan. Even the emergence of Arab nationalism after

the First World War did not blur some Moslems' acknowledgement of the justice of the Zionist cause. King Hussein
of Hejaz wrote ..."We saw the Jews streaming to Palestine
from Russia, Germany, Austria, Spain, America... The
cause of causes could not escape those who had the gift of
deeper insight; they knew that the country was for its original sons, for all of their differences a sacred and beloved
homeland." Thus there were Arab leaders and villagers
who accepted the return of the Jews to Palestine as a
natural event, although some regarded them as intruders
and usurpers.

Jerusalem was the national capital and soul of the Jewish
nation. It is mentioned in the Old Testament hundreds of
times and its meaning and importance to the Jews has no
parallel in any other nationality or religion. It is holy to
Moslems mainly due to the presence of the El Aqsa Mosque
and Dome of the Rock on the site of the Temple where it is
believed Abraham offered his son Isaac in sacrifice. There at
the Jewish Holy of Holies, Mohammed's legendary horse
Burraq rested as a sign of respect, before it carried him on
the last stage of his journey into heaven and it is this shrine
that renders Jerusalem sacred to Islam.

Neither Jerusalem the city nor Palestine as a country has
any equivalent national or political significance to Arabs or
Moslems. Even when Israel was part of a small province in
the Arab empire, the regional center was not Jerusalem but
Ramle. Jerusalem, the city where Jesus preached, died and
was resurrected, is of great importance to Christians in the
religious and theological sense, but has never had a political
or national meaning to Christianity as a whole or to any
Christian nation.

Sinai, where Moses received the Ten Commandments
during the wandering of the Hebrews, was not part of historic Egypt. It was conquered by the Turks and later at Brit-

ish persuasion, conveyed by them to Egypt, then one of its colonial possessions. When Egypt became independent in the present century, Sinai remained under its dominion and control, but was administered as a separate entity. Other than exploitation of its mineral wealth and serving as a staging ground for invasions of Israel, it was never completely developed or integrated into Egypt proper.

Even Gaza, standing on the Way of the Sea, the main route connecting the extremities of the Fertile Crescent, was never actually Egyptian. It was seized by force in 1948 and controlled by a military government until the Six Day War. The hundreds of thousands of Palestinian refugees living there were never permitted to receive Egyptian citizenship or be absorbed into Egypt proper.

In another example on divide and rule colonialism, Britain transferred to French control substantial territories in northern Palestine. After the withdrawal of France from its colonies in the Middle East, these areas were presented to Lebanon and Syria. They included the Golan Heights which became Syrian territory.

This is the factual and historical justification and rationale of those Israelis whose frank goal is the permanent retention of territories conquered — they would prefer "liberated" — and their complete integration into Israel. Most would reluctantly agree to the return of Sinai and Gaza to Egypt, if this is the price of peace, and even abandon the isolated settlements in the Pitha area south of Gaza. These were established in the sand dunes as a land barrier between Egypt and the teeming masses in Gaza and Israel and are assumed to have military and strategic value.

More Israelis are hawks about the right of Jews to settle in Judea and Samaria and some insist on imposing Israeli sovereignty there. It is clear that the Israeli case is much stronger here and the Jewish connection to the West Bank is not merely one of pre-Arab (biblical) or post-Arab (the Holocaust) history. The historical moral ideological connection of the Jews to the land of Israel is also inevitably bound up with the 13 centuries of Arab Jewish relationships.

In another of Israel's numerous paradoxes, many of these hard liners are not the warmongers some feel they must be. They are regarded by most Israelis as highly motivated idealists, mainly youth, who have abandoned the comforts and safety of life in the big cities for a mystical, messianic, emotional brand of pioneering. The most militant faction is the small but vocal *Gush Emunim* (Bloc of Believers) led by yeshiva students and their Orthodox supporters. The knitted skull caps have become a sign of zealous youth devoted to what they unconditionally believe is the God given and inalienable right of Israel.

As though in response to Gush Emunim, a rival, so called Peace Now camp is emerging to return the ship of state to what they feel is a sane Zionism and a rational interpretation of Jewish pioneering values. They have no parallel religious ideological common ground or political organization. Their views have not made the startling impact on the international media that Gush Emunim has achieved. Nevertheless, they are heard on the campus, in kibbutzim and on every city and village street corner. They are likely to form the silent majority that will prevail when the crucial test comes.

Some respect or at least understand the motivation of Gush Emunim and are cognizant of the alleged security advantages inherent in Israeli presence and control over the disputed territories, but believe that retaining them will prevent any possibility of peace and that the immediate solution of the conflict and real security lies in the establishment of good neighbor relations with the Palestinians. In their view, policies that idealize Jewish rights and perpetuate Israeli rule over more than a million refugees who will not settle for less than self-determination, will only jeopardize the future of all.

Although there has never been a national referendum on this matter, most Israelis would return nearly all the areas to Arab control as part of a peace agreement. Everyone talks about minor border adjustments for security and demographic reasons and few would agree to tear reunited Jerusalem apart again, by turning the eastern portion over to Jordanian control. There is hardly anyone who would agree to abandon the Golan Heights again to Syrian artillery and tanks. The ultimate question for Israel is: How small and Jewish should the country be? Can and should any of the new areas, with their total of over a million Arabs, become integral parts of Jewish Israel?

Cutting through these vital questions, is a popular gut feeling that the Arabs will never accept and recognize Israel, even if it were to return all of the territories. This stiffens the resolve of those opposing Arab autonomy in Gaza and the West Bank. These sceptics bolster historical and religious arguments with warnings that a Palestinian state would be a continuous threat to Israel. It would enable expansion of Soviet control, establish a base for continued Russian trouble making in the Middle East and encourage continuation of Arab terrorism, that evil genie born in Palestinian refugee camps, now the plague of the civilized world. It would again give Arab armies the strategic and topographical advantages that have encouraged their wars against Israel.

Strategically and even statistically, Arab terrorism is of relatively minor significance in the Middle Eastern conflict, but killing and wounding of innocent civilians is a continuous blow to national morale. It is also a perpetual reminder of the existence of Palestinian Arabs who will stop at nothing to hurt Israel and prove that they must be taken into account. After many incidents there is an Israeli military reaction to punish those responsible and deter others. More lives are taken and new vows of revenge are made in the vicious circle of political terror.

The key to the quest for peace is the Palestinian refugees and demands for an independent Palestinian state. Many who abandoned their homes have found new livelihoods and built new lives in the Arab world and elsewhere. Others live in slums and camps built for them in Gaza, Jordan and Lebanon, wards of the United Nations and private charities and serve as cannon fodder for terrorist bands and Israeli counter-attacks. Objective evidence confirms that many refugees left voluntarily, before and during the War of Independence to facilitate the expected Arab blitzkrieg that would drive the Jews into the sea. Some fled in fear for their lives or under order of Jewish soldiers and irregular forces. Others left to join the massing Arab armies and guerrilla forces or to avoid being branded collaborators of the Zionists.

All awaited the openly expressed promises of their leaders of a massacre that would enable them to share the spoils of a "Judenrein" Palestine within a few weeks. When Israel surprised the Arabs and everyone else by successfully defending themselves and then advancing to drive out the invading armies, still more Arab leaders fled and the frightened and bewildered masses followed. Assurances by the Jewish leadership and armed forces that Arab lives and homes would not be harmed could not stem their flight.

Since Independence, Israel has admitted and resettled thousands of refugees under a family reunion scheme. It has taken in more than half a million Jews who fled for their lives from Arab states as a result of the war in Palestine. Contrary to expectation, urbanization and modernization of Arab society in Israel has not reduced its birthrate, one of the highest in the world, and eight, ten and twelve children per family is typical. The national average is 8.5 children among Israel's Arabs as compared to 2-3 children in the Jewish families, and it is believed that this Arab population explosion is politically motivated.

Even if present Arab birth trends eventually slow down, and on the other hand, Israel attracts an average of 30,000 immigrants annually — approx. the present number — the demographic projection for the 21st century is grim. Under the most optimistic forecast, the country that is supposed to be the Jewish national home, will have only a small Jewish majority. It would then only be a matter of time before Israelis become a minority in their own country, even without admitting any more Palestine refugees to the country.

If Israel continues to retain the West Bank and Gaza or enters some confederation with them, the Jewish predominance would end even more quickly. With more than one million refugees and their descendants outside of Israel, many of whom were born only after the war, they still insist on "returning" to homes and villages that no longer exist and that most have never even seen. Large tracts of cultivatable land and almost unlimited quantities of water available for resettlement are available in the Arab countries in which they are living, but the Arabs refuse to consider this solution.

All Israelis hope and pray that the Yom Kippur War was the last one, as Sadat and Begin have each declared, but if it be their duty and destiny, this and future generations will rise in the hour of crisis to defend their country. From the farthest kibbutz in the Galilee to Eilat on the Red Sea, there is a deep and abiding faith that the Jewish homeland will live forever. To what extent does the nation possess this determination and readiness for further sacrifice to hold set-

tlements in the hills of the Golan? Must the ancient pro-
vinces of Judea and Samaria with their teeming hostile Arab
population form a part of Israel?

How will Zionists resolve historical, religious and
strategic considerations in the light of global-political
realities and the maneuvering of the super powers? In the
innermost recesses of his soul, can any Israeli who loves his
country deny there are Palestinian refugees who will
sacrifice no less for the right to live in an Arab Palestine?
Will the proud Arab people ever cease to find fault with
history and fate? Will their bitterness and hatred of a small
nation that has humbled them in battle fade with the passing of time, or shall still more wars be the heritage of the
next generation?

These are the burning ideological, moral and political
issues that must be resolved together by Israeli and Arab. If
the decision is a bold one and leads to peace, it may gener-
ate a new golden era in the Middle East and the entire
world. Now is the time for soul-searching for the Zionist
movement and lovers of Zion. After one hundred years of
struggle and accomplishment, the children and grandchildren of the founding fathers have come to a crossroads and
must decide what they are to be in the coming century.

Todays dilemmas are related to several obscure, nearly
forgotten milestones of Zionism. The movement which
resulted in the rebirth of Israel gave rise to unusual events,
dialectics and dogma. They are interesting in the mere fact
of their occurrence and several of them in particular, are
relevant apropos the search for Israel's identity. With the
spreading popularity of Zionism in Eastern Europe at the
turn of the century, Jewish nationalists looked for ways to
breach the gap between Jewish national revival and the
parallel awakening that was taking place among Gentiles
they lived with.

"Yiddishists" for example, claimed that Yiddish was the national language of the Jewish proletariat in the ghettoes and shtetls of Russia, but that Jews were only one of many minorities in Europe struggling for emancipation and autonomy. Their roots were in Eastern Europe and not in some far away land in the Levant where once their distant forefathers lived. The Jewish national identity would reach fruition not through Zionism, but through the Bund — the League of Yiddish-speaking Jewish Socialists. Thus would the down-trodden lumpen Jew become a respected partner in the brotherhood of international socialism and humanism led by Russian Communism.

These were the "Autonomists" who were elated by Zionism but rejected it and who were aptly gibed by Plekhanov, the father of Russian Communism as "Zionists who are afraid of sea-sickness". The "Diaspora" Zionists among them also opposed what they considered an obsession with a physical return to Palestine and even the cultural, elitist Zionism that Ahad Haam espoused. Their ideal was a national renaissance of Jewish pride and culture in the lands of the Diaspora and especially the new world.

Later events in Europe — the Russification of the Communist revolution, Soviet-led anti-Semitism in the east, fascist-led anti-Semitism in the west and the Holocaust, put an end to Yiddishism, Bundism, Autonomism and their adherents. Only those who had left for Palestine, America or elsewhere, escaped to abandon their illusions of autonomy within world brotherhood, for assimilation or return to Orthodoxy or Zionism.

A totally different concept was developed by the "Young Hebrews" or the "Canaanites" as they still are erroneously referred to. They were not only inspired by Zionism, but carried it to what seemed to them, a logical extreme which was rejected by mainstream Zionism. Their basic premise was that there never had been a *Jewish* nation or national-ity. It was the *Hebrew* predecessors of the Jews who were a people with a land, national culture and a nation they had forged out of nomadic Canaanite and Hebrew tribes. Juda-ism, on the other hand, was a religion consisting of a defense mechanism of defeat and exile of Hebrews.

From this rationale, the Young Hebrew view of Zionism envisioned a return by the Jews to Zion based upon a total break with that malady of exile, Judaism, its mores, liturgy and culture that were not part of pre-exilic Hebrew national life. A return to Israel was not enough if it only meant the continued practise of Diaspora ways. It was in Canaan and the Semitic world that Zionism must establish its new state. Two thousand years of dispersal had only brought about a rabbinic-dominated codification of the Oral Tradition of the Prophets, Synagogue in place of Temple and a ritualization of the free and natural ways of the Hebrews.

Israel could be the basis of renewed nationalism, but not if it was simply to bring western-oriented, Diaspora Orthodox cum-Judaism to the Middle East. The Canaanite version of Zionism was the converse of Autonomism and far different than the modern Jewish homeland which arose. In a curious and ironic — some would say perverse way — they anticipated what the PLO and Arab countries declare. If Jews have a right to national existence in Palestine-Israel, they must de-Judaize and become part of the Semitic Levant rather than serve as a vanguard and headquarters for World Jewry and western culture.

When seen in the perspective of numbers, the Zionism that has prevailed in what is Israel today, has been a very small success. Unkinder observers would say that a move-ment which has brought only 10% of the total population of the exiles to the homeland in one hundred years is a fail-ure. Those who do not come may be at best, *Hovevei Zion*

(Lovers of Zion), but not Zionists or Israelis — and certainly not Hebrews. The most extraordinary achievements of Israel *have* in fact been original, Hebrew creations to suit the needs of the old-new nation — the secular and religious kibbutzim, the moshavim, the Histadrut, Zahal.

Should Israel not consider new and daring paths to national redemption? Should it not take from the Diaspora only that which is relevant, positive and meaningful to the new nation? Should it not uncover and reexamine the universal ethics and values to be found here? Must it inevitably and totally be interdependent and related to Jews and Jewry, their institutions and values wherever they may be? This too is the challenge of Israel.

We have come to the Land to build and to be built there
(pioneering Zionist folk song)

Chapter Seven

THE ODDEST TRIBE

THE ANGLO-SAXONS

American settlers, like any others, are individuals and do not constitute types. Nevertheless, for the sake of those who have not visited Israel, the author will offend the fundamental rule of logic that all generalizations are false, including this one. With this apology the reader is invited to become acquainted with some of the English speaking immigrants one is likely to meet in Israel. Sceptics can take a walk around Dizengoff Street, the Old City of Jerusalem or visit the American Embassy or offices of the Association of Americans and Canadians in Israel. There he will surely see many of the following Americans.

The PIONEER is a Yiddish-speaking veteran of the First or Second Aliya. He was probably born or lived in East Europe before he arrived in America during the European emigration to that country. Pioneers helped build villages such as Ra'anana, Emek Hefer and Rosh Pina. Few in number, but strong in Zionist consciousness and idealism, they paved the way for those who followed and raised in the new land a generation of children that would later do their share for Israel. One was the father of General Itzhak Rabin.

The FIGHTER was a GI and fought against the Nazis and Japanese before he joined the thousands of Jews who volunteered to fight for Israel in the War of Independence. These became the men and women of *Machal* (Foreign Volunteers) in the *Hagana* underground. They took part in the major battles of a war that seemed doomed to defeat and provided an important part of the fledgling air force and technical services of the infant State. Former American army officer and Judge Mickey Marcus became one of Israel's first generals and modern folk heroes and died on the Latrun front near Jerusalem. His body was returned to the native land he had also served so bravely and was buried at West Point. Others fought and lived and stayed on in their adopted country.

The SENIOR CITIZEN is a pensioner from America. Some come with or to be near their children in their golden years. Others are attracted by nostalgia for the *yiddishkeit* of the Old World or the American Jewish communities of 40 and 50 years ago, which they rediscover in Israel. With lots of Israeli pounds per dollar, they find that Social Security and pension checks can go much further in Tel Aviv and Jerusalem than in New York or Miami Beach.

In Israel they do battle with the ravages of old age in an atmosphere that gives them renewed vigor. Many become active volunteers in youth or welfare work and give of their time and energy to help less fortunate immigrants. They make friends with other old-timers and some may even find love or marriage. A few live in comparative luxury such as the residents of *Neve Avivim* (Oasis of Spring) near Herzlia, but most get along modestly on their monthly checks from America. Many are lonely and ignored in a land that glorifies the young and the hardy.

The IDEALIST has been an enthusiastic member of Israeli kibbutz and Zionist movements in America. Raised in Young Israel, Young Watchmen or the Builders, coming to Israel is the natural culmination of years of preparation and anticipation. He has a real knowledge of and love for the land and the language. He quickly and happily adjusts to his new life, to the mixed pleasure of proud but anxious parents, many of whom are active in the Zionist establishment in America, yet refuse to move to Zion, a paradox only they understand.

The RELIGIOUS is a Jew carrying out a basic tenet of his faith by "ascending" to *Eretz Hakodesh*, the Sacred Land of Israel. Religious Jews form perhaps 20% of the total Jewish population. Sometimes entire families follow these young members of *Bnei Akiva* and other religious youth movements, and the *Mizrachi*, as they are called, with their knitted skull caps, settle down to participate fully in the national life of the country, while holding to their observance of religious Jewish law. The Hassidic Habad village is very well known, and the dancing, singing Hassidim are popular and well liked. The Ultra-Orthodox come to reestablish their yeshiva and Torah centered lives in places such as the Kiryat Sanz village near Netanya, led by the Rabbi of Klausenberg. Some head straight for the Mea Shearim or Bnei Brak communities, but these Jews usually prefer to stay in the Williamsburg section of Brooklyn and their other tiny enclaves in the US, where life among the Gentiles does not demand the compromises necessary in "secular" Israel.

The SCHOLAR is a student, teacher or professor. Perhaps he came over as an expert, adviser or participant in a research project or archaeological dig. When he finishes his work or study, he decides to remain in Israel. The brain drain flows in both directions and the US has also absorbed many such emigrants from Israel. Greater material rewards and opportunities in America continue to attract scientists and the intellectuals of other countries, and some are Israeli emigrés returning to their former country.

An unusually large number of professors and instructors at Israeli universities are Western immigrants. They are regarded by optimistic Israelis as the first of the one million Jewish American students, faculty and intelligentsia who could be the pioneers of tomorrow. Positions are available for qualified instructors and students are invited to continue their studies. Special reception centers have been set up to help them in their adjustment to Israel. Each year more courses are offered in English or especially designed for the English-speaking student. Some universities offer full baccalaureate programs recognized by institutions of higher learning in the US.

The MIXED MARRIAGE includes, for lack of a better term, the who knows how many Americans who find Israeli husbands or wives and come here to live with them. Some have no Zionist background or inclination and, but for the fortunes of love and marriage, would never have come. Many become enthusiastic and happy Israelis, while others leave after what turns out to be only a honeymoon and return to the US where they and their Israeli spouses can join America's Israeli colony.

The INVESTOR is a middle-aged or middle class Jew who comes here to represent some company or to start his own business. They bring a little part of the West with them and Israel has not been the same since. A noble tradition of the Good Old Days was the *makolet* (family grocery) found on every street corner. Israelis welcomed buying on credit and accepted the dirty floors, newspaper wrapped purchases and long lines as inevitable. Thanks to the insight and stubbornness of the Canadian-American Super Sol chain and the cooperative supermarkets, drab little groceries have spruced up or been forced out of business. Today Israelis are "Super" crazy and more and bigger supermarkets and shopping centers are opening up.

Quick service and junk food restaurants, cocktail lounges and even Coca Cola have come to Israel, where they are thriving. The government tries to encourage American investment by easing the complicated regulations applying to foreign investors but investors remain uneasy about mediocre management practices, lack of initiative in Israeli business life and Arab boycott threats. Still, these newcomers have discovered that one can find profits and affluence in Haifa, Jerusalem and Tel Aviv as well as in the cities of America.

The SECOND CHANCER also fits into other categories, but his real motivation is to make a new beginning after having undergone some personal crisis elsewhere. Moving to Israel makes them believe that they can "start again" and often they do. There are unhappily married couples trying to change their luck and survivors of broken marriages. Like the pensioner, the divorcée or estranged wife finds that her alimony or maintenance check from America may go much further in Israel. Others soon move over to the "mixed marriage" category, confirming the wisdom of those who declare their faith in the permanence of marriage by counselling that everyone should be married once or twice.

There are Second Chancers who are dropouts from unhappy homes, tensions of life in the megalopolis or studies in the megauniversities of America. Some have abandoned jobs which have become intolerably boring or a way of life which is no longer rewarding. If they were not Jews they might have moved to Alaska, Hawaii or Paris but they come here and discover their Jewishness. While some are no happier in Israel, others find the peace of mind they lacked and a worthwhile new life.

The VOLUNTEER comes from one of dozens of countries and probably for as many reasons. They are young and old, Christians and Jews, idealists and adventurers and many are from the US. A large number are students while a few are professional drifters. Some came "to fight," but for most the war is always over by the time they arrive.

A Volunteers Department in the Jewish Agency handles the reception, assignment and needs of these newcomers. Many stay for only a few months and return home. Some have started Volunteer or Aliya clubs in their own countries and pledge to settle in Israel at the conclusion of their studies or preparations for settlement. Others wander around aimlessly and become members of the next group.

The ADVENTURER is often sandaled, bearded or beaded and looks a lot like the Jewish and Gentile hippies from Scandinavia, England, Germany, Holland, Tel Aviv or Haifa. Adventurers fill the beach at Eilat and in the Sinai, and when the winter rains come build colorful huts or tent colonies in the sand. Others live in deserted buildings or in the youth hostels and hospices around the country.

Their original and often weird appearance and hip or punk costumes look strange in contrast to the dress alike, look alike, young Israelis. They are a regular part of Eilat, downtown Tel Aviv and the Old City of Jerusalem and can be seen strumming banjos and guitars and singing songs few passersby understand, or chalking their version of pop art on the pavements, hoping for contributions from appreciative Israelis. They usually have enough money to eat, drink and tour around the country and those who are interested know where to find a friendly Israeli to sell them a little hashish.

When their well hidden travellers checks run out or their parents are late in cabling funds, they tell friends they are going to the desert to meditate. Then they hitch a ride to a kibbutz or somewhere in the Negev or Eilat where they can work with no questions asked for that despised commodity called money. Once they have been photographed on the back of a camel or reading a newspaper while floating in the Dead Sea and have tried their luck with the sabra girls, they are ready to move on.

Somber Israelis consider them too way out but are a little sorry to see them go. They add a touch of lightheartedness and nonsense to a land where most people are too serious and busy to be eccentric. When the Adventurer is a Jew, his Israeli acquaintances encourage him to shave, bathe and marry some nice Jewish Israeli girl. This invitation is usually declined and after a while, he travels on in search of greener pastures, to prolong an adolescence that starts earlier and ends later than in any other society. When he returns home to become a proper member of society, he may be the first to mock what will be the hippies of the next generation. At least he does not cause the embarrassment of the last, smallest and most peculiar group of Anglo-Saxons.

TRA-LA-LA is sabra slang for *very lo normali* and include extra-hippie black sheep who are bad news both in Israel and abroad. While it is no secret that every Jewish (and Christian) community has its strange Aunt Shirley who never goes out of the house or Cousin Harry, whose activities are a bit of a mystery, some of these eccentrics are also psychopaths, criminals and drug addicts and sometimes they end up in Israel. Their coming here pleases only their anxious families and often they arrive just a step ahead of an extradition, arrest order or law suit in America. Israel, which, for its part, has no shortage of local *meshuganers* would prefer that this type of "Zionist" stay where they are or join the Foreign Legion.

The Law of Return is the legislative fulfillment of the Zionist dream of a national homeland open to every Jew. In the past too many wanted men and cranks have taken advantage of this law and joined the hundreds of thousands of genuine immigrants. While asylum is granted to the sick, the poor and the hopeless, Israel no longer admits those who come only to escape the law or to make trouble for the Israelis. The Minister of the Interior is authorized to refuse entry to or to expel a Jew who has "engaged in an activity directed against the Jewish people or who is likely to endanger the public health or security of the State".

Israeli tra-la-las, believing in giving an eye for an eye, rather than in turning the other cheek, have tried to correct this injustice, and are doing so admirably by flocking in droves to the shores of America where they have become a national embarrassment for both countries.

FIGURES & STATISTICS

According to official data of the government Bureau of Statistics, the total population of Israel at the beginning of 1979, was 3,730,000, including 3,135,000 Jews and 595,000 Arabs, excluding the administered areas where about a million Arabs live. During 1978, natural increase and immigration added 77,000 Jews or 1.9% while the Arab population increased 19,000 or 3.3%. Approximately 26,000 Jewish immigrants arrived compared to 21,300 in 1977 and this upward trend is expected to continue in the 80's with greater numbers coming from western countries following the signing of the Israel-Egypt peace treaty.

Reliable figures and statistics about American immigration

170

and emigration are sparse and in constant flux and dispute. AACI, the US Embassy, Jewish Agency and Absorption Ministry refer to different numbers and percentages but some raw data and general trends are accepted by most observers.

1. The figure most frequently cited is approximately 60,000 American citizens permanently residing in Israel. Not all are registered at the Embassy and some are not holders of Israeli citizenship. A few manage to retain formal status as "Temporary" residents, "Students", "Businessmen" and even "Tourists" for years, although they have long since become de facto if not official Israelis.

2. Approximately 2,500-5,000 Americans arrive every year, with the declared intent of settling in Israel and only cynics point out that far more Jews from any large northern city in the US move every year to Florida, California and even Hawaii.

3. The percentage of settlers who return to North America is extremely high, with speculation ranging from 20% to 70% returnees, the highest rate of dropouts of all the immigrant groups (except possibly for the Russians), with most leaving within five years.

4. The exact number of settlers and returnees cannot be accurately verified for several reasons. "Settlers" include those who become Israeli citizens and those who do not, but statistics regarding the latter are limited. Furthermore, some returnees to America come back again while others are not genuine *Yordim* having left only on business, study or official missions to return later to Israel. Some Olim on the other hand, arrive for a limited or specific period and should be classified neither as settlers nor returnees.

5. Approximately 4,000-7,000 Americans live in kibbutzim and moshavim on a permanent or semi-permanent basis with the rest residing in cities and large towns. Jerusalem

has become an increasing favorite especially with the young and single, but housing is scarce and expensive. Metropolitan Tel Aviv gets most newcomers — despite the criticism that the quality of life has sharply deteriorated, something familiar to former Americans. Yet it is still first choice especially with businessmen, marrieds and retirees. Beautiful Haifa unaccountably ends up with the least newcomers along with small towns like Rosh Pina, and Nahariya.

6. Each year there are greater percentages and numbers of American born settlers in Israel, confirming that more younger people are immigrating than before. Previously more settlers were older and European born.

7. The number of American immigrants has remained fairly steady both in total figures and percentage breakdown except for brief spurts after the Six Day War. This tends to prove that their Aliya is really a totally voluntary act. Immigration from other free countries in affluent Europe, South America and South Africa fluctuates greatly, depending upon political, social and economic conditions there. While there has been only a small rise in American settlement from year to year, the numbers are stable.

8. Most of the available data indicates that a primary motivation of American settlers is a response to feeling Jewish and a desire to lead a more Jewish life. Many have been involved in Aliya groups, Zionist organizations and/or have had some Jewish education however brief. They come "to study", to "find myself", "start a new" or "better life", "for the children's sake" or "to retire". Some settlers are not sure if they want to remain permanently in Israel, but almost all consider that possibility when they arrive.

The drastic breakdown in the quality of life in the big cities of America — social tensions, crime in the streets, unemployment — has led to an unease among American Jewry and more are thinking about alternatives than in earlier decades. Were it not for anxiety about the security of Israel and its own smaller but similar social internal problems, some might consider the possibility of Aliya.

Veteran Anglo-Saxons know that near-revolutionary changes are necessary to prepare the foundations for large-scale American settlement in Israel. Those who have successfully settled know that the problems of every new immigrant from planning the big move to follow up stages of integration constitute a single process. A single non-political organization should deal with immigrants, run by those who have lived the problems and speak the language of the new arrivals. Settlers from the same city or country should be helping the greenhorns in their first difficult days in the new country.

In practice, the government sponsored and controlled Jewish Agency and Ministry of Absorption are the official institutions that deal with immigration and social adjustment of new settlers. Their activities are carried on in cooperation with the Jewish National Fund, which was established to finance, acquire and prepare the land in Palestine for Jewish settlement.

Throughout the years the JNF has purchased large areas of land, holding them in trust as the inalienable property of the Jewish people. It engages in soil reclamation, afforestation and development and in providing the land basis for Jewish farming has done much to prepare the infrastructure of the Jewish State. Its holdings amount to about a million acres and most of it has been given to immigrants for settlement. The JNF's accomplishments are impressive — a quarter million acres of rocky, swamp or sandy wasteland transformed into productive arable soil, 1000 miles of roads blasted through mountains and deserts plus 100 million trees, some in areas where there has been nothing green for 2000 years.

173

The Fund, the Jewish Agency and the Ministry of Absorption in Israel and abroad function through the same politization, factions and coalitions as other institutions in Israel. Many of the key officials and ideologists like those of the national leadership, are western, European Ashkenazi immigrants and more than a few were old-timers even when the State was born. It is the job of these seniors to encourage young Americans to settle in Israel but they do not always understand them or speak the same language either literally or figuratively.

Each department head is appointed by a political party whose interests and policies were subconsciously shaped by experiences in the towns and villages of Russia and Poland 30, 50 and 70 years ago. Few American voices are heard on the top levels, and claims that they are better qualified to deal with immigration from their native country are usually ignored with professional and political Zionists remaining firmly in charge.

A related anomaly is the failure of the vast majority of Israel conscious, American Jews to make Aliya. This has contributed to another interpretation of the term "Tsionut" (Zionism) to mean insincere or hypocritical polemics. It has hardened the professionalization of US Jewish leadership and the camp followers for whom Zionism is essentially a cushy job, prestige and trips abroad. The interfaction argumentation, intolerance of dissident voices and boring meetings and congresses have turned off a great majority of the Jews whom they are supposed to represent. Only one out of every 10 American Jews has even visited Israel and perhaps only one out of 300 has tried to live here. Very few give their children a Jewish education or teach them Hebrew.

Eighty years after the founding of the Zionist movement, a fresh look at traditional attitudes and activities in America is imperative to provide viable goals and activities. School-children and students in significant numbers are not study-ing Hebrew, or Jewish and Zionist history. Programs enabl-ing young Americans to spend time in Israel during vaca-tions or in study courses are not widespread. Israel and Aliya desks and information centers are not found on the campuses, in Jewish Centers, or in Synagogues and Tem-ples to answer questions about Israel and encourage interest in the challenge of Aliya. Substantial financial assistance, loans and mortgages are not available for Americans who settle, though funds for local Jewish, Gentile and minority causes are not lacking. Only a myopic or cynical Zionist can deny that the movement in America is floundering.

Nevertheless party hacks and idealists continue to work together within this difficult framework and atmosphere. With their cumbersome sections and sub-sections, created to accommodate the needs of political rivalries, coalitions and jobs for the faithful, these institutions stagger on. Infinite glasses of tea and lemon — the Zionist beverage — are sipped by a multitude of clerks and petty officials at endless meetings in Jerusalem, Tel Aviv and New York (though many might prefer beer or whiskey). Only some-what less than in the political arena, they are distracted by political intrigues, quarrels, splits and coalitions. Like a good natured *golem*, the clumsy giant moves on and in one of Israel's many miracles, remains the outstretched if shaky hand that has brought in and absorbed more than a million immigrants in a monumental feat of trial and error.

In spite of confused policies, long lines and complicated forms, the race from office to office and clerk to clerk, few newcomers can justifiably place the blame on the Agency or anyone else for not getting along in Israel. Just when Olim may reach the end of their patience, they usually receive the encouragement, advice, loan or mortgage they have

175

been waiting for, are admitted to Hebrew School, University, Absorption Center or their new apartment.

Veteran immigrants received little or no help at all when they came while today's arrivals, especially professional and academic settlers, are given considerable material assistance to make their first years in Israel easier. No other immigrant country has anything to compare to Israel's doting, chaotic and frustrating Jewish Agency and Ministry of Absorption. The product of historical developments, political compromises and Zionist dogma, run on an inadequate budget and by a not always qualified staff, they have served the nation loyally though not always well.

PROBLEMS, CHALLENGES

New arrivals are usually excited and apprehensive. They may want to write to relatives or friends: "Have arrived and conquered" but almost immediately they are undergoing hurdles and challenges that test their faith and fortitude. Just clearing household belongings from the port can be a Kafka-like maze of visits to shipping agents, customs authorities and warehouses. Seemingly endless examinations of passports, forms, declarations and guarantees whittle away at their enthusiasm and soon they will sign anything placed in front of them by the overworked port officials. Finally — success! They are seated in the cabin of a precariously loaded truck containing their lifts and crates and racing at frightening speeds down the highway to their new home, with the driver telling them in some strange language what they will continually hear when everything seems so difficult: *"yihiye be'seder"* — "Everything will be OK".

The first lesson for the naive is that in Israel a home is not a house. Houses or "villas" as they are somewhat inac-

curately called, are few and their prices limit them to diplomats and the near wealthy. Small, two family houses,
similar to country cottages back home can cost $150,000 if
they are located in choice urban areas. Attractive three bed-
room, garage and lawn, American style suburban homes
are sold for $200,000 and more! In a country no larger than
New Jersey where most of the land is desert, there is
nowhere or way to build popular priced American type,
suburban housing estates. Most available land is owned by
the Jewish National Fund, kibbutzim, moshavim or Israel's
Arab citizens and the search for a small lot on which to
build a dream house is often unrewarding.

The owner of land plus the equally invaluable permit to
build a house — perhaps one in every 50 — pays dearly for
what is usually no larger than one-eighth of an acre (half a
dunam) and building costs are expensive. With moderately
priced private homes available only in distant villages or
small towns and rental housing equally rare, the city bound
newcomer frequently ends up the owner of an apartment in
a *shikun* (housing project). Some are small, modern apartment houses that look much like those in American cities.
For others home is the large, uniform looking apartment
buildings built row upon row all over the country. A family
buys its apartment and becomes a joint owner with the
neighbors of the tiny garden (where the kids play tag and
soccer) and building air raid shelter (used by everyone as a
storage room for a variety of junk).

Small, out of town flats cost as "little" as $35,000. Mod-
ern, three bedrooms in town may be double. Larger and
luxurious four and five room flats cost $75,000 or $100,000
and even $200,000 in prestigious sections like Jerusalem's
Rehavia or North Tel Aviv. All that the builder, often a
government owned or controlled company, requests is
approximately two-thirds of the purchase price as a "down

payment". Mortgages are granted at interest rates that would be criminal in other countries. Since it is almost impossible to evict a tenant or owner in Israel, the banks insist on three or four respectable citizens to guarantee payment of the loan. In this ultimate test of trust the newcomer learns who his real friends are.

Finally the *Oleh* (new immigrant) moves into what will be his new home. It may be plush by any standards with steam heat, elevator service, incinerators and luxury kitchens and appliances. *Shikunim* like Jerusalem's *Naot* (Oasis) or *Shikun Amerikai* in Herzlia are filled with former Americans, and accents and furniture suggest apartments in Long Island and points west. Time and Vogue magazines lie about and paperback books from the US fill the bookcases, while furnishings from Macy's and Bloomingdale's add to the impression that this is America.

When they finally settle down, the new family has a comfortable home and more than friendly and/or inquisitive neighbors. All they have left to worry about are annual state and municipal taxes plus gas, electricity, water and water-heating bills, and monthly house dues (someone has to pay for cleaning the building stairs and entrance and taking care of the shikun garden). "Extra" dues are imposed for major repairs and upkeep in the building and miscellaneous expenses such as gifts for the Goldberg party or the new Cohen baby (they have eight already).

Sooner or later the settler sets himself to what seems like a truly impossible goal — learning Hebrew. Its classical form was spoken by Jews 3000 years ago and it is the only language ever to be successfully revived after having ceased to exist as a living language. It is the tongue the Bible was written in and that of great writings in many fields of human endeavor, particularly during the Golden Age of the Jewish Renaissance in medieval times. Almost all Israelis speak Hebrew and for the sabras it is the language in which they study, work, argue and make love.

The newcomer is helped by an institution called *ulpan* (studio). This is the government supervised, intensive, Hebrew language school where students are taught to speak, read and write the tongue of the prophets in anywhere from six months to two years. One sits in a classroom five hours a day with other new immigrants, often for the first time since youth, and there is homework in the evenings. With no language spoken but Ivrit, the first few days are a human comedy of sign language and misunderstandings, but almost every graduate of the ulpan manages to learn Hebrew. Only for some does this challenge prove too difficult, resulting in total discouragement and abandoning of the goal.

Others go on to further study in preparation for careers as actors, teachers or lawyers and succeed in what once seemed mission impossible. Perhaps the sweetest victory is that of the typist who must learn to use a typewriter where the letters are strange and the carriage moves "backwards"! This achievement is a dubious one for the Anglo-Saxon office girl who later learns that an English language typist is paid a better salary than her counterpart in Hebrew.

Many Americans, especially the young at heart, prefer to learn Hebrew at a kibbutz run ulpan where they study in the morning, work in the afternoons and have evenings free to practice their Hebrew with the kibbutz girls and boys. The favorite test is often an Israeli version of "Me — Tarzan, you — Jane" in which they are not always thwarted by the cool but curious sabras. This type of social absorption has become an additional attraction of the kibbutzim for young and single newcomers and a steady source of mixed marriages and new hands for the kibbutz movement.

Once Hebrew has been learned, all that is left is to find a

job and make a living. This is *the* test for veterans as well as newcomers, but the monthly battle of the budget is particularly acute for those spoiled by the affluence of America. In Israel some learn to give up much that was taken for granted back home, while others may not have to. The womb to tomb benefits of Israel's social welfare system are considerable. No family need fear for instance, that illness will wipe out the family savings or be beyond its means since almost no one has savings and almost everyone is a member of a Sick Fund (*Kupat Holim*), Israel's version of Blue Cross/Blue Shield.

Medical fees depend on family size and income, but this is always a bargain since coverage includes complete medical and hospital services. Immigrant families are insured at nominal or no cost. To make the whole arrangement typically Israeli, there are different Sick Funds, some affiliated with none other than those Israeli political parties. Every Israeli family is able to receive all the benefits of modern medicine except tender, loving care. For Americans, the bureaucracy, revolving door treatment and lack of real patient doctor relationship makes Sick Funds a mixed blessing.

Generous sick and maternity leave, holiday allowances and cost of living allowances are granted to employees, and zealous workers' committees exist in every office and factory to protect their legal rights. Some developing countries are plagued by population explosions and bonuses are paid to volunteers for sterility operations. In Israel a Jewish population explosion would be a blessing and government bonuses and a monthly "children's allowance" (*kitzvat yeladim*) are paid to parents for each new baby, in addition to all medical and hospital bills.

When he leaves work to join his unit in the reserve army, the worker's position is protected and he is kept on nearly complete salary. At vacation time he receives two to four weeks paid leave and can spend it at a subsidized holiday resort or rest at home. If his employer is late with the pay check, stiff penalties and fines can be imposed and added to his salary. If he is discharged from his job and in government employ this is often as difficult as evicting a tenant and a major cause of Israel's bloated bureaucracy, he is given a severance bonus equal to a month's salary for each year of employment. When he dies, the government and his employer share in the funeral costs and pay an allowance to the widow, through the National Insurance Institute (*Bituach Leumi*).

The worker contributes his share towards the cost of these benefits and he is the most heavily taxed citizen in the world. When the Finance Minister asks for higher rates or voluntary taxpayers' loans to the government, Israelis grumble but pay up. They understand the imperative need for a modern army and the great expenses involved in its upkeep. A huge part of the national budget is drained away each year by the costs of defense but Israelis accept this burden, knowing it is another case of *ein breira* (no alternative).

Salaries are relatively small and the average worker earns no more than $350 to $850 per month (before tax, which may reduce the amount by one third or one half). "High" income brackets start at $900 monthly and few Israelis *net* more than $1,200 per month. They are not paid in dollars but in Israeli currency, and the cost of living is attuned to the same standard.

Once wages were more egalitarian and a bank manager who happened to be a bachelor was paid no more than the father of 10 who was the cleaning man. Today, disparities in salaries are greater than in many developing countries. Socialist equality has given way to the law of supply and demand and the same bank manager now earns four or five times the salary of the porter. Top professionals such as technocrats, scientists and professors are paid monthly salaries and benefits of $2,000 or more, while clerks and common laborers can expect no more than a quarter or less.

Salaries conform to wage scales based on skill, tenure and number of dependants that are the result of government and *Histadrut* (Labor Federation) wage policies. Even such individualists as rabbis, disc jockeys, journalists and museum directors are subject to labor contracts between their representatives and the Histadrut. These policies have assured relative labor stability and economic growth and while the affluent West has many living in conditions of poverty, Israel's poor, although possibly poorer, are fewer.

With all of the social benefits the purchasing power of the Israeli salary is limited. The new Chevy or Ford within the reach of almost any working man in America, costs more than $30,000 in Tel Aviv and is almost always driven by a tourist, ambassador, gangster or rich man. The one out of three Israeli families fortunate enough to own a small European car has to pay $15,000 plus additional sums annually for vehicle and license taxes.

Quality clothing is very costly and a man's suit runs about $300 while electrical appliances can be triple with a new refrigerator that sells for $750 in New York is $2,000 in Israel. If one wants a telephone installed he must pay a $250 fee, as well as substantial taxes added to the monthly bills for its use. Even the question one asks the information operator is charged as a call, if the number is listed in the telephone directory.

In addition to relatively low salaries, the most alarming economic problem is the ever spiralling inflation. Thirty years ago, the once proud Israeli "Lira" was equivalent to a British Pound (Sterling); today it is worth less than a nickel and is going down all the time. The annual inflationary rate hovers at a sky-high, three-figure percentage that is devastating the economy and the average family's budget.

For all Israelis, and western newcomers in particular, low wages and rapid inflation means a net income equivalent to two thirds or three quarters of what is needed to maintain an adjusted but reasonable standard of living. The solution is overtime, double time, moonlighting, a working wife and for many not paying income tax on whatever they can get away with. This in turn has contributed to the decline in morality and added to the invisible and potentially dangerous "Black" money phenomenon.

In spite of this economic vicious circle, Israelis somehow live surprisingly well even compared to back home. Statistics confirm what any discerning tourist can see, that life in Israel is more comfortable than in Western countries such as Italy or Greece and for some immigrants, very similar to their former life style. It is more comfortable and surely more exciting than the highly industrialized and highly ideological nations of the communist world.

There is a growing middle class in Israel and the problem of how to keep up with the Goldsteins and the Levys is affecting more and more Israelis. Country clubs, resorts and night clubs are packed with merry making Israelis and even psychiatrists are becoming popular. The latest disco gyrations have easily replaced the hora national dance and fashion plate teenagers are attracted by pop records and discotheques as they were just a few years ago by songfests around a bonfire. Stores and boutiques are crowded with Israelis buying things they don't need, with an "It will cost even more tomorrow" rationale.

Even those doctrinaire bastions of the simple life, the kibbutz and moshav, have been affected by the new emphasis on materialism and the good life. Swimming pools, tennis courts, espresso bars and cafés now flank the cotton fields and communal dining halls. Some settlements send their members to the city to learn Chinese cooking or beauty techniques to satisfy demands of kibbutzniks and moshavniks interested in eating and looking better. It is clear that while patriotism and sacrifice are national traits in emergencies, the austere and unpretentious Israel of yesterday is all but gone.

Surprisingly few see anything inconsistent between material comforts and the building of a just and happy society for all. Israel has been Spartan long enough and after four wars, and the tensions and frustrations of three generations, the time has come to relax and to be like other people. With life and liberty more or less secure in the cities of Israel, Israelis are now engaged in the uninhibited pursuit of fun and happiness.

Some deplore the new emphasis on materialism and hedonism. They view the ostentatious weddings, gadgets and trips to Europe as serious challenges to the moral and social values that built up the country. Many expect an economic "earthquake" unless Israel returns to the simple ways of yesterday. With the ever present threat of new depressions and wars hovering over Israel and payments continually due on government bonds and loans, it will again be forced to tighten its belt. Others decry the faltering quality of life and the inroads made by the problems of other countries such as pollution, crime, moral decay and scandal in public life, now Israeli problems.

Many Israelis are not unduly concerned about this social and economic criticism. Having faced more difficult struggles, they are not dissuaded by what they consider prophets of doom and defeatists. There is a middle class aspiration in the country that has affected every level of society and while people are willing to work harder and longer, they will not give up what they now consider the good life. They go to work at an hour when most Americans and Europeans are still sleeping, do their job, come home for a quick lunch and nap if they can, and still have time and energy for moonlighting or an evening out that can last into the early morning hours. They may be somewhat sorry that they didn't stay home, but the next day will be very much the same. They grumble and curse their lot but do so in an almost "what the hell" attitude.

This becomes the life of the Anglo-Saxons and most thrive on it. Brass bands do not meet them on arrival and they suffer disappointments that are difficult for some to endure. Those with health, financial or personal problems often do not get through successfully. While American families have adjustment pains moving from New York to Illinois or even from Brooklyn to Westchester county, Western settlers must adjust to a new world and totally new way of life.

A few do so only partially and remain on the periphery of Israeli society. Those who do not succeed in learning Hebrew have only limited and superficial contact with the world around them. Some choose to live in the familiar and comfortable surroundings of the English speaking colony, not unlike those in the dozens of lands where Americans live abroad. With diplomats, tourists, transient businessmen and others like themselves, theirs is a play world Israel that is really an extension of the US. Few share real friendships with Israelis or become personally integrated or emotionally involved in the country and its life.

Others are fully and successfully Israelized but are disturbed by negative aspects of Israeli life. Western immigrants are annoyed each time veterans ask them that surprising question ..."*Why* did you come to Israel?" It is usually asked in a tone of incredulity that suggests that Zionism is

185

nonsense and that American settlers belong to the naive adventurer category. No matter how you struggle to explain they shrug and say, "But why would you want to leave America?" Serious problems are rationalized away by Israelis with the familiar "...but we're still a young country." This is offered in good faith as an explanation for such prosaic faults as dirty streets or the inability of bus passengers to wait in line. Just let there be a national achievement of any kind and the same sidewalk philosophers will confidently wink and tell you, "What did you expect, we are one of the oldest countries in the world."

Moshe Dayan declares that an Israeli paratrooper is the "bravest Jewish soldier since Bar Kochba", the leader of the last Jewish rebellion against the Roman Empire. The generally keen Israeli sense of proportion is affected by the same considerations. An Israeli weight lifter becomes the "strongest Jew since Samson," and at an automobile assembly plant one almost expects to hear: "This is the first Jewish car since the days of King Solomon." The national soccer team beats a pickup squad in a practice workout in New York and Israeli sports pages rave as though the New York Mets or Mohammed Ali has been humbled by athletes from Zion.

Even justifiable remarks by newcomers about sullen waiters, noisy movie audiences or needless red tape often bring the rejoinder "Things were worse when we came." The embarrassed American is sure that they are also saying, "*We* don't need *you* to tell us how to run the country." Just a few years ago one had to stand in line at a bank each month to pay utility and other bills. Some western immigrants refused and their stubbornness paid off. Today one can pay bills by mail and companies and stores are glad to accept checks and credit cards. Still, old habits die slowly for the faithful. Stand near the teller's window in banks and post offices and you will see Israelis of every background awaiting their turn to pay bills of every type, something that was once a national tradition.

A few years ago one could hardly get a good meal except at home or in a luxury restaurant. Israeli cuisine bore the taste of the pioneer heritage and the English influence. Food was rationed and prepared and devoured quickly in order to get on with the task of building a country. Today things have changed and so have Israeli waistlines. A new cult has sprung up among the Israeli masses and it is aptly named *zollallanut* (gluttony). *Steakerias* compete with Chinese, Vietnamese, Italian and French restaurants. An annual "Queen of the Kitchen" is elected and the Tourist Ministry operates a training school for chefs. In pre-Independence and Israel of the fifties this could not have happened and though a few still prefer borsht and sour cream at Tnuva dairy buffets they are the last of a dying and slimmer generation.

Sometimes the Israeli penchant to be *normali* and like other people seems not so normal to confused newcomers, as familiar values are rejected for new ones. Several real life vignettes dramatize the quaint differences between Jews and Israelis. While Jewish doctors, merchants or comedians in Israel are nobody's fool, they hardly enjoy the status in this society that they have in America. Israel's élite are apt to be paratroop colonels, cotton farmers, soccer players or Bible champions, endeavors in which American Jews are hardly expert. Biochemists, physicists and writers in Israel are quietly making new discoveries and winning Nobel prizes; it is almost expected of them. But when a developing country asks for a Dan or Egged bus driver to explain the fine points of driving Israeli assembled buses — that makes headlines and is deemed a national achievement!

The daily newspaper has a different meaning in news-hungry Israel and it is not bad manners to lean over a stranger's shoulder on a park bench or bus and read along with him. It is almost rude not to offer the onlooker a page or two if he asks for it and chances are he will say, *slicha* (pardon me) and "borrow" it before you can reply. At first one is shocked, especially English Jews for whom this experience may be almost traumatic. After a year or two in Israel you find yourself "borrowing" someone else's newspaper or reading along with him.

There is considerable indifference to good old Hebrew words such as *bevakasha* (please) and *toda* (thank you) and the shoving, pushing and rudeness is irritating. Perhaps the biggest shock is when Israelis rationalize "...after all Israel is a pioneering country," while others claim decent manners and politeness are hypocritical and unnecessary leftovers from the Diaspora. For some Olim these are disappointments they will never adjust to, while others quickly learn to do as the Romans do. Unfortunately, manifestations of aggressiveness and gruffness — and they can be crude — have become synonymous with the ugly Israeli at home and abroad.

Noisy, levantine, elitist, tough, selfish, inconsiderate are some of the descriptions used to define the negative side of the Sabra personality and it is not flattering. This same behavior affects the average Israeli in his relationships with family, neighbors, friends and the man in the street. Tensions have risen rather than disappeared as Israel grows up and with them an increase in marital discord, divorce and emotional disorders.

One should point out that these national traits are related to an egalitarianism that is a pleasant contrast to class consciousness prevalent in other countries and cultures. An Israeli waiter will no longer indignantly return a proffered tip, but he will not be servile to the customers as he might

n Europe. He will do his job without being charming and
s not disappointed if the diner seems dissatisfied. Israelis
are simply not at ease in circumstances requiring formality
or positions of service and their behavior reflects this
attitude. It is the rare post office clerk or waiter who is as
courteous as his counterpart in Europe or America.

For Israelis who don't own cars, riding buses is the only
way to get around. Having braved Arab guns to deliver the
mail, provisions and citizen soldiers to the front in four
wars, the Egged or Dan bus driver is no mere mortal. He
gives change, punches tickets, sorts coins, drives faster,
brakes more suddenly and scares more passengers to death
than anyone else on wheels. Just dare to interrupt him
while he is flirting with a woman soldier or arguing about a
soccer game with an acquaintance. When he is at the steering wheel, few are the passengers or drivers who will challenge him. He is not a mere bus driver, but part owner of a
powerful Cooperative with its own representative in the
Knesset and a salary double the average clerk or teacher.

This rugged individualism and freedom of expression is
typically Israeli. Perhaps a neighbor in the shikun, at the
beach, or the sherut or bus driver is listening to his radio —
often a Greek or Arab love song — at full earsplitting volume. Try smiling and asking him to change the station or
turn it down a little. Heads shake and people stare as if to
say, "Relax, greenhorn, you're in Israel now." With scores
of ethnic groups, behavior patterns and customs, new
Israelis soon learn to live and let live. The wise settler
learns the ways of the other tribes and survives when
nothing else seems to work.

Conscious of racial and social injustice in other countries,
Olim are surprised to discover slum-suburbia conflicts also
exist in Israel. Those who come to escape the fleshpots of
the West are saddened to find a possibly even greater or at

189

least similar stress on materialism. There is more authoritarianism and less popular manifestations of personal and political dissent. The merger of religion and politics are a continuous enigma for non-Orthodox Jews weaned on a tradition of separation of Church and State. Liberals are embarrassed to learn that Israel's best friends are evangelical Christians and the radical right in America and the government of South Africa. Idealists and Zionists alike are upset that the rest of the western world is indifferent or unenthusiastic in their support while those whose viewpoint is to the left, must live with the fact that their idols, Tito, Che and Fidel, as well as much of the third world today, demonstrate hostility to the Zionist cause.

Israel has no blatant racism, menacing junkies, inner city blight, unpopular wars or poverty stricken masses. Relieved at once of these onerous problems, the Anglo-Saxon soon learns that Israel is not the land of milk and honey he had hoped for. This sobering revelation is the greatest crisis in the making of an Israeli. To come to grips with it, the Anglo-Saxon must be able to view Israel in the greater perspective of the enormous problems it has faced and the light that shines on its achievements.

In spite of political blackmail and extortion, Israel has made loyal friends in the community of nations and gained strength by leaps and bounds. It has usually cordial if not friendly relations with non-Moslem countries and many would quickly warm up were it not for the fear of the Arab oil and petrodollars. It has secret admirers and some warm relations with the third world. There are many in Africa, Asia and Latin America who empathize with this small country struggling with similar problems and challenges — the role of tribalism in nation building, patriarchal and religious forces against secular and modern strivings, molding a society with the best from capitalism and socialism,

There are American settlers (kindred souls to the early American pioneer), who have tried and then abandoned other adopted countries. For most who give up and go back it is an ambivalent and often traumatic decision that haunts them for years. The struggle to learn a new language and adapt to unfamiliar job habits often becomes overwhelming. Some return to their homes and lives in America with renewed faith in their Jewishness and wonderful memories and stories to tell their grandchildren and who knows, maybe some day...

The culture conflict usually reaches its climax three to five years after the euphoric first days in Israel. By then the new family will have encountered most of the problems and disappointments awaiting them and they may have begun to think seriously of going back. Savings have been depleted and some have gone into debt to finance purchase and furnishing of their home in Israel. In spite of sincere efforts, the monthly battle of the budget has proven too formidable an adversary. Tax and financial concessions granted after arrival have expired, to be replaced by new and alarming realities that prove insurmountable to many.

Having a pleasant home and making a decent living — once taken for granted — are now major obstacles. The parallel struggle to Israelize or even simply get along with the neighbors and make friends are difficult and frustrating, especially for those who cannot be as fluent in Hebrew as their Israeli counterparts. The day is won only by those who learn to cope successfully — the acid test for every new settler of every background and tribe. Those who manage will survive and go on to become Israelis with all that implies for better or worse.

The key element is simply whether one really believes that their Jewishness is important and that Israel is the center and focus of the Jewish people. If so, they know that their future is here where it is happening, and this becomes more compelling than any other consideration. If one has this faith, the disappointments and frustrations are a price that is not too high to pay. When this gut feeling is not really there, it is only a question of when the Anglo-Saxon will give up to return to the carefree, uninhibited, easier-to-get-along-in America even though the old restlessness, alienation and what-do-I-really-want-out-of-life problems will pop up again very quickly.

A few blame everyone but themselves for not succeeding. They may write bitter letters to friends or the Editor of the Jerusalem Post to explain — the officials were horrid, the salary ridiculous, the neighbors provincial, the apartment small. Some are really second chancers for whom Israel was an impossible cure-all for problems they took with them to the new land. It is always everything but their own reluctance to become Israelis, with the serious commitments and onerous obligations that implies.

Some never get used to the new country and while they came because they felt Jewish elsewhere, they return conscious of how American, English or Australian they actually are. A number of otherwise successful Olim find it hard to burn their bridges behind them in America. They have personal, business and emotional ties which they cannot easily sever. It is less difficult for the Algerian, Iraqi or Russian Jew to make a total commitment to Israel. They rarely have a real choice or anything left in the old country.

There are Anglo-Saxon settlers who have a real emotional involvement with Israel but hesitate to become its citizens and this contributes to their alienation from their neighbors. They are confused about accepting a new nationality and the personal, emotional and legal implications it involves, and this increases their ambivalence. The timid look for a way not to serve in the regular or reserve army with their neighbors, and this cop-out is humiliating for most men. They become a generation wandering in the desert of indecision, and only their children, like the followers of Moses, will really see and know the Promised Land.

Americans are fortunate in being members of a returning tribe that is one of the best liked. Just ask directions on the street or try to find tickets to a movie that is supposed to be sold out. When one starts to mumble Hebrew in that accent Israelis find so quaint, he has discovered the secret to instant charm.

Even those who do speak Hebrew fluently somehow cannot avoid sounding as though they have marbles in their mouths. When they start talking in Ivrit, smiles break out and Israelis who would be indifferent to another stranger are showing them where to go or helping them in whatever they are doing. Ordinarily shy strangers who bump into an obvious Anglo-Saxon start gabbing away "helpfully" in their no less amusing and limited English.

This pleasant encounter has another explanation, for the initial goodwill seems to be a subconscious recognition of the generosity of American Jews to the Stae through the Bonds and the Jewish Appeal. Israel desperately needs their contributions to enable the Jewish Agency to assume almost the entire national budget for health, housing and higher education and provide half of the funds for agricultural settlement, welfare and unemployment benefits. They know that many schools, hospitals, factories and social services would not exist but for this unparalleled support.

They know that Americans and their government are genuinely friendly and constitute their firmest and possibly only major ally. Israelis also understand that life in America is pleasant and comfortable and that Anglo-Saxon Aliya is an idealistic act. Paradoxically the contrast with their own economic situation coupled with the Anglo-Saxon hesitancy in becoming totally Israelized, create an undercurrent of jealousy and resentment.

It is ironic that Americans arriving in Israel should be concerned by problems of citizenship and national loyalty when there is hardly a true expatriate among them. Few are the countries, especially in Western Europe and Latin America without their Yankee permanent residents and dual citizens. More than a few have proven to be American haters or baiters and not at all adverse to criticizing their motherland, its institutions and government or acting against its interests. Some are political or social outcasts who openly give aid and comfort to its enemies.

Israel on the other hand is one of the few countries where there are no America haters or at least no more than a handful. While Israelis are critical of different aspects of American life and policies, there are no anti-American riots or marches against its embassy. An Oleh struggling in beginner's Hebrew with an unseen telephone operator might suddenly be asked, "Why is your State Department making so many problems?" Israelis of every political affilia-tion deplore the Pentagon's stinginess or White House anti-Semites but are proud members of the Israeli America Friendship Society or the Library and Information Center of the US Embassy.

American Jews are also pleased the two countries are friends and allies. They have been impressed by Israel's startling military prowess and strength and because of it, enjoy a new stature and pride. Aware of the great freedom and success they enjoy, they are America's loyal citizens no less than any other minority group, in spite of their affec-tion and support of Israel. Ben Gurion said he was more concerned about what the Jews did than what the Gentiles might say. While American Jews are thrilled by the exploits of Dayan, they are more concerned with what Carter says

and does. They are somewhat anxious about Palestinian terrorists and Arab war threats, but vitally concerned about
the price of gasoline, inflation and crime in America.

They are in brief, personally and primarily involved in
the events and issues of America, with Israel becoming
their major concern only when its existence or security is
endangered. Their youth and intellectuals are involved in
social movements and issues in America. The vast majority
will never live in Zion but many arrive as enthusiastic tourists, in groups, conventions or congresses. They come to
see the Promised Land and shed a tear or two on arrival
and at the Western Wall but are only slightly less sentimental in the presence of the Statue of Liberty or Barbra
Streisand. They adore kibbutzim and Eilat, but home is
Shaker Heights, Forest Hills and Grossingers. Still, they
good naturedly submit to the inevitable discussions and
comparisons of Israel and America that can be called the
"Dialogue".

THE DIALOGUE

For Israelis the Dialogue is an important part of
their connection with the Diaspora and American visitors soon become somewhat reluctant participants. It is a
climactic and inevitable personal confrontation between an
irresistible force (Israelis committed to convincing, charming
or frightening the American Jews to settle in Israel) and an
immovable object (visiting Jewish Americans who are just
as adamant about returning to their lives in America).
Sometimes it happens during a conversation in the street or
in a shop. Often it is just a few words exchanged between
the visitor and a local relative, acquaintance or taxi driver.
Periodically it is a planned get-together where both sides
deliver speeches on subjects connected to American Jewry
and Israel.

195

Each side expresses the basic themes and hypotheses heard before in countless such meetings. Discussion usually proceeds politely at first and then the tempo picks up as the other side refuses to be convinced. They exchange harsh words that contain some truth, but all will soon be forgotten and the Dialogue in fact rarely accomplishes anything concrete.

Israel is a world tourist center and the site of international conventions, symposiums and meetings of every type. Occasionally these are specifically arranged for the purpose of holding the Dialogue. The Americans in these meetings might be delegates at a Jewish Writers Conference or Congress of Jewish Intellectuals. Sometimes they are young and modest members of Young Judea of Detroit, or a "Summer in Israel Work and Study Tour" by the venerable Sisterhood of Lodge 92 of Bnai Brith or the good ladies of Hadassah. The Israeli participants are their peers whether students, professors or members of Rotary or a Jewish dentists' association.

The protagonists may start in a casual way by reminiscing gaily about the good time had by all during their tour or convention. If this is a diplomatic encounter, they might sing the Star Spangled Banner and Hatikva. A Zionist politician will bless the proceedings and offer a toast to the health of the noble Israeli President. An Israeli will rise to the occasion and express the sincere wishes of the Israelis for the continued prosperity and happiness of the great American people and their esteemed President.

Glasses of orange juice or Israeli wine are raised to a strong and peaceful Israel and all applaud the hope that Jewish values and ideals everywhere be advanced. The crescendo is reached when someone cries out, "Let there be a spiritual bridge between New York and Tel Aviv!" This is a sign that the Dialogue is about to begin. An Israeli fires the first round by declaring: "Why can't we build a real bridge from America?" An imaginary, but fairly typical, Dialogue might continue like this:

Israeli: When are you going to realize that we are your people, this is your homeland and that you cannot be Jewish without identifying with us and our future?

American: In a religious and cultural sense yes; but physically and politically we are Americans and we have the same confidence in the future of the US as you have in Israel.

Israeli: You are what they call "whistling in the dark" in your country. American Jews are in a constant decline and other ethnic and racial groups are taking over in areas where you were once prominent. Only Jewish nationhood can provide Jewish destiny.

American: Our position in America is secure and well rooted. We might even have a Jewish President or Vice-President in the next few years.

Israeli: That's all we need! The first thing he'll probably do is to break off relations or declare a blockade of Israel just to show the Gentiles and the Arabs how evenhanded he is. Anyway, everyone knows the WASPS run America.

American: Wait a minute, you must have also read somewhere that the Jews are only 3% of the population in America. If we had any more influence and success, it wouldn't be fair to the WASPS.

Israeli: All we want is that you give us 3% of your youth, your idealism, your know-how...

American: And our dollars.

Israeli: The dollars you give help us, but they also help your conscience and it's tax deductible. What we really want is you and not your charity.

American: When are you going to understand that America is a melting pot as well as a great democracy and that Jews are full partners in it with the Gentiles? I don't see you taking any Arabs home for dinner.

Israeli: At least I don't claim that some of my best friends are Arabs. As for your melting pot, American Jews are being melted by indifference, assimilation and intermarriage into a slowly disappearing species.

American: If it's so bad with us, how come so many Israelis end up settling in Chicago and Miami, including people *you* send over to encourage *us* to settle in Jerusalem and kibbutzim!

Israeli: Israelis who leave their country are dropping out of being Jewish like you are by refusing to settle here. Marxism! Black Power! New Left! American Jews have been thrown out of every radical movement they joined that wasn't theirs. The only Jewish revolution is Zionism and the State of Israel.

American: What about a social revolution in Israel for the poor Sephardim or to provide freedom of religion and separation of synagogue and state?

Israeli: *We* don't have a Nazi Party and Ku Klux Klan!

American: What about Protektzia and Jewish prostitutes?

Israeli: Let's look at the facts. The main lesson of history is that man is basically a tribal creature. He may belong to a national, ethnic or religious group, but if it has a common history, rituals and behavior, it is a tribe no matter what it calls itself and *you* belong to *our* tribe.

American: Today's need is for universalism. Tribal concepts only lead to chauvinism and wars. Israel is necessary for someone who needs to be rescued, but we just want to visit once in a while. Whether you like it or not, we are Americans.

Israeli: Are the Armenians Russians? Look at Lebanon, Cyprus, Northern Ireland, Belgium, even Quebec. Everywhere else in the world the minority wants to be a majority and live with his own people. By refusing to acknowledge the peoplehood of the Jews, you are denying your own Jewishness and spiritual existence.

American: We are more Jewish in America than you are in Israel. We have a richer cultural and religious life in our towns and cities than you do. How many of you go to synagogue? How many keep kosher kitchens? You don't have a single place in Israel where you can get a good kosher knish.

Israeli: With your Jewish jokes and your Jewish food you only prove the point. You live in a spiritual wasteland and gilded ghetto. You have not really become Americans, nor are you real Jews. Your weddings and bar mitzvas lack real Jewish content and meaning. Practically none of you know Hebrew or Jewish history. Being Jewish in America is Jewish chic — eating pastrami sandwiches and taking steam baths in Jewish Centers.

American: Your values are the same as ours. You just wish that you could eat a good steak or pastrami every day instead of humus and felafel. Instead of us building schools and libraries for you, you would be happy if we built you country clubs and steam rooms.

Israeli: We don't want anything from you except to share our problems and joys. We are grateful for the money you contribute and lend us, but it is we who must spill our blood in battle to preserve the Jewish State and to strengthen the Jewish position in the countries of the world.

American: We don't have sleepless nights worrying about our position. We're just worried that Arafat will get an atom bomb some day and drop it on Tel Aviv.

Israeli: *We'll* worry about Arafat. *You* should worry about the erosion of American Jewry, about the indifference of your youth to being Jewish and their attraction to "Jews for Jesus", the hippie life, drugs...

American: You have your share of dropouts and hippies in Israel. We have intermarriages, but a fair number of our *Shiksas* (Gentile girls) convert, and anyway, one Sammy Davis Jr and Liz Taylor are worth a hundred Jewish dropouts...

At this point the participants begin to weary and the great debate is about to draw to a close. Each side gets in one more "argument" and the Dialogue will be over at least until the next time.

American: I'd like to continue our discussion, but our tourist guide is waiting. Would you like to join us? We're off to tour the slums of Tel Aviv and a real underworld hashish party.

Israeli: Thank you, but my friends are waiting for me. Don't forget to mail me the book I asked for, unless of course your downtown stores have been burned down again by rioters or you have a blackout or curfew in your city.

(To himself: He's not a bad fellow for an Anglo-Saxon. Too bad a *few* like him don't settle here. Of course, if *too* many came, what would we do with them?...)

American: I've really enjoyed touring Israel and meeting you. Look me up if you get to the States. I'd love to show you all those nice little restaurants and cafés those Israeli *emigrants* have opened up everywhere.

(To himself: He's not a bad fellow for an Israeli. It wouldn't hurt to have a few Begins or Weizmans in America. Just imagine, Moshe Dayan President of the United States...)

SUMMING IT UP

Why Jews elect to settle in Israel and why they remain is, in the last analysis, a personal and complex matter. Motivations and reasons are individual and subjective, but there are tangible and definable attractions. It is the only country in the world where anti-Semitism, that constant specter of the Jews, does not exist. There are jealousies and frictions among the tribes but it is never "Cohen, the Jewish embezzler" or "Schwartz, the Jewish plumber" or the "Jewish controlled newspaper." All the embezzlers, plumbers and newspapers in Israel are Jewish and the freedom from seeing things through a constant Jewish mirror can be exhilarating.

Conversely, when everyone else in the whole world wants to be tribalistic and chauvinistic, there is something rewarding and reassuring when you are Jewish in Israel. Other religions and nations have perpetuated their separate cultures and development, so why shouldn't Israelis enjoy being themselves? Newcomers are soon captivated by the spirit and feeling of Jewish peoplehood and it becomes more than just a religion or country or people or place to live. It is everything, a raison d'etre that cannot possibly be fulfilled anywhere else. For pious or emotionally involved Jews of every denomination it is the only country where they can live complete and natural lives in their own milieu. Only in Israel can the ancient prayer, "Next year in Jerusalem" become a reality.

Devout Jews in the Diaspora busy themselves with synagogue oriented ritual, but they cannot really live the dynamic substance of the faith they hold so dear anywhere else. A truly religious life for a Jew means more than worship of the God of Israel. It means to laugh and cry as well as pray in the language and in the land where Judaism originated, developed and was reborn. Archaeologists, anthropologists, sociologists and just plain people have found it to be an emotion awaking, pioneering wonderland. Joining in has given new goals and direction to those who were jaded and indifferent in other societies.

With all their hang-ups and problems, Israelis are neither boring nor brooding and their country is an exciting and interesting one. They are probably no better or worse than any other people, but surely they are not quite like them. Their children are not alienated from their parents nor are they addicted to a television wasteland or turning on in

unior High. There is no ennui, few alcoholics or sexual
evolutionaries. They deny they are religious or idealistic,
yet in every crisis prove their selflessness and faith in their
neighbors and country.

They talk fast, loud, too much and rudely, but are not
concerned someone might notice. They are full of *chutzpa*
owards others, but criticize themselves mercilessly. They
have lost much of the traditional Jewish pathos, but laugh,
sing and dance as they seldom do elsewhere. A simple out-
ng or get together becomes a holiday of cheer and celebra-
ion. There are no strangers here and all who wish to par-
icipate are invited. Whether one fancies the Bible, Bartok or
beach games, he can find companions to share them with.

Tiny Israel is a giant in contrasts. On the same day there
may be a snowfall, a heat wave and hail storm. It has the
only Precious Stones Exchange (emeralds, sapphires,
rubies, opals, turquoises, topazes, Eilat stones and agates)
n the world, a prehistoric stalactite cave, Crusader castles,
Turkish baths actually built by the Turks and the oldest
(Jericho) and lowest (Sodom) cities in the world.

It has an offbeat movement for the restoration of the
Israeli monarchy, in which the royal Pretender, naturally an
immigrant from America, and allegedly a descendant of the
ancient Israelite Kings, promises prosperity and peace upon
his return to the throne. There is a small village in the
Galilee called Amirim. Some people have never even heard
of it and many who have consider its inhabitants a little
crazy. For Amirimites it is the noblest place in all Israel with
no other comparable settlement in the world. Every man,
woman and child living there is vegetarian or a naturalist.
Several are settlers from the West and some are American
Christian Seventh Day Adventists. The naturalists live on
raw fruit, vegetables and nuts, while the vegetarians can
eat anything — except of course, meat, fish or eggs.

203

Sheik Idris is the uncrowned king of the country's seers, healers, fortune tellers and self declared prophets. He lives in an Arab village called Baka Al'Garbich not far from Amirim. For 20 years Baka was divided in half by the winding Israel Jordan ceasefire line that ran through its streets and alleys. Weddings and funerals were attended by villagers from the Jordanian side, looking through the barbed wire fence. Following the Six Day War the fence was torn down and the village reunited under Israeli administration. Strangers are invariably directed to the Sheik's house. To most Israelis and his own neighbors he is a false prophet, exploiting the hopes of the foolish. To others, including not a few educated Jewish "westerners", he is a final hope. The loveless, the barren, the desperate and the dying, they come from all parts of Israel. In a country where people pride themselves ·on rationality and good sense, there is a Sheik Idris and those who seek him out.

The heart and soul of Israel is this too — the panorama of saints, hermits and sinners. Christian, Jew and Arab, in city, village and kibbutz. It is the extraordinary babble of voices and sea of faces. Look at them. Here is an elegant gentleman reading a Rumanian or Hungarian newspaper on a park bench. Maybe he is only a petty clerk in an office and his impressive briefcase contains a few sandwiches and a book of poetry. Who knows what memories he has brought with him from the old country. Here is a housewife from a development town returning from market. Her shopping bags and cartons spill over as she laughingly struggles with a cackling chicken. Making her way home to feed a dozen children, in the evening she and her husband will learn to read a newspaper in the language of Abraham and Jacob

A Moslem villager with fierce moustache and sweeping headdress passes by on his way to a business meeting or from some government office. Here is a group of young Yeshiva students with long sidelocks, dressed in black coats and hats. They are arguing in Yiddish about a fine Talmudic point and do not notice the giggling schoolgirls in their blue uniforms walking right by. An Oriental beauty makes her graceful way down the street and is subjected to the keen scrutiny of a western student, while he devours a felafel as eagerly as he once downed hamburgers and malteds.

Who can resist staring in delight while a class of two and three year olds walk by hand in hand to their nursery? Carrying little knapsacks filled with cookies and crayons and wearing the *kova tembel* caps on their heads they are singing a song about the loves and glories of David, King of Israel. Is there a Jew who can watch without a tear in his eye as young boy and girl soldiers of the Israeli Army pass by on parade? Who can live here and not share the pain of Israel's mourning or the joy of its triumphs? Who will resist being swept into the rhythmic and spontaneous dancing of the celebrants on a national holiday, festival or wedding?

This is part of the *havaya* — that special mystique of those who share the experience of Israel. Here the spirit transcends laws of reason and logic, and the intangible memories, scenes and impressions overcome pragmatic doubts and challenges. There is an indefinable and immutable essence that makes some decide their real home is here and not in that rich and secure land where they grew up.

One may come to visit and tarry awhile, to learn about Israel and find, through it, the meaning in their own lives. Here one can study, pause, work, contemplate, clarify goals and broaden vistas; here skills and ideals can be shared and new challenges and horizons discovered.

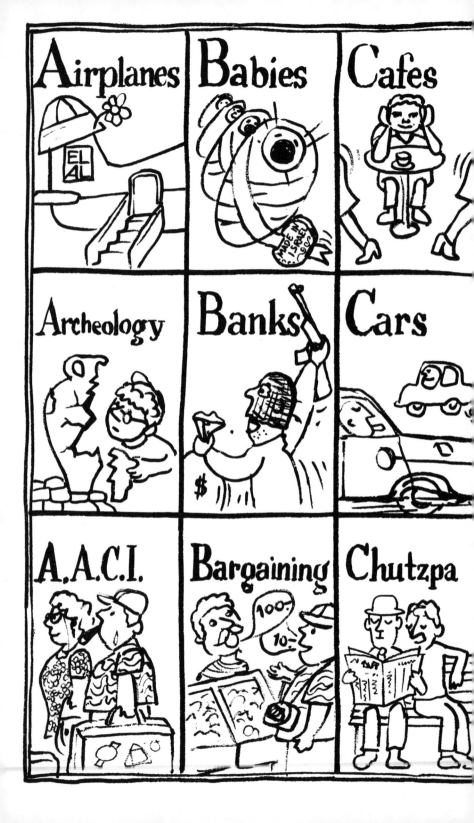

The real "Jewish" question is this —
from what can a Jew earn a living?
(Shalom Aleichem)

Chapter Eight

THE PRACTICAL ISRAEL

This Lexicon does not include everything *you wanted to know about Israel and were afraid to ask. Such a work would require an encyclopedic approach and style not in keeping with the purpose of this book.*

The alphabetically listed entries that follow are subject to change and only intended to whet the appetite. The logical next step is reference to the bibliography and other sources about subjects of particular interest, or better yet — come to Israel to find out first hand.

The entries include subjects mentioned in passing in earlier chapters, plus topics, expressions and helpful hints the average tourist and newcomer to Israel would want to know about.

Airplanes Most of the major international airlines have flights to Israel. If you fly El Al, it's safer, but expect more tumult and delays. The plane is apt to be filled to capacity and may seem like Saturday night on Dizengoff Street. Everyone talks to everyone except the pilots and it is not uncommon to bump into relatives and acquaintances you least expect to meet. A favorite pastime of El Al passengers is walking around to see who else is there. Youngsters prefer trying to count everyone on the plane, guessing who the security guards are or just running wild. After a few hours of noise, confusion and all the meals that are served, people get sleepy and there is peace and quiet for a while. When the plane makes its usual safe and smooth landing, its passengers (only on El Al) often spontaneously break into applause and if there are Hassidim, song and dance as well. It's a lot quieter on the other airlines. Arkia, the inland flight carrier, flies between most cities, the Galilee, Eilat, Sharm el Sheikh and Sinai. Charter and rental flights can be arranged, including air tours of Jerusalem. Check with tour guides.

Airport (Ben Gurion) First and last impressions of Israel take place at its international airport near the town of Lod, and they may be unpleasant. With a million plus tourists arriving every year at a terminal building that was put up during the British Mandate, no improvements and expansion can 'possibly provide the conveniences and services travellers may be used to. Like many other international airports, there is overcrowding everywhere and inadequate facilities are apparent, especially during the tourist season, which is most of the year. Israelis add to the near bedlam by insisting on taking the whole family to welcome and see off every relative and friend. Porters are no longer officially permitted entry to the passenger hall, but some may still hang around and be a nuisance. If you accept their services

— and some give you little choice — agree on the price in advance. Don't let any luggage get out of sight until it is checked in and whenever possible insure it, especially if you have valuables. Further delays and standing in line is caused by intensive passenger and baggage searches and security procedures. Going through the airport can be a rough experience and it is a good idea to bring a few books and whatever to help pass the time. You can check in baggage for El Al flights, at their Air Terminal at the Arlozorov Railway Station, in Tel Aviv, the evening before departure to cut down on the airport hassle. If things really get out of control, walk up two flights in the administration building and raise hell at the airport manager's office, it's about time someone did. Don't forget to reconfirm return flights three days in advance and again before scheduled departure time to make sure there are no unannounced delays, changes or strikes.

Arab Countries Israel's enemies of today will inevitably become the good neighbors of the future. Jordan in the east, with its population of two million composed of Bedouin tribes and Palestinian refugees, is enjoying stability and prosperity under "Hoossy" as Israelis call plucky King Hussein. Egypt in the south was one of the ancient world's great civilizations. Its nearly 40 million inhabitants live in hundreds of poor farming villages along the fertile Nile River and in the teeming cities of Cairo and Alexandria. It is a hot desert land with few natural resources and all the problems of an overpopulated, developing country. Nevertheless, by virtue of its size, technological and military strength, it is the leading Arab nation and pacesetter of the moderate Arab camp in peace and war. Lebanon in the north is about the size of Jordan and the home of feuding Moslems (Sunni and Shia), Christians, traditionalists, progressives and revolutionaries. Until the outbreak of the six year old civil war that has brought anarchy, bloodshed and widespread destruction to Lebanon, it was the peaceful and gay entertainment, banking and business capital of the Arab world. Now, it is ravaged by continuous feuding and violence and divided in a de facto partition between Moslem and Christian. It also harbors competing terrorist groups within and around the refugee camps who constitute a threat to Israel and the Christian Maronites who are friendly with it. Syria on the northeast has five million Moslem inhabitants and large Druze, Kurdish and Christian minorities. It is ruled by the militantly anti-Israel *Ba'th* (Arab Socialist) party who are part of the hardline, Arab "refusal" camp. Its no peace, no recognition, no negotiation stand, is supported by its even more militant and Marxist rival – now ally — to its southeast, oil rich Iraq. Saudi Arabia to the southeast of Israel across the Gulf of Aquaba like Iraq, has no common border with Israel. The wealthiest in the Arab world, it is a western oriented, feudal monarchy with strict Islamic moral and legal codes. Recently it has played an increasingly active, though vacillating role in the Middle Eastern conflict.

Archeological (digs) are usually open to volunteer participants. Israeli and foreign universities sponsor summer excavations and IGTO (Israel Government Tourist Office) and student organizations are helpful. The government run Department of Antiquities and Museums conducts surveys and maintains records of excavations. It also protects, preserves and exhibits important finds like the Dead Sea Scrolls from the pre-Christian era. Other discoveries cover the history of mankind going back as far as one million years. Make sure to bring a hat, water canteen and insurance policy. Even Moshe Dayan cracked a few ribs in a cave-in while out on a dig — and he should have known better.

Army Duty Receiving an induction notice from the Israel Defense Forces provokes mixed feelings among Israeli veterans and newcomers alike. It is both a vital obligation and proud privilege of citizens and permanent residents, as well as a substantial personal burden on the soldier and his family. Because of Zahal's unique and unusually close relationship with the people, it has retained much of its pre-state militia atmosphere and informality but is very much a professional army with all the bureaucracy, discipline and genuine hardship that involves. The Security Service Law requires every 17 year old to register for the draft. Following induction processing at mobilization centers (*lishkat gi'us*), conscriptees are sent for basic and advanced training before they are assigned to units and jobs that may continue for 30 years. Male immigrants over 29 only do basic training and reserve service that averages 30 to 60 days annually. Pregnant women and mothers are completely exempted from military duty while some married women are called up for the reserves. Enlistment in the police and Border Patrol is usually accepted in lieu of army service. Full-time Yeshiva students and Orthodox women are entitled to full or partial exemptions or can elect to do national service as teachers, hospital or welfare aides in lieu of military obligations. Conscientious objectors are rarely exempted by the military authorities whatever their motives or beliefs may be. New settlers are permitted to postpone conscription, especially students and participants in the *atuda academai* (academic cadres) for a year or so. Older immigrants and those who have already been in a foreign army are entitled to a reduction of their period of service.

Association of Americans and Canadians in Israel (AACI). This is one of the first places North American settlers visit after coming over. They drop by when they're in the neighborhood and want to make sure it's there in case they need it. Often it's where bewildered or uncertain Olim can find out, in American accents, if the assistance and explanations they are getting at government ministries and official institutions are what they should be. The staff of professionals and volunteers were once Olim themselves and usually know when and how to cheer up or calm down the new folks in town. For years AACI headquarters were surprisingly drab with one of the smallest elevators in Tel Aviv, but they are big-hearted, and they have now moved to larger offices in a better part of town. Activities for members include newcomer hospitality receptions, visits to absorption centers and hostels, publications (bulletins, newsletters, information booklets), pen pals, small loans and second mortgages at low interest rates, blood bank, cemetery plots, seminars, social and cultural programs, guided trips, consumer awareness and civic projects, and special interest circles including the largest Anglo-Saxon singles group. There is an information desk which deals with the problems and inquiries of tourists and potential settlers and brings newcomers together in person and by mail, with veteran settlers. A similar service in slightly different accents is provided for people from other English speaking countries at their immigrant associations and they join forces in matters of common interest to lobby in the Zionist Establishment on behalf of all Olim.

Babies Giving birth in Israel has no disadvantages except Junior will not be able to run for President of the US. He or she, on the other hand, will receive free, high standard medical hospital care, stand a better chance of becoming President of Israel and baby's parents receive a $75 bonus. Expectant mothers are looked after at the *Tipat Halav* (literally "Drop of Milk") clinics at Kupat Holim but can engage the services of a private obstetrician. Routine deliveries are performed by experienced, professional midwives at government and Sick Fund hospitals. Those interested in having an obstetrician deliver and attend their baby at a private hospital can arrange it at a cost of $300 to $600 inclusive. Obstetricians are always in charge at caesarian or complicated deliveries and mother and baby care in general is as good as anywhere. After discharge — usually within three or four days — a pediatric follow-up is given by the Fund doctors. Again, many Western and Israeli families prefer paying extra for a private pediatrician who makes home visits and devotes more time and individual care than is customary at Kupat Holim. Abortions are free and legal when approved for medical or personal reasons by medical committees. Illegal abortions are also available with the authorities turning a blind eye and moonlighting gynecologists and small private hospitals who cater to them are rarely harassed. Arrangements cost around $300 to $500. Israeli birth certificates are issued to all parents and appropriate changes must be made on ID cards at the nearest office of the Ministry of Interior. Americans may also want to register their baby as an American citizen and receive a birth certificate issued by the US Consulate.

Baby Sitters — Maids There is no reliable, commercial service and looking for domestic help usually involves asking friends and neighbors. Sitter rates depend on the age of the person and whether you live in one of the big cities where such services are more expensive. Anyone who will be looking after your kids will probably check *you* out, so the least you should do is to confirm whether *they* are trustworthy and when necessary, would she know how to keep things under control in English. A maid (*ozeret*) and children's nanny (*metapelet*) is always problematic for the average working wife and mother and it is the rare female who admits she is pleased with her help. There are not enough responsible women available for this type of work and the result is that household helpers are tough and independent. Experienced housewives stay home when their ozeret comes in, to pamper and work along with her. Payment is in cash and amounts to a small fortune if you have maid service more than once a week, especially in the better neighborhoods. Pay the extra sum necessary to the National Insurance Institute (*Bituach Leumi*) or you may have trouble if she has an on-the-job accident or demands severance pay some day. If you find a babysitter, maid or nanny you are happy with, tell everyone how horrible she really is or one of your best friends will surely try and steal her away.

Banks For a struggling, developing social welfare country, Israel has an amazing number of banks and they seem to have branches everywhere in the country. Larger ones have offices in Europe and the US for those who want to do their banking in Hebrew. Make sure you slash your sevens (7), European style or it (7) will be taken for a one (1). Services include foreign currency exchange, savings and checking accounts in Lira and dollars, loans, mortgages, investment and estate planning. Not all have tellers or computerized methods and some transactions require a few conferences across the counter before it's over. Banking hours are from 8:30 am to 12:30 pm and 4 pm to 5:30 pm Sunday, Monday, Tuesday and Thursday and on Wednesday and Friday from 8:30 am till noon only. Interest rates are high on loans and overdrafts and low on deposits compared to back home. To avoid misunderstandings these matters should be discussed with the bank manager and agreed in writing before opening an account. There are no bank guards in most branches but that doesn't mean Israel doesn't have holdup men. Bank deposits are partially insured but valuables in safety deposit boxes may require an extra insurance policy for theft or loss.

Bargaining is an ancient tradition in the Middle East and Mediterranean. It is expected in the outdoor markets and bazaars and you can try your luck in smaller shops and hotels. It is the essential element of a visit to those outdoor, circus-like character full Flea Markets found in the large cities. Shopping in Israel is both an art and an adventure, but can be disappointing for unwise or naive buyers. Consumer protection and better business practices are not well established yet and even respectable stores are often reluctant to refund purchase money, though exchange of merchandise is common. So shop carefully and insist on dated receipts for questionable and large purchases.

Bible (The) Israel the land and people and much of their history are what the Old Testament is all about. In Hebrew, the Jewish Bible is called *Tanach*, the acronym of its three major sections — *Torah* (the Law), *Neviim* (the Prophets) and *Ketuvim* (the Writings). Its 24 books were written, compiled and canonized over a period of 10 centuries, from about the 7th century BCE to the 2nd century CE. The interpretations and commentaries of the Old Testament by later generations of rabbinic scholars became known as the *Mishna* (Repetition), and in turn were the subject of further amplification and commentaries that are the *Gemara* (Supplement). Together, Mishna and Gemara constitute the *Talmud* (Learning), consisting of some 15,000 pages, in about 35 volumes written in Hebrew and Aramaic. They include complex analyses of legalistic principles called *Halacha* (Law), philosophical dissertations on morality, ethics and human behavior, *Aggada* (Narration) and the marvelous wise and piquant sayings, tales and passages of the *Midrash* (Sermons). The Talmud is probably the only sacred book whose readers-believers are permitted and even encouraged to question, debate and render different interpretations of its age-old values and principles.

215

Bills for gas, electricity, water and telephone can be aggravating when they are so high, especially when they contain unusual expressions, calculations and small print and are written in a strange language. Unlike some utilities, gas (in Hebrew it is "gaz") for cooking and home heating is supplied by private companies (*Amisragas, Pazgas, Petrolgas* and *Supergas*). All utility prices and services are subject to regulation and supervision and complaints can be filed with the ministries in charge or the consumer organizations. Electricity is a monopoly of the national Electric Company (*Hevrat Hahashmal*) and charges are based on kilowatt rates and the size of the dwelling, with a "users" fee, defense tax and VAT adding another 20% or so. Water is strictly controlled by the authorities, but is not rationed. It is allocated to cities and towns for home consumption on a multiple tariff basis, with families of five or more eligible for reduced rates. Water used by tenants in apartment buildings for the lawn, washing cars, etc. is billed to all on a proportionate basis. Phone service and repairs are handled by the Telephone Department (*Mador Hatelephonim*) of the Ministry of Communications. Most utility bills are mailed or delivered to consumers bi-monthly. Reminder letters and grace periods are not customary and service cut off can be quick and painful, not to mention expensive and time consuming for restoration of service. Bills can be paid by check or at banks on an individual basis or sent directly to one's bank with instructions to make automatic payments which are deducted from the consumer's account. Just for variety, municipal and national taxes on apartments and homes are payable annually, and TV sets and radios are billed on a semi-annual basis. To avoid problems with someone who may buy or rent your home some day, the utility computers or the men from the Broadcasting Company (*Rashut Hashidur*) — they can show up for spot checks and try to take away your TV or radio if you don't have proof you paid — you had better keep a *permanent* record of *all* bills and receipts.

Black Panthers (Israeli)   There may be a black panther in Jerusalem's Biblical Zoo, which has most of the 100 odd animals mentioned in the Old Testament. The Israeli *Pantherim* are a real life protest movement and political party, and they are serious. It began as an intentional imitation of the people with the same name in America; most were young, Oriental, school and army dropouts and delinquents, but supporters and admirers now include factory workers, slum residents and middle-class Ashkenazi sympathizers. During the first few years they organized street demonstrations that often turned disorderly and violent, but it brought them and the problems they raised to the front pages of the daily press and they have been a controversial issue since then. The *Pantherim* have had some success in local council and Histadrut elections and one of their leaders, Charlie Biton, is a Knesset member as part of the Arab led *Rakach* Communist list. They are another reminder of the social and ethnic gap in Israel.

Cafés   Outdoor café sitting and people watching are part of the social life and there is a *beit kafei* (coffee house) for every type and crowd. Clientele and prices may change from morning to afternoon and evening, but the important thing is the atmosphere and the view of the passing parade. Food and beverages are usually served, but the main standby is, naturally, coffee, prepared in seven different ways: *"nes"* — instant coffee with milk; *"espresso"* — French coffee in tiny cups; *"hafuch"* — espresso plus milk; *"shachor"* — all black; *"turki"* — strong Turkish coffee with or without "hel" (it's the Hebrew word for the wild mint condiment called cardamon); *"kar"* — iced coffee without ice cream and *"ice"* — the same, with ice cream.

Cars The average "private", as non-commercial vehicles are called in Israel, does about 10,000 miles a year and the total annual cost (gas and oil, maintenance, repairs, insurance, taxes and depreciation) is stupendous, around $3000 or $250 a month, for medium sized European vehicles such as a Ford Escort and $2500 annually for small cars like a Volkswagen beetle. Volvos, Peugeots and other "large" automobiles run about double the latter and giant, gas guzzling products of Detroit nearly triple! Buying a new car takes one to five years total income, plus what amounts to a full-time salary to keep it up. While some can really afford it and others get total or partial reimbursement from employers, nobody can figure out how the rest manage. In other developing countries including the Communist peoples paradises, only a few or minority can ever enjoy this privilege. In Israel there are approximately 400,000 "privates" — one for nearly every other family — and how they do it is another miracle of the Jewish State. Newcomers can bring or buy a new or used car locally with tax deductions, provided they hold a valid driver's license at least one year before aliya. All vehicles in the country must be registered at the Motor Vehicle Bureau and carry third party insurance. The Oleh's spouse and children over 18 may drive cars, but usually only one per family is allowed. If it is sold soon after arrival to someone not eligible for this benefit, Customs insists on payment of the entire balance due and this can easily equal the price of the car. Annual vehicle taxes, maintenance, parts, gas and insurance bills are based on size and horsepower and most Israelis prefer small or medium sized European models. Rental cars can be had by the day, week or longer with or without a chauffeur guide at fairly expensive rates including *kilometrage* (mileage). Larger companies have offices at the airport and in major hotels.

Checks   Credit cards and charge accounts are not widespread in Israel and a personal check is still the most important and popular way to pay for things. Tourists, Olim and diplomats can open dollar or local currency checking accounts. Most banks only have what would be "Special" accounts in America where a minimum balance is not required, but no interest is paid. You can write and sign checks in English or any other language. If you send any by mail, take some security precautions by making them payable to payee only and "cross" checks, i.e. you add two parallel lines to the upper corner so the payee will have to deposit it for clearing first before he gets the money and make sure you send it by registered mail. Post-dated checks are confusing in Israel where everyone does it, even though technically speaking it is not always binding. Under Israeli law you cannot simply cancel checks after receiving goods or services on the grounds that what you received is inadequate, not what you ordered, in breach of contract, etc. The law says you have to let the check go through and all you can do is sue. So never buy anything in Israel without checking it out thoroughly and don't give anyone a check unless you are certain you and your bank will honor it.

Churches   There are dozens of Christian denominations in Israel, with the largest the Greek Catholic, Greek Orthodox, Latin and Maronite. Roman Catholic and Protestant Churches are found in the main cities and at Christian Holy Places and tourists and newcomers are usually welcome. Pilgrims can retrace the path of Jesus from the Church of the Nativity in Bethlehem to Nazareth, the Sea of Galilee, Jerusalem and along the path of the Via Dolorosa. Church locations and particulars are available at IGTO and foreign embassies. Christian hospices and communities also offer worship and fellowship for believers. Like the synagogues and mosques, Israel's churches are not community centers and the emphasis is on prayer and liturgy. Some Holy Places of all religions are afflicted with noise, dust, dirt and commercialism while others are inspiring. Churches usually have their main religious service on Saturday rather than on Sundays.

Chutzpa   is what keeps the country going full steam ahead and it pays to learn a little about the local variety if you want to survive and prosper. When it is overdone, as unfortunately is the case many times, chutzpa turns into arrogance and aggressiveness in which Israelis are also proficient. Chutzpa is a combination of self-confidence ("I'm *here*, everyone!"), self-assertion ("*I* was before you in this line!") and, especially, curiosity ("What are *you* doing here?"). Only in Israel do neighbors who meet at the corner grocery store, bus stop or restaurant ask each other such a question. But the main thing is to ask *everyone*, strangers included, *everything*. "What do you do?" ... "How much did your flat cost?" ... "How long has your wife been pregnant?" ... "How much do you really earn?" ... "Are you having an affair with your secretary?" If you are too sensitive for this sort of thing, you probably will not like life on a kibbutz or shikun apartment house and should keep away from Israeli "parties"; they frequently turn in to free for all verbal combat. If you must have privacy, there are wide open spaces south of Beer Sheva.

Citizenship (more about)   This is a privilege for Zionists, but for some suspicious or "practical" Anglo-Saxons, it is to be avoided as long as possible. A Jew can accept the automatic citizenship granted to Olim under the Law of Return and retain American or any other citizenship. You are usually permitted to hold and use two passports and enjoy dual nationality, as in fact more than one million Americans of every religion are doing all over the world. If you "opt out" of receiving Israeli nationality, you may have that unpleasant feeling of not quite belonging, and will not be able to vote, run for public office or qualify for government employment in many positions. If you reject Israeli citizenship initially and later change your mind, the State Department may regard the subsequent acquisition of nationality as a "voluntary naturalization," which can result in loss of US citizenship.

Clothing and shoes are expensive and not always up to the selection, quality or style Americans are used to and the system of measurement used is different. Many families prefer to bring a large supply with them and have friends and relatives mail over clothing packages later on. If they are marked "used clothing — no commercial value" or "not intended for sale" and new items have been in the washing machine before shipping, customs let them in without payment.

Comfort Stations Public conveniences are not very convenient if you insist on a minimum of cleanliness and facilities. The best are in the good hotels and at tourist sites like museums, but even these can be disappointingly dirty. Toilets in most cafés, restaurants, stores and gas stations are either non-existent or too dirty for anything except urgent visits. Public toilets are apt to be marked W.C. or by large, double zeros, English style. They are not what you would find in Buckingham Palace and some strange people might be loitering around. In conclusion, don't wait till it's too late to do your thing.

Credit Cards Diners Club, American Express, Carte Blanche and other cards are accepted in better hotels, restaurants and stores, but expect some delay and red tape. Local banks and entrepreneurs have initiated a similar service for Israelis as well as charge account buying but it hasn't caught on yet. Personal checks drawn on American banks may be refused or payment delayed for weeks pend-

ing clearing, unless you have convincing local references
Visitors who intend to stay a while and are not interested ir
working or living on a kibbutz, should bring sufficien
travellers checks or a bank letter of credit to cover their
stay.

Crime There is no Mafia or drug culture as such but Israe
has its underworld. It is probably the only country in addition to the US, that has officially admitted the existence o:
organized crime. Rising statistics are not only due to the
usual causes in affluent societies. Israel also has specia
problems of a brand new society with each ethnic community bringing different mores and standards of behavior. Culture shock, breakdown of traditional values and alienatior
of children from parents have all done their damage. Criminals have not penetrated the government and people are
safe in the streets but there is burglary, rape, assault anc
teenage rowdyism. Hundreds of millions of dollars ir
"Black money", profits from illegal drugs, extortion, pros-
titution and widespread income tax evasion form an alarming, invisible economy. Some of it involves law abiding citizens who help criminals launder it back into legitimate
businesses and investments. Tourists should be on the
lookout in hotels for burglars, luggage thieves, and cor
men and women who specialize in gullible tourists and
immigrants, particularly the lonely and aged. The Israeli
expression *chashdehu-ve-kabdehu* "be respectful but wary" is
apt, till you become better oriented. If the poet laureate o
pre-independence Israel, Hayim Nachman Bialik really
lamented ... "We will not become a country like all other
countries until we have our first Jewish prostitute and first
Jewish thief...", he would turn over in his grave if he could
see just how much Israel has become like all the others.

Customs Most import and export regulations are similar to
those in effect in Europe and America. The passenger halls

at Ben Gurion Airport and Haifa Port have a "Green Line" (nothing to declare) and "Red Line" (for declaration of goods and payment of customs duty). Smuggling goods into Israel or foreign currency abroad can end up in confiscation plus stiff fines, imprisonment or both. For Israelis the onerous duties and purchase taxes on foreign goods are an unpleasant but routine fact of life. Tourists and new immigrants are granted substantial exemptions from duties and taxes on their cars, personal belongings, home appliances and furniture.

Dating The singles game in Israel has some unique variations and rules and newcomers may want to play it cool till they catch on, to avoid unpleasant surprises. Once you've been around a little it can be fun and good vibrations. Getting friendly with certain ethnic, married or religious types requires honoring local customs or having terrific chutzpa or charm. Otherwise things are pretty much like most American and European cities. There are no singles bars, but it is simple enough to meet Israelis — all you have to do is say "Hi". If you're going to make your move in Hebrew, it's *"Shalom"* and don't forget, *"hu"* means he and *"he"* means she. Except for teenagers and steady couples, the man is expected to pay but Israeli girls are not used to dinner and night spot dates (yet). Going to a movie, friends, parties or just meeting in a café is still standard procedure. Unless you are absolutely sure this is it, don't make marriage promises; in Israel you can be sued by a slightly pregnant or jilted lady for breach of promise and support.

Divorce in Israel is surprisingly simple for the couple who have worked out all their problems — property settlement, child support, custody and visitation. If so, they can submit a joint petition for an uncontested termination of their marriage based on "incompatibility." When there is no clear

223

agreement between them or some complications arise, the procedure can be lengthy and very unpleasant. Once a couple is divorced in the Rabbinical Court, the decree is valid abroad under the full faith and credit principle affecting foreign judgments. Unfortunately, the reverse is not always true and Jewish couples who have divorced elsewhere (except before Orthodox Rabbis) may find that in Israel they are still regarded as man and wife. If either thereafter remarries without a "get" (rabbinical divorce) and the first spouse objects, they may have trouble in Israel regarding their marital status. Couples who are in the process of considering divorce and settling in Israel should consult a knowledgeable attorney about this combination of happenings and their rights and obligations.

Driving Israeli licenses are issued without road tests to holders of valid international drivers licenses and tourists can use their foreign licenses for up to six months. Motoring in Israel is a serious and often a dangerous affair. There is a 50 mph speed limit and almost no drunken driving, but statistics confirm that the country has one of the worst road accident rates in the world. Approximately 12,000 drivers, passengers and pedestrians have been killed in traffic accidents in the past 30 years, the same number that have lost their lives in all the wars and terrorist actions! Local drivers can be inconsiderate, impatient and habitually fail to keep proper or any distance from the car in front. They speed, go through red lights and dash in and out of traffic both on the left and right. It is hard to believe, but driving in city traffic and reading a newspaper at the same time is openly indulged in! If that's not enough, even when nice, law abiding citizens get behind a steering wheel they may shout and curse other drivers and pedestrians *"chamor!"* (ass!) and *"idiot!"* (self-explanatory), with heated references to the sexual organs of one's grandmother or mother not unusual.

The price of gas is shocking and insurance payments to victims of accidents low especially since Israel has gone over to "No Fault". So take a bus, *sherut* (service taxi) or train or better yet, walk.

Drug Stores are called pharmacies and they don't sell ice cream sodas or sundaes. Some are open nights and holidays as listed in newspapers under emergency services. Sick Fund members pay only nominal fees for prescriptions and their low cost plus the daily tension has caused an over dependency on medicines and a pill hoarding-using phenomenon. Israelis also visit their family doctors far more often than necessary and the overload adds to the long lines and in and out style of already over-burdened Sick Fund clinics. But then Israelis explain: "Even hypochondriacs can really get sick living under such conditions".

Ecology The pollution scene is not too bad, but it's getting worse fast. Like other developing countries Israel has emphasized material progress and technology and is beginning to pay the price of indifference to ecological considerations. The Council for a Beautiful Israel, Nature Reserves Authority and many citizens have good intentions, but they are fighting a losing battle against government, industry, indifference and hordes of picknickers, visitors and school children who should know better. Some public beaches in the coastal areas especially in and around Tel Aviv and Haifa, are closed to swimmers. Even the air in these cities occasionally approaches pollution levels, due to traffic and factory fumes as well as the giant Reading Power Station which is located right within Tel Aviv and the heavy industry and petrochemical plants in the Haifa port area. Another offender is noise and it is going on nearly everywhere. Under the Abatement of Nuisance Law, certain types of noise like yelling, rug beating, playing radios and musical instruments are supposed to be forbidden during the 2:30-4

225

pm rest hour and between 11 pm and 6 am, but some people couldn't care less. Israelis might slowly and surely be going deaf and decibel-mad without realizing it and it is definitely a cause for frayed nerves.

Electricity   is expensive and also shocking. Unlike the 110 volts, 60 cycle system of America, Israel uses high power 220 volts 50 cycles and this is why there are no outlets in Israeli bathrooms. On the other hand, blackouts and dim-outs are rare and there is never any looting or rioting in the streets when it happens. Hall and stairway lights only go on if you push the round red button on the wall. If you are a slow walker you may have to push often, because the lights go off automatically after 30 seconds or so. Most families keep flashlights and candles handy for use during power failures. Some American appliances may not work in Israel even with transformers or converters. When in doubt, ask your electrician.

Elevators   come in different sizes, shapes and personalities and can be as obstreperous as the Israelis they serve. Don't expect to find them in older buildings or if there are less than four or five floors. Usually there is no inner door and caution should be exercised. If there is one, make sure it is firmly closed or the elevator won't go anywhere. In some apartment buildings they only stop at the top floor and you may prefer to walk up or down to get where you are going. If your elevator stops in mid-flight, which can be a fairly common occurrence, there is no cause for panic and never any babies nine months later. Local elevators are much too small even for nimble and romantic Israelis. Just push the emergency button or holler and a passerby or neighbor will lower the elevator manually in a little while. The Shalom Tower outdoor elevator, Haifa's *Carmelit* subway and the cable lifts at Massada and Rosh Hanikra are special treats.

226

Embassy (American) is located in a modern, impressive building with fancy antennas on the roof and Marine guards at the entrance. Don't expect the Ambassador or Consul General to see you; they may be too busy with other problems. The Consulates in Tel Aviv and Jerusalem and their staff are available from 9 am till noon or thereabouts, Monday to Thursday and few departments are open to the public Fridays. All are closed Israeli and American holidays. Consular services for visiting Americans are limited by both American law and sovereignty of local authorities as well as budgetary considerations. The Citizenship Section is where most Americans visit when they have problems. People from the States living in the country are invited to register in case of a future personal or national emergency. Consulates can replace a lost, mutilated or expired passport, issue a birth or death certificate, send or receive urgent personal messages, provide liaison with local authorities regarding missing Americans and accept absentee votes in national elections. They will not ordinarily lend money or interfere in legal or other problems of its citizens. In exceptional cases they assist in repatriating people in serious distress or those whose immediate departure from Israel is deemed absolutely necessary. The Embassy has a book, record, periodical and lending library and there are library facilities for the business minded including old New York Times and Wall Street Journals in the office of the Commercial Attaché. Important Israelis are invited to cocktails at the Ambassador's house. "In" people go to the Marine Guard "happy hours" Friday afternoons. Everyone can take part in the annual July 4th holiday picnic at the American School in Kfar Shmaryahu.

Emergencies IGTO branches at the airport, major cities and tourist sites assist tourists, provide advice, brochures and maps and deal with complaints about tourist services.

Hotel personnel, policemen and telephone operators are generally English speaking and they or almost any Israeli will help in an emergency; if you start yelling *atzilu! atzilu!* (help! help!), that will get things moving. Doctors, dentists and *Magen David Adom* (Israel's Red Cross) also have night and holiday service; check at hotels or the *Jerusalem Post*. There is no Travellers Aid Society but US Consulates and AACI provide counselling service for American citizens and deal with passport and visa problems. If nothing else helps, dial 100 for police emergencies or 102 for the fire department. When worst comes to worst and if you are feeling suicidal or really depressed, call 253-311 in Tel Aviv for emergency, on the phone psychiatric counselling.

"Emergency Regulations" (Takanot Hahagana) were originally enacted by the British Mandatory authorities in Palestine to further their struggle against the Jewish underground groups — *Hagana, Irgun* and *Lehi*. After independence the Israeli government adapted the same regulations for use against Arab terrorism and threats to the security of the new State and its people. They are a strict and not very civil libertarian application of laws pertaining to arrest, detention, court procedure and censorship affecting persons charged with espionage or terrorist acts. Israelis and foreigners can be tried and sentenced even for crimes committed outside of Israel, such as illegal contact with enemy organizations including PLO, Popular Front for the Liberation of Palestine, etc. Today the government is considering abandoning some 'emergency' regulations to rely on the ordinary criminal laws and procedures.

Employment is officially permitted only for those with "Temporary" or "Permanent" resident status or holders of special labor permits. Anyone can register at the local labor exchange (*lishkat avoda*) but they look more like offices of the *lishkat ha sa'ad* (Welfare). Some exchanges do place professionals and skilled craftsmen, but Israelis who are not domestics, unskilled farm or factory hands usually look elsewhere. A separate department deals with elderly people and those in need of rehabilitation, so where does that leave the average newcomer who doesn't fit into these categories? One job opportunity for an enterprising Israeli would be to open a private employment agency catering to immigrant academicians and professionals. Diligent job seekers generally follow the want ads, especially in the Tuesday and Friday editions of the Hebrew afternoon newspapers, or apply directly to personnel managers of large companies and institutions. The Absorption Ministry and immigrant associations are tuned in to the job market and offer personal counselling as well as information bulletins dealing with some occupations and professions. The Labor Ministry, Histadrut and Manufacturers Association operate retraining programs to encourage white collar employees to shift over to export geared, production line jobs that need filling. Flexibility is the word and even educated immigrants have found fulfilling new management and other careers once they are Hebrew speaking and learn to adapt.

Inadequate preparation for that most important part of life *parnassa* (making a living), can spoil an otherwise happy and successful adjustment to the country. It makes good sense to go to Israel first on a pilot tour to meet as many prospective and potential employers and colleagues at work as possible. Bring professional portfolio, photostats of diplomas and licenses for evaluation and approval by local licensing authorities as well as curriculum vitae and local references. Good positions are available according to the law of supply and demand and there is no legal duty on the part of the government to find anyone a job. Individual initiative and personal contacts are still almost always the main factors in getting a good job. Ability to adjust to a new occupation or ways of doing things are equally important criteria for succeeding once you do find suitable employment. Sooner or later you will have to — there is little unemployment in Israel, although there may be seasonal fluctuations.

Entertainment walking, looking, listening and talking are Israel's major tourist attractions plus sun, sea and scenery and it's all free. You can have interesting encounters in any sidewalk café or bus if you aren't shy. If you are, IGTO arranges home hospitality and visits with Israeli families. They also have listings of night clubs, discos, theaters, vaudeville, opera, museums and all current social events. If you read Hebrew, check the street posters on the circular kiosks in downtown streets. Nightlife runs the gamut from Beethoven to belly dancers to the especially Israeli art-culture coffee clubs whose programs include music, theater, exhibitions, films and lots of atmosphere, genuine and phony. The area around Yermiyahu Street and the old Tel Aviv port is bustling with off beat bistros, galleries, tea houses, cafés and Greenwich Village-Soho atmosphere. Hamlin House has lectures, folk and social dancing and draws an older, largely Yiddish speaking and Anglo-Saxon crowd. There are community centers called "*Matnas*" (Culture, Youth and Sport Centers) in the cities and towns, where you can join in or watch Israelis doing their thing. Every other Thursday evening there is an English-American hootenanny, folk music and socializing for singles at the Cellar Club in the school across the street from the *Payis* (lottery) Building in Tel Aviv. Other popular Tel Aviv night spots are located in Old Jaffa, Dizengoff and the Atarim tourist center near the Municipal Marina. Check weekly tourist guides for other cities and newspapers for current events and guided tours.

Firearms Unlike most of the States and some foreign countries, Israel has very strict laws regarding possession or use of firearms including pistols, shot guns, rifles and ammunition and they apply to local residents *and* tourists alike. Application for a license is usually approved for adults without a criminal record. If you don't have a license you are not allowed to hold or use weapons even for hunting or as a hobby, If you are caught you may get involved in an unpleasant police investigation and prosecution.

Food Basic items are reasonable and plentiful the year round, due to government subsidies and the miracle of Israeli agriculture respectively. Junk foods and eating out is relatively new but have proven as elsewhere that they can be habit forming. With the emphasis on home cooking and so many ethnic backgrounds, it is no wonder Israeli cooking is diverse and tasty. You can find almost every international and Jewish food (except a good pastrami sandwich). There are even local cows and cowboys, but most beef comes over on refrigerated ships and is both expensive and not as tender as the cuts in Europe and America. The hot climate is another reason meat eaters cut down on steaks and roast beef or prefer poultry. Typically Israeli snacks and dishes include *felafel* (small balls of fried chick peas spiced with pepper) and served with coleslaw in *pitta* (flat, pancake shaped Arab bread), *humus* (ground chick peas and olive oil spread and slurped from a plate with chunks of pitta), *techina* (looks and is eaten like humus, but is made of sesame seeds), *shamenet* (thick sour cream), *leben* and *eshel* (thin yoghourty milk products) and natural fruit flavored yoghourts.

Foreign Currency can be openly held and exchanged by Israeli residents and illegal and street money changers are to some extent, no longer the only way to get dollars or other hard currency. One may hold limited sums in cash per family member, so for Israelis who want to hide more under the mattress or really need dollars (for instance to buy a flat listed in foreign currency), the illegal, down-town street corner 'banker' is a temptation and sometimes a necessary evil. Israelis are allowed to deposit dollars in a local savings account, but interest is low (3 to 6% net) and withdrawals in dollars is limited. In spite of recent liberalization in currency regulations, citizens and permanent residents are supposed to keep their foreign currency and assets here, unless they have special permission from the Treasury. Hotel bills paid in foreign currency are exempt from VAT. Tourists can pay for other services and purchases in American dollars or any other freely exchangeable Western currency (Canadian or Australian Dollars, English Pounds, Swiss, Belgian or French Francs, Dutch Guilders, German Marks or South African Rand). If a store or tourist facility is unable or unwilling to accept or give change in foreign currency, tourists must pay in Israeli Lira.

Gas (Cooking) Unless you bring or buy American cooking ranges you'll have to do without fancy, automatic, push button microwave oven and stove. Local families use good old-fashioned wooden matches (there are no match "books"), but friction lighters to turn on the burners are becoming popular. Newer buildings have central butane (cooking) gas which reduces costs and eliminates the need for delivery service and unsightly gas "balloon" containers that clutter up many apartment entrances and gardens. With good restaurants expensive and decent fast food service and TV dinners rare, some Anglo-Saxons have rediscovered a new joy in Israel — healthy, tasty home cooking. *be'tayavon* — "Bon appetit".

Gas Stations are usually just that and nothing more. You can find a *Delek*, *Paz* or *Sonol* station open just about anywhere any time, even on the Sabbath and holidays, except for Yom Kippur. Local petrol comes from the Haifa and Ashdod refineries and the 83 and 94 octanes are OK for all European and American cars. Make sure the pump marker is at zero before they fill you up, or Israel's ridiculously expensive petrol will cost you even more. Larger stations provide ordinary grease, lubrication, ignition, tire and minor repair service. Attendants do not clean windshields or check battery, oil or tires even if you ask nicely, unless you look like a big tipper or a Hollywood star. Forget about free road maps, clean rest rooms and smiling attendants.

Geography Israel is situated at the eastern terminus of the Mediterranean Sea and is 265 miles long from Kiryat Shmonah on the Lebanese border to Eilat on the Red Sea. It is 70 miles wide in the Negev south but only 10 miles wide in the heavily populated coastal plain near Netanya, just north of Tel Aviv. Its 8,000 square miles lie on the same latitude as the state of Georgia and would easily fit between Plains and Atlanta. Israel is 5,000 miles from New York and half that far from London.

"Good Fence" (The) is the section of the Israel-Lebanon international frontier which has been opened to help the nearby beleaguered Christian villagers in their struggle against marauding Moslem terrorists and the "peace making" Syrian army now permanently stationed in Lebanon. For a year or more, Israel quietly gave arms, medical and other equipment and aid to the Christian population of its northern neighbor. Now, it is an open alliance and tourists can ride right up to the Good Fence and see smiling faces and two way traffic that symbolize the cooperation possible when there is goodwill and a common interest on both sides.

Green Line (The) refers to the international borders of Israel from the War of Independence in 1948 until June 5, 1967. It is "green" because that was the color of the armis-

233

tice lines on Israeli maps. The areas captured in the Six Day War beyond the Green Line are "administered," "captured" or "liberated" territories, depending on one's political views. They have been administered by Israeli military government together with local Arab authorities, except for East Jerusalem which has been officially incorporated into the State and reunited with Israel's Jerusalem.

Hatikva (The Hope)   is the title of Israel's national anthem and a well chosen expression to describe the country. Its author was Naftali Imber, a poet who lived briefly in Palestine. At first it was the theme of one of the Zionist organizations, later of the entire movement. Since independence it has become the national anthem of Israel. In English and Latinized Hebrew the Hope is:

> So long as still within our breasts the Jewish heart beats true;
> So long as still towards the East, to Zion, looks the Jew,
> So long our hopes are not yet lost — two thousand years we cherished them,
> To live in freedom in the land of Zion and Jerusalem.

> Kol od balevav, penimah, nefesh yehudi homiyah;
> Ulfatei mizrach kadimah, ayin le tziyon tzofiyah.
> Od lo avdah tikvateinu, hatikva shnot alpayim,
> Lihyot am chofshi beartzeinu eretz tziyon virushalayim.

Health Funds, Sick Funds (Kupat Holim)   provide essential medical and hospital services for most of the population. There are four major funds — or more accurately, medical clinics: *Ammami, Maccabi, Mercazit* and the largest by far, the *Histadrut*. Most operate modern neighborhood clinics and medical facilities which involve revolving door treatment and a lot of waiting in line. Some have panels of doctors who see insured patients at their own homes or offices. Average monthly cost for full coverage is about $15 for singles to $40 for families, but most employers pay the bill or part of it. Newcomers sometimes find the drastic change in climate, food and way of life can cause a temporary increase in complaints and illnesses, actual and psychosomatic, and thus in visits to the doctor during the first few months in the country.

Heating Except for Jerusalem, hilly regions of the Galilee like Safed, Rosh Pina and the Golan, Israel winters are not very wintry. Rare snowfalls melt quickly and the friendly Israeli sun never goes away for too long, but there are some nasty, wet and cold winter days and temperatures go down fast after dark. Furthermore, Israeli homes and buildings with their stone walls and tiled floors, are not built to keep out the cold. Just a decade ago, the standard and cheapest home heating was a kerosene-fed controlled flame heater or "Friedman", after the name of the largest manufacturer. Push cart peddlers with their ringing bell and singsong, "neft"!"neft"! (kerosene) were as familiar as the neighborhood *Alte Zachen* man. Today, Friedmans are a big export item to developing countries in Africa and Asia and most Israelis use more convenient, odorless gas or electric heaters even though they cost more. There is central heating in some buildings but the heat doesn't always make it up to the top floors and it only goes on when the House Committee says so. Newcomers may want to install a reliable home gas or electric heater. Hot water is solar supplied and requires some waiting during cloudy days. An oil burner system with 24 hours, instant hot water can be installed in almost every house and flat.

Hebrew (Ivrit) One curses in Arabic, grumbles in Yiddish and gets along in English, but Hebrew, an ancient Semitic language related to Aramaic and Arabic, is Israel's national language. Its successful revival is one of the most unique social-linguistic achievements in recorded history. There are no regional dialects, but every immigrant group has its own slightly different pronunciation. It is taught everywhere in schools, community centers and Ulpan. The temptation is strong to put off the study of Hebrew to some vague date when it may be too late, but Israel is more exciting and meaningful in *Ivrit*. Street signs are in English as well as Hebrew, so you can't really get lost. You can also go a long way with *"Shalom"* (it means Hello, Goodbye, Peace and Hi), *"slicha"* (Sorry), *"yoffi!"* (Wonderful) or *"Ani midaber rak Anglit"* (I can only speak English), not to mention old standbys such as *"allo!"*, *"fantasti!"*, *"ze lo fair!"*, and *"OK"*. These are only a few of the gems in the language where *"hu"* means he, *"he"* is she, *"me"* is who and *"ha"* means it and it's not funny. Sabras also use a body language slang where a click of teeth against palate ("tsk!") means no, forefinger to bottom of eye means "who are you trying to kid?," rotating an open hand from left to right in imitation of a mixer means "What's going on?" and holding thumb to index and middle fingers and shaking means "Hold it," or "Wait a minute." The Mediterranean tapping of a forefinger against a forehead signifies "You're nuts". *"Nu"* and *"oy!"* are two Yiddish expressions that are part of spoken Hebrew and constantly used with different accents and meanings; try them when nothing else works.

Historical Milestones Any attempt to condense 4,000 years of Jewish history to a few pages takes real chutzpa. The following summary is only an approximate capsule glance at the major highlights, trials, tribulations and triumphs of the Jews throughout their amazing history. For thirty centuries, most of what happened took place outside of their own land. They faced and somehow survived such challenges as Paganism, Hellenism, Rome, Christianity,

Islam, Medieval Ages, Secularism and Assimilation. In the Modern Era they have had to cope with Enlightenment, Fascism, Nazism and the Holocaust. During the present generation some have returned once again to the Land of Israel while the majority remain in exile in the Old and New worlds.

BCE (Before the Common Era)

Bronze Age	Prehistoric Civilizations form in Jordan, the Hula Valley and around Haifa and Beer Sheba. Pagan tribes and idol worshiping cults dwell in Canaan amidst Nomadic incursions.
2100	Noah boards the Ark with his family and some friends.
2000-1800	Abraham the first Hebrew leaves Ur of the Chaldees in present day Iraq, to bring the Hebrews and Monotheism to the place of the Seven Wells in Beer Sheba, followed by the Patriarchs.
1800-1500	Jacob's progeny go to Egypt, where the Israelites are accepted and then enslaved by a Pharaoh who knew not Joseph.
1300-1200	Exodus of the Israelites from slavery, led by Moses who takes them on a wandering sojourn through the desert towards Zion, and receives the Ten Commandments on the way.
1200-900	The Twelve Tribes spread out and settle in the Land followed by the First Jewish Commonwealth with self-government by the Judges and then Saul, David and Solomon. Israeli Kings rise and fall, as the Jewish Monarchy disintegrates into mini-kingdoms of Judah and Israel and again, dispersion of the Twelve Tribes of Israel.

800-500	The Age of the Prophets.
500-300	Coming of the Persians, destruction of Solomon's Temple and the exile of the remaining Tribes to Babylon. Then under benevolent King Cyrus the return to Judah, Israel and rebuilding of the Temple. Alexander the Great conquers and forcibly Hellenizes the Land and the Hebrews.
200-100	Judah Maccabee and his followers defeat the mighty Greeks and restore Jewish rule.
100-0	All-powerful Rome and its Legions end the Second Jewish Commonwealth.

CE (Common Era)

0-300	Roman Emperors send the largest army in all history to finally crush the Jewish rebellion. In genocidal fury they slaughter more than half a million Jewish residents of Jerusalem, destroy the Second Temple and raze and plow under the capital of ancient Israel. The Fall of Massada symbolizes the beginning of the Diaspora in the Mediterranean world. A shattered Jewry holds together united by growing liturgy, synagogue and the *Minyan* (brotherhood of Jews) in every city and land where they find refuge.
400-500	Byzantium rules the Holy Land, the cult of Christianity becomes a Religion of the World and the Wandering Jew becomes a universal Pariah. Jewish suffering in Europe reaches new heights with forced conversions, feudal enslavement and degradation.

500-1100   Judaism encounters militant Islam and growing anti-Semitism but is strengthened by a common fate and the growing force of the Talmud, the invisible link between the scattered communities.

1100-1300   Seljuks conquer the Land followed by Crusaders and 200 years of Christian-Moslem wars and feudal principalities in Palestine. Pogroms, ritual murder charges, massacres and banishment in Europe as the Jews in exile become Ashkenazis and Sephardics.

1300-1500   Now the Mamelukes rule Palestine. Some Jews have never left while others will trickle back in every generation. In Europe the Inquisition brings still new forms of misery to a battered Jewry.

1517-1917   Four centuries of neglectful rule by the Ottoman Turks and steady return of more Jews to the ancient homeland. In the Diaspora, Moslem and Christian oppression continues as Jews withdraw to ghetto life. Still new challenges confront them in secularism and the Age of Enlightenment brings false Messiahs and false hopes for Jewish emancipation in the Old World.

1896   Theodor Herzl assumes leadership of the Zionist Movement and a year later convenes the first meeting in Basel of the World Zionist Organization. While masses of East European Jewry are sailing to the New World, others are making a more perilous voyage southward to disembark at Jaffa port. More and more are looking eastward and some are returning to Zion.

1898   Founding of *Petach Tikva* (the Gateway of Hope), the first Jewish pioneering village in Palestine is followed by growing waves of pioneers who begin the redemption of a wilderness and new life and spirit to the ancient homeland now in ruins.

1917   The Balfour Declaration confirms the legitimacy of the Zionist goal of restoration of a Jewish National Home in Palestine. One year later the 'War to end all Wars' ends, even while the forged Protocols of the Elders of Zion is circulating in Emancipated Europe.

1922   The League of Nations Mandate confers responsibility for encouragement and protection of Jewish settlement in Palestine on the British Government, as growing Arab nationalism clashes with Jewish aspirations. Throughout the centuries-long struggle for rule in Palestine, only the Hebrew-Jews and now the modern-day Zionists will live there as a self-governing, independent nation.

1933-1945   Rise of Fascism and Nazism fan dormant anti-Semitism in modern Europe and culminate in the greatest national disaster in Jewish history. One third of an entire people are purposefully destroyed and Holocaust takes on a new meaning for the civilized world.

1947-1948   Survivors of death camps become displaced persons and illegal immigrants and Britain leaves Palestine. Israel achieves Independence as the Third Jewish Commonwealth arises and defeats invading Arab armies in the first of four wars. Sephardic and Oriental Jews flee Arab and Moslem countries for Israel while Arabs flee Palestine-Israel to become refugees.

1949-1980   Israel grows stronger and strives for fulfillment of Jewish history. It faces serious challenges at home, global intrigues, geopolitics, petrodollar realities and thorny problems of the peace making process as it approaches the 21st century.

Hitchhiking is legal and a must for many young soldiers and reserve army civilians throughout the country who have no other quick way to get home for a brief visit or back to the base. It has been known to be an unpleasant experience and even worse for female tourists and soldiers and is definitely risky at night and when alone. If you have to hitch (its called *"tremping"* in Israel), don't thumb a ride — you point your extended arm towards the road in a downward motion. Be careful walking or jogging on roadways if there are Israeli drivers around.

Hotels are officially supervised by the government and are divided into five categories depending on location, size and facilities. Four and five stars assure de luxe, fully air conditioned, plus private bathroom, all on international standards. Three stars mean a smaller, less pretentious but comfortable hotel. One and two stars could be a decent, family pension or sleazy dive and caution is advisable. High season rates and crowds are the rule during the main holidays. The Galilee and mountain resort areas are fuller and more expensive in summer and Eilat, Sinai and the Dead Sea are during winter. For budget minded and the adventurous,

241

there are youth hostels (all ages), Christian hospices (all religions), and outdoor camping sites (tents, bungalows and caravans) as well as Israelis who will rent a room to a tourist. Details at the Youth Hostel Association, Pilgrimage Division of the Ministry of Religion, Camping Union and IGTO respectively.

House Committee Try to get along with your *Vaad Habait* because like it or not, the committee has the authority to decide things like when the heat goes on or off, what building repairs will be made, how much it's going to cost each month, etc. If you make structural changes (install an air conditioner, knock down an interior wall, extend your porch), open an office, give piano lessons or hold wild parties without inviting the Vaad, they can say no or make you sorry you ever moved into an apartment house. Serious disputes with neighbors or the house committee are supposed to be resolved by a special representative of the Justice Ministry (*misrad hamishpatim*). If you have the dubious honor of becoming a member of your Vaad, it will help you understand this interesting institution, and like they say, "when you can't beat them, join them".

Housewife (for the) The ladies will have to get used to some changes but becoming an Israeli housewife, if you really want to, is not all that bad. For instance there are almost no walk-in closets and wall shelves of the kind found in every American apartment and home. In Israel you buy ready mades or have a carpenter build and install them to order. Kitchens are just empty rooms the first time you see them unless you buy your housing second-hand or rent someone else's home or apartment. Shopping, cooking and cleaning are more or less the everyday routine they are everywhere else after you learn the ropes, products, spices, weights and measurements, and how to say it all in easy Hebrew. Don't worry about heavy packages, dish washing or garbage disposal; that's where husbands come in handy in Israel.

Housing (or more about where to live) There are few apartments and houses for rent and they are very expensive. So if you are not headed for kibbutz, moshav, monastery or Yeshiva, you will have to consider buying a house or more likely, an apartment. Prices have gone up 100-300% in the last three years and are still rising. They can cost from $15-40,000 per *room* these days, depending on location. The near impossibility for so many slum dwellers and young couples of ever being able to buy an apartment of their own in a decent neighborhood is one of the most serious, if not *the* national problem. If some solution is not found it may become Israel's most explosive domestic issue. Houses (*"Villas"*) of any type are beyond the budget of most Israelis who usually end up in housing projects or small apartment buildings where one buys and gets title to a flat. It is exactly like buying a condominium apartment in America (as distinguished from "Co-op" apartments, where one buys shares in a corporation that owns an apartment building and land with the number of shares depending on size and desirability of the apartment). "Key money" is a hybrid between rental and purchase with tenants paying a one time sum to acquire the key, i.e. possession and thereafter only nominal rental. The landlord retains ownership and receives a share of the key money paid by each new tenant to the outgoing one. It is the Israeli way to enable a person or couple of limited means to acquire a small flat which they could otherwise not afford. Used apartments are often better buys since you know what you are getting and that you are getting it, especially since there have been cases of builders and contractors going bankrupt before completion and occupancy. Never buy anything, don't even sign a binder, without consulting a lawyer and appraiser.

There is one consolation in this grim picture; villa and apartment prices have consistently been one of the best and most secure investments you can make in Israel. If you sell, you almost always make a profit.

Identity Cards (tiudat zihut)   are issued by the Ministry of Interior to every citizen, resident and *Oleh*. They are in addition to the *tiudat Oleh* (Immigrant Certificate) which is the official confirmation of one's immigrant status and a supplement to the ordinary ID card. The latter is required as proof of identity for all official purposes and legal transactions. The law requires Israelis to carry it with them and to register changes in address and family status at the Ministry. It is symbolic of the multitude of forms and documents that confront citizens and newcomers. Never having encountered the need for an official ID card, Anglo-Saxons may find it a little strange or even unpleasant, but in a new country populated by immigrants and surrounded by hostile neighbors, it has become an absolute necessity.

Immigrant Associations are voluntary organizations of established settlers like the Landsman societies in melting pot America. They provide invaluable encouragement and advice that supplement official aid and counselling of the Jewish Agency and the Ministry of Absorption. AACI has offices in the USA and throughout Israel and veteran Israelis who speak your language who are ready to help. There is a similar association for newcomers from most of the other returning tribes. If you haven't been to your immigrant association for a long time, it's a sign that you are making it on your own or are no longer an *Oleh hadash*.

Investments (foreign currency) are welcome and encouraged by the Government and there are lots of success stories from Coca Cola and oil prospectors to those who have brought supermarkets, computer dating and personalized T-shirts to Israel. Convenient loans, tax exemptions and other incentives are granted to "Approved Enterprises" such as dollar earners, export industries and investors who bring a plant or business to a development area. Newcomers who want to go into business in Israel should proceed with caution, bearing in mind how different laws, customs and procedures are here. The ethics and mentality of competitors, customers and even business associates may not be what one is used to and professional advice should be sought before getting involved or making important decisions. There is a "Law for the Encouragement of Capital Investments" and Investment Centers that advise potential investors. They also assure everyone that those bitter warnings — "How can you make a small fortune in Israel? ... just bring over a big one", or "It's easy to end up with $100,000 after only one year, all you have to do is come over with $200,000" — are only sick jokes. Healthy reasons for doing business here are intelligent, skilled labor at relatively low wages, advanced research and development capabilities, modern transportation and communication facilities, convenient location astride three continents and Israel's associate status in the European Common Market. More than a few, smart, hard working entrepreneurs with good ideas and management and a little mazal have turned small fortunes into big ones, (well, bigger, after taxes) in Israel. Further details at Israel-America Chamber of Commerce, US Embassy Commercial Attache, Tour Ve'Aleh offices and Investment Centers.

Islam which swept the Middle East in the 7th Century AD, is one of the great religions of the world. It has two main denominations, Sunna — which follows the traditional practices of Mohammed as set forth in the Hadith (Traditions) and Shia (the Faction), which declares that only descendants of the Prophet Mohammed and his son-in-law

245

Ali could be leaders of the faith. The Sunnites are the majority in most Middle Eastern countries except Iran, Iraq and Yemen where Shia prevails. Islam is the most prevalent, but not the only religion in the Middle East. It is monotheistic and for Moslems there is no God but Allah and his Prophet Mohammed and his words as recorded in the Koran. The Jewish Patriarchs and Jesus are esteemed and the Old and New Testaments are accepted as Holy Books, but all is subservient to the Koran. Devout Moslems pray five times a day, facing Mecca in Saudi Arabia to which they are required to make a pilgrimage at least once during their lifetime. Israeli Moslems may not marry four wives as they are permitted elsewhere in the Arab world.

Israel Government Bonds   have helped a lot in the growth of the country and many projects and accomplishments would not have been possible without the Bonds. Visitors who are original registered Bond owners can redeem certificates at local banks without restriction for the first three years in Israel. Others may receive limited sums in dollars or vouchers which entitle tourists to exemptions from local surcharge, service and Value Added Tax (VAT) on bills. Details should be clarified upon purchase or at Bonds offices.

Israelis (When do you become a real one?)   You *know* it is happening when you drink *Turkish* coffee at breakfast, *nap* after lunch and turn on the TV news report *every* evening, even though you've already *heard* it on the radio once or twice in the office or on the way home. It's when the phone rings and you answer *"allo"*, when you talk *back* to your kids in Hebrew, curse in Arabic and someone you grew up with points out how sloppy your *English* has become. It happens when your neighbors put *you* on the House Committee, you buy an electrical appliance and have to pay full customs duty, wear your shirt with the top buttons open, sign checks in *Hebrew* and can't remember the names of the teams in the play-offs back home; you've forgotten the *players* long ago. You are a 100% Sabra when you *enjoy* felafel and *shesh besh* (backgammon), start smoking again (local brands), click your tongue against your teeth instead of saying no, race an old lady for an empty seat on the bus, peel, chew *and* spit sunflower seeds *and* talk all at the same time *without* choking and tell some greenhorn how tough things *really* were when *you* first came to Israel!

Jew (Who is a?) The dictionary defines a "Jew" as a member of the tribe of Judah, one whose religion is Judaism, an Israelite. The word comes from the Patriarch Judah, son of Jacob, later the name of one of the ancient tribes of Hebrews. The latter is English for *Ivri*, meaning one who comes from the other side, i.e. Abraham and his descendants, who came from the other side of the River Euphrates. When the monarchy formed by Hebrew Kings David and Solomon divided into two parts, the northern kingdom became known as Israel and the southern one Judah. Israel fell and then Judah and in the centuries that followed dispersion of the Hebrews into the Diaspora. They were called Jews by the Gentiles, meaning inhabitants of Judah and descendants of Jacob's sons. The name was accepted by the Hebrews and thus they became those stiff-necked people who are Jews to this very day. The religious definition of who is a Jew according to *Halacha* (Orthodox religious code or law), is a person whose mother was born a Jewess or is an Orthodox convert. Secular Jews and adherents of Conservative and Reform Jewry reject this narrow definition. So do the courts and government authorities, who regard as Jewish anyone with at least one Jewish parent by birth or converted by any Rabbi. Ben Gurion and others have contended that anyone who wishes to be regarded as a Jew should be one. The dilemma is acute regarding the right to Israeli citizenship, which under Zionist ideology and the Law of Return, is granted automatically only to a "Jew". Many Israelis couldn't care less about the matter; they have enough problems of their own. Some would even prefer to be considered "Hebrew" or just "Israeli". The enemies of the Jews never seem to have trouble identifying and finding them. Perhaps the best solution would be for the Gentiles to convert to Judaism and end this thorny problem once and for all.

Jewish Agency (The) can't get you a good job or into the movies or the modeling profession. It is the government supported organization of the Zionist movement on behalf of Jews everywhere who support the State of Israel, immigration and the successful absorption of new immigrants. Through its offices and representatives, it has helped more than a million *Olim* and established hundreds of towns and villages and there is nothing quite like it even in immigrant oriented countries such as America, Canada, Australia or South Africa.

Kibbutz (visiting a) Tourist buses and guides include an in and out visit to some kibbutz as part of most regular tours of Israel. For an especially unique educational experience combined with an exhilarating holiday, a kibbutz rest or guest home may be the answer. Amenities are similar to a small country resort or hotel; they are clean and often have swimming pool or beach facilities. The Kibbutz Rest and Guest Home Association supplies information and suggestions. For more serious students of one of the most extraordinary wonders of Israel and the 20th century, there are kibbutzim that accept volunteers and visitors for extended or even indefinite periods, free of charge. All that is required is to get along with everyone and to do some part or full time work in the fields, workshops or dining hall. Any able bodied tourist, Jew and Gentile, can try life on a kibbutz but should make arrangements first at the Tel Aviv offices of the kibbutz movements.

Laundry There are a few Chinese Jews in Israel but they don't operate laundries. Laundromats are almost non-existent and expensive. Israelis usually do their laundry on their home washing machine after adding a special softener for the tough Sabra water. Then it's out to the porch clothes line where there's sunshine most of the year; only a very few have clothes dryers. Singles and working mothers may prefer laundry and/or ironing service provided by *"mangle"* laundries — what a lovely name! Some cleaning ladies — not all — also do laundry and ironing. Newcomers learn that Israel's household help are the most independent, sulky and scarce people around. Almost nobody can afford or put up with them more than once a week even if they have strong nerves, and mother's helpers are just as hard to handle. For spoiled mothers and infants there is a diaper rental service and disposables are sold at larger pharmacies.

Libraries in English are hard to find. Most municipal libraries are small and English selections are apt to be limited and dated. The magnificent Hebrew University library English language section is open to the public. So are the libraries at the US Information Center and British Council. Better book stores have large English lists and there are inexpensive used paper back book shops in the cities where you get back half price when you return the book.

Liquor Stores There are none. Beer, wine and the hard stuff, both domestic and imported, are sold to all comers and all ages at grocery stores, kiosks and supermarkets with no government regulations or limitations. A few years ago, no one drank alcoholic beverages, except for the Sabbath wine benediction. Today, Israeli beers and wines are export items and international prize winners. Social drinking has become acceptable and Israel now has home grown alcoholics whose downfall is usually attributed to unsuccesstul social and economic integration, and the emulation of western life styles. Still, it is rare to see a drunk in the streets and martinis with lunch or whiskey and soda after work are also unusual. There is no such thing as a neighborhood bar or pub and most Israelis do their drinking at family or social functions. Except for larger hotels, many big city bars are often patronized by the local jet set, underworld-type characters and prostitutes.

Lotteries Tickets are sold from booths and kiosks all over the country and for about seventy-five cents everyone has the chance to become a Lira millionaire if you hit the big winner. Proceeds support schools, hospitals, youth and old age homes and other worthy projects. The *Payis* and *Lotto* lotteries provide employment for hundreds of elderly and crippled ticket vendors who would otherwise be unemployable. There is a *Toto* lottery for the young and armchair athletes based on prediction of *"futbal"* (soccer) results. All other gambling is illegal, but shady card clubs and card sharks are around for the addicted. Some Knesset members have recommended building a fancy casino for tourists only, in Eilat or somewhere too far away to tempt the local inhabitants. The secret plan *after* peace with the Arabs, is for a desert casino with Jewish belly dancers to bring in Arab sheiks and royalty and help recoup some of the petro-dollar fortunes they have piled up.

Mail If you don't have a permanent address in Israel, you can receive mail temporarily care of the Consulate, AACI, Meditrad (the local representative of American Express) or "Poste Restante" (General Delivery) at the Post Office. Personal or important letters and those containing checks or money orders should be sent registered, cabled or by inter-bank transfer. Cash should never be enclosed in a letter. If you want your in or outgoing mail to arrive in a hurry, add "Express" (special delivery) postage. Local postal rates are about the highest in the world and are always going up but air letters cost much less. Overseas cables have a cheap and expensive per word rate — depending on whether you want overnight (LT) letter-telegrams or quick service and you can send them from any private telephone. The main Post Offices in Tel Aviv, Jerusalem and Haifa have a public telex service open to the public.

Manners (and etiquette) This should be a blank page if some commentators and sociologists are to be believed. A lot of Israelis are abrupt, rude or totally indifferent to the niceties of good manners. Menahem Begin's courtliness and Abba Eban's articulation are the exceptions and even they are as often ridiculed as admired. Generally, leaders of society and the average person do not display much old world charm or elegant speech. It can be depressing to encounter yelling, pushing and impatience, but Israelis can also be among the most friendly and helpful people you will ever run into. They go out of their way to help someone in real need or trouble, in situations where the average person in urban America would bury himself in his newspaper or discreetly disappear. Social introductions are usually on a first name basis unless a Mr. (*mar*) or Mrs. (*gveret*) so and so is clearly called for or it is someone of unusual rank or standing (Colonel ... Rabbi ... Judge ...). Otherwise it is almost always "*korim li*" so and so, ("I am called...").

Marriage In Israel this is the most important family affair by far and there is plenty of *Simcha* in the catering halls, photography studios and bridal accessory boutiques, where business is always booming. Marriage registrars are situated at the Rabbinate and when couples register they must present proof of age — 18 for both, but 17 is enough for girls with parents' consent and even younger with Court approval, (like when there are slightly pregnant girls and very angry fathers). *Olim* must also produce evidence they are single, widowed or divorced and Jewish. The registry procedure requires brides to receive sex and religious instruction from a *Rebbitsin* (Rabbi's wife) and to undergo a *mikva* (Orthodox ritual) cleansing bath, even if all this doesn't turn her on. There is no real choice, since Israel has no legal civil marriage and inter-faith weddings are even more complicated and difficult to arrange. The nearest alternative possibility is Cyprus which gets mixed marriages and Jewish couples the Rabbinate won't marry, like a Cohen and a divorcée, but such wedding ceremonies might not be recognized by the authorities upon return to Israel.

Medical Care Visitors who need a doctor due to chronic or sudden illness or accident will be in good hands and there are well trained, competent English speaking physicians and dentists all around. Emergency ambulance service, hospitals, *Magen David Adom*, private nursing and pharmacy are all nearby when necessary, 24 hours a day. Extensive care for serious medical problems can become expensive and tourists and settlers should consider arrangements abroad or in Israel for accident and health insurance or Sick Fund coverage. Compared to other countries with the same high standards, medical and hospital bills are substantially lower in Israel. In recent years, European tourists in need of dental or medical care, have been coming over for week's holiday plus some bridgework or a few days at the spas and hot springs, all for the price of one. Israeli doctors advise tourists to take it easy in the summer, especially during the sunny midday and to drink plenty of liquids (use straws at street stands and vendors). People with sensitive stomachs should keep away from local junk foods, spices and grubby restaurants. Faith healers and acupuncture specialists are also around if anyone is interested.

Mezuzah Gentile visitors are frequently curious about those small, rectangular pieces of wood, ceramic or metal nailed to every apartment and building doorpost. This is the *mezuzah* or ritual door post, mentioned in two Biblical injunctions, and the Children of Israel take it very literally. Some families prefer artistic or avant garde mezuzahs while others are content with simple ones. All contain a small piece of parchment containing the Jewish credo *Shema Yisrael* (Hear O Israel), handwritten by a scribe.

Milestones (Social) When invited to some social occasion you can show up on time or up to half an hour late, unless you have been specifically asked to be punctual. The main family occasions are the *chatuna* (wedding), *brit* (bris — circumcision), and *levaya* (funeral) and they are usually late in getting started. Informal dress is generally OK; at the sadder occasions women would be wise in covering their heads and wearing something modest, men should have on a skull cap at funerals, condolence calls to a family sitting *shiva* or when attending memorial services (*haskara*). Weddings and brits call for a gift and Israelis for the most part give and prefer to receive a check. Flowers are a gracious gesture for almost any occasion or get together. If you want to bring along a friend, you should ask your host first. Unescorted women are permitted everywhere but some find it more pleasant if they have a male companion. If it's a party you can bring a bottle of wine or liquor, though drinking is not a popular social custom even at parties and celebrations. Getting drunk is rare and bad form, unless it's Purim or you have won the top prize in the national lottery.

Money For more than thirty years Israel currency was called the Lira (IL) or Pound, since it was once equivalent to the British Pound Sterling. Continuous devaluations reduced it to less than the lowly nickel. Just as this book went to press, the government decided to make things

more Sabra (and confusing) by issuing new legal tender
with the good old Hebrew name, *Shekel* — after the ancient
unit of weight, mentioned in the old Testament, for weigh-
ing gold and silver. The new currency is equivalent to
exactly one tenth of the Lira: one thousand Liras being now
one hundred Shekels. The latter have the same appearance
as the Liras except that they are called Shekels and have
one zero less. For example, David Ben Gurion's portrait still
appears on what was a five hundred Lira note, but this is
now fifty Shekels. The former coins have been replaced by
new coins of one, five and ten Agorot and one-half Shekel.

Mourning (and funerals)   have special symbolic meaning in
a country that has suffered the Holocaust and four wars in
a single generation. Death in Israel evokes a widespread
response because people live in close proximity, so each
death becomes a neighborhood if not national loss. There is
little of the commercial exploitation of the American way of
dying and the Orthodox run *Chevra Kadisha* (Burial Society)
looks after all Jewish funeral arrangements and ceremonies.
It is customary for the immediate family to stay home in
(*Shiva*) mourning for an entire week, with friends, relatives
and neighbors coming by to pay condolence visits. Thirty
days later there is a memorial ceremony (*haskara*) at the
grave site and on the annual anniversary mourners go out
again to the cemetery. On top of all their other troubles,
Israelis have an unusually high mortality rate from road and
industrial accidents, heart attacks and strokes. Their extraordinary penchant for living every moment with such gusto
and spirit may be their reply to the anonymous adage that
death is only nature's way of telling you to slow down.

Newspapers *The Jerusalem Post* is Israel's only English
newspaper and appears daily except Saturdays and holidays. It has a large Friday weekend edition which includes
special supplements; Hebrew newspapers usually contain

from eight to fifty pages. Except for matters of military security there is no censorship. There are nearly a dozen Hebrew dailies and numerous foreign language papers including French, Rumanian, German, Hungarian, Polish, Yiddish, Bulgarian and Russian. The Herald Tribune European Edition is flown in from Paris one day late and news stands also carry Time, Newsweek and the other American and European weeklies and monthlies for the nostalgic. The weekly tourist magazines, "Tel Aviv Today", "This Week in Israel" and "Hello Israel" are distributed free of charge in hotels and tourist centers. Hebrew students can try *La Matchil* (For the Beginner) weekly in simple Hebrew using vowel signs or the more advanced *Omer*, a regular, serious but fully voweled newspaper, or tune in to the *Ivrit La Am* (Hebrew for "the People") daily radio program in beginners' Hebrew. Programs include interviews, reviews, news round up and Hebrew lessons. Daily broadcasts are scheduled at 11:35 to 12 am and from 7 to 7:15 pm.

Not in Israel There are lots of things you took for granted you won't find here — TV dinners, Miami Beach, TV commercials, Zen Buddhism, Moonies, 42nd Street, Con Edison, sleet and blizzards. On the other hand you'll just have to get used to living without the New York Times, sleeping late Sundays, the Staten Island Ferry, Macys, Disneyland, Dr. J., Howard Johnson ice cream cones and one, two and three martini business lunches.

Office (Life in the) is both similar and different than the nine to five routine back home. First of all, it's never nine to five and only a lucky few don't have to work Fridays. Office hours are not uniform and every job and company has its own set up. There is a growing tendency for a switch-over to the straight eight or nine hour work day instead of the split shift still the rule in stores, private offices, banks, etc. Practices like office and lunch hours, coffee breaks, sick leave, severance pay, vacations and how do you address the boss, etc., depend on the place and the people who work there. In government employ and large industrial and commercial companies, much has already been negotiated and decided in collective bargaining agreements, between the government, Histadrut and a committee representing employers' associations. Job security is more secure when you receive the officially accepted status of *kviut* (tenure). Even then, you had better get along with the others in the office and especially the number one man or woman, or you're in trouble. Government employees who have *kviut* but are not very productive or necessary are the bane of the civil service system. Getting fired is especially unpleasant because Israel is a small country and word can get around quickly if you are considered a loser or a trouble maker, and you won't have that nice paid-in-dollars unemployment check to keep you in felafel till you get another job.

Oleh (Olim in the plural) to be distinguished from *ole* (bull fights), *yodelei* (Swiss yodelers) or *oy veh*, is Hebrew for what happens when a Jew moves to Israel. There is a different word (*hagira*) for Gentile immigrants or when Jews immigrate anywhere else. *Aliya* means the seven main waves of immigration to Israel since the days of Herzl and in its literal as well as ideological sense — to ascend — to Israel. Immigrants from Israel are therefore *yordim*, descending, as it were, to a less lofty existence. Zionist terminology aside, an *Oleh* (settler) whatever his motivations or destination in Israel, is the lifeblood of the country. Inquiries at the Aliya Centers and Israeli Consulates abroad and at the Absorption Ministry, AACI and Tour Ve Aleh, all of whom answer questions and provide information.

Packing If it's your first trip, you won't need neckties or high heels — evening wear to the average Israeli means pyjamas. You'll get funny stares if you insist on wearing Bermuda shorts; they are called Zalmans which is also a nickname for a jerk. Bring a hat or cap for beach and synagogue scarf or kerchief for women, good walking shoes, sun glasses, lots of film and a thermos, because you'll be thirsty often and sometimes it may be convenient to have a cold or warm drink handy. Pack paper tissues. since restaurants and toilets may not have any napkins or tissues, or be otherwise up to your standards. Insect repellant is necesssary for summertime mosquitoes and flies, especially in desert areas. If you are on special medication, bring along a good supply plus the prescription, as you might need to have it refilled. Dungarees and a sport shirt plus sweater in the evenings is what Israelis usually wear and is good enough for almost everywhere except fancy restaurants and meetings with Menahem Begin. American cigarettes, whiskey, shirts and sweaters are gifts Israeli friends and relatives would probably appreciate. Baggage weight is no longer important, but make sure you get it all into two pieces of luggage plus one carryon bag or package; Check in baggage must not exceed 62 inches in total length, width and height or you pay heavy charges.

Parking in congested downtown streets is as frustrating as driving, riding a bus or being a pedestrian. Some municipalities use coin operated parking meters, while others have hourly or monthly tickets you're supposed to stick on your car window, but who knows where you can buy them? Private parking lots are pretty expensive and not always safer than parking on the street or sidewalk. Be on the lookout for a round blue sign with a diagonal red stripe which means you are in a tow away zone. If your car is not where you left it, call the police to find out whether you've been towed away. If so, they'll tell you which garage your car is at and you can pick it up if you pay the fee and ticket and prove ownership. If you are not lucky, it's only been stolen and you may never see your car again. Owners of late model automobiles should install an alarm and other anti-theft devices and be sure you're insured for the full replacement price. Never leave valuables or documents in your car.

Pedestrians (What again?) Yes. Walking in Israel is as dangerous as driving and even walking on or near a street or road is not really safe, if you don't learn the basic rules. There are clearly marked pedestrian crossings but be warned in advance, they are extremely hazardous if there is an Israeli driver in the vicinity. Most pedestrians are just as undisciplined as the drivers and cross anywhere, like in the middle of a highway, sometimes together with a donkey or two or a few hundred sheep or camels. Israel has official traffic observers, student and police traffic patrols, a National Council for the Prevention of Road Accidents, Careful Driver and Courteous Driver Contests, and it's all a waste of time and money. Some day a brilliant sociologist or psychologist may figure out why Israeli drivers and pedestrians are so meshuga.

Pets If you are going to bring him/her/it, your pet (animal) should have an up-to-date vaccination certificate, plus a letter of introduction from a vet and whatever else the Israeli Consulate in your area may suggest. If mootsy-pootsy is a monkey, alligator or other off-beat, non-human get written permission in advance from the Israel Ministry of Health, or they may put you and your baby lion in quarantine till everything gets straightened out.

Photography With its bright sunshine, clear skies and wonderful contrasts in photogenic people and scenery, Israel is a photographer's delight. Shops carry modern equipment and film and do black and white and color developing at rates higher than abroad. Expensive cameras should be insured and kept covered against dust, sun and heat. Arab women, Orthodox Jews and Druze do *not* like having their picture taken because of the 'evil eye', modesty or the commandment forbidding "graven images". If you must take their picture, don't let them know it or use a telescopic lens to avoid unpleasantness. Photography is strictly forbidden in border areas, military bases and installations. Photo stores may not develop risqué shots even if you explain it really is modern art or a second honeymoon. Soft or hard core pictures from Copenhagen or elsewhere enroute should remain in your suitcase between the Bermuda shorts and neckties. They might break box office records in Tel Aviv and some kibbutzim, but if the word gets around the Israeli vice squad will probably confiscate them and later, but not too quickly, destroy them and possibly file criminal charges.

PLO are the initials of the Palestine Liberation Organization, which came into existence in the sixties as a loose federation of Palestine-Arab political, military and terrorist groups and organizations. It is the funnel for receipt and distribution of funds from Arab countries and alleged representative of the Palestine Arabs, although they were never appointed to office by vote or referendum by the people they claim to represent. The largest, strongest and best known is *Fatah*, whose leader Yasser Arafat is the PLO spokesman.

The word is an acronym derived from the Arabic meaning movement for the liberation of Palestine. Its initials (HTF) means death and in reverse (FHT) conquest. In its most popular form it is FTH, pronounced Faht or El Fatah. Their common tactics have been to harass and bleed Israel and provoke Arab countries into continuous wars; which will wear it down until a "secular, democratic Palestine" has been established. Fatah is considered relatively conservative and western oriented, compared to *A Saika* (the Thunderbolt), which is Syrian-based and hard-line. The third large faction is the Popular Front for the Liberation of Palestine (PFLP), supported by Libya, Algeria and Iraq and has been responsible for most of the despicable and cowardly terrorist attacks in Israel and elsewhere against innocent children and civilian victims. PFLP has broken up into three branches; a relatively conservative group led by George Habash, the pro-Chinese Communists headed by Naif Hawatma and a terrorist-guerrilla unit led by Ahmed Jibril.

Policemen All 7,500 of them are overworked, undermanned, underpaid and sometimes under qualified, at least in the lower ranks. They work under a centralized, national police force divided into districts, sub-districts and stations. Many are FBI types (Foreign Born Israelis) and some are brand new immigrants. Lab, technical people and the top brass are as good as the best anywhere and the force is doing a reasonable job under unusually difficult circumstances. They are assisted by the 100,000 or so citizens who serve as volunteers in the Civil Guard (*Hamishmar Haezrachi*). Most work in pairs, patrolling the streets and crowded areas. Their guard duty is an important aid in protecting lives and property against crime and terrorism. With rare exceptions the police are incorruptible and it doesn't pay to try to bribe a traffic cop or call a policeman a *hazir* "pig". Insulting Israel's finest, the national flag, State or Jewish People are criminal acts. Cops wear beige summer and black winter uniforms resembling British Bobbies.

Post Offices sell the usual things as well as telegrams and cables — there is no Western Union in Israel. The Post Office can be identified by the blue sign with the leaping deer and some think it should be a turtle or some animal more appropriate to slow mail deliveries, but the service is

no worse than anywhere else. Larger branches stay open
from 8 am to 7 pm; smaller stations take a three hour afternoon break and close earlier. Every branch has a pay
phone, but many are out of order and telephone tokens are
not always available due to hoarding.

**Proclamation of Independence (Hachrazat Ha'atz-
naut)** was read out to an astonished world by David Ben
Gurion on May 14, 1948, the last day of the British Mandate. That date became Independence Day for the new
nation and thirty years later the proclamation is still a stir-
ring, summing up of what Israel was and is for its people,
world Jewry and all mankind. It is revealing and important
enough for those interested in Israel to want to read.

"Eretz Israel — The Land of Israel — was the birthplace
of the Jewish People. Here their spiritual, religious and
political identity was shaped. Here they first attained statehood, created cultural values of national and universal
significance and gave to the world the eternal Book of
Books.

After being forcibly exiled from their land, the people
kept faith with it throughout their dispersion and never
ceased to pray and hope for their return to it and for the
restoration in it of their political freedom.

Impelled by this historic and traditional attachment, Jews
strove in every successive generation to reestablish themselves in their ancient homeland. In recent decades they
returned in their masses. Pioneers, Jewish immigrants who
came in defiance of restrictive laws, and defenders. They
made deserts bloom, revived the Hebrew language, built
villages and towns, and created a thriving community, controlling its own economy and culture, loving peace but
knowing how to defend itself, bringing the blessings of
progress to all the country's inhabitants, and aspiring
towards independent nationhood.

261

In the year 5657 (1897), at the summons of the spiritual father of the Jewish State, Theodor Herzl, the First Zionist Congress convened and proclaimed the right of the Jewish People to national rebirth in its own country.

This right was recognized in the Balfour Declaration of the 2nd November, 1917, and reaffirmed in the Mandate of the League of Nations which, in particular, gave international sanction to the historic connection between the Jewish People and Eretz Israel and to the right of the Jewish People to rebuild its national home.

The catastrophe which recently befell the Jewish People — the massacre of millions of Jews in Europe — was another clear demonstration of the urgency of solving the problem of its homelessness by reestablishing in Eretz Israel the Jewish State, which would open the gates of the homeland wide to every Jew and confer upon the Jewish People the status of a full member of the community of nations.

Survivors of the Nazi holocaust in Europe, as well as Jews from other parts of the world, continued to migrate to Eretz Israel, undaunted by difficulties, restrictions and dangers, and never ceased to assert their right to a life of dignity, freedom and honest toil in their national homeland.

In the Second World War, the Jewish community of this country contributed its full share to the struggle of the freedom and peace loving nations against the forces of Nazi wickedness and by the blood of its soldiers and its war effort, gained the right to be reckoned among the peoples who founded The United Nations.

On the 29th November, 1947, The United Nations General Assembly passed a resolution calling for the establishment of a Jewish State in Eretz Israel; The General Assembly required the inhabitants of Eretz Israel to take such steps as were necessary on their part for the implementation of that resolution. This recognition by the United

Nations of the right of the Jewish People to establish their State is irrevocable.

This right is the natural right of the Jewish People to be masters of their own fate, like all other nations, in their own sovereign state.

ACCORDINGLY, WE members of the people's council, representatives of the Jewish community of Eretz Israel and of the Zionist Movement, are here assembled on the day of the termination of the British Mandate over Eretz Israel and, by virtue of our national and historic right and on the strength of the resolution of the United Nations General Assembly, hereby declare the establishment of a Jewish State in Eretz Israel, to be known as the State of Israel.

WE DECLARE that, effective from the moment of the termination of the Mandate, tonight, the eve of Sabbath, the 5th Iyar, 5708 (14th May, 1948), until the establishment of the elected, regular authorities of the State in accordance with the Constitution which shall be adopted by the Elected Constituent Assembly not later than the 1st October 1948, The People's Council shall act as a Provisional Council of State, and its executive organ, the People's Administration, shall be the Provisional Government of the Jewish State, to be called "Israel".

THE STATE OF ISRAEL will be open for Jewish immigration and for the ingathering of the exiles; it will foster the development of the country for the benefit of all its inhabitants; it will be based on freedom, justice and peace as envisaged by the Prophets of Israel; it will ensure complete equality of social and political rights to all its inhabitants irrespective of religion, race or sex; it will guarantee freedom of religion, conscience, language, education and culture; it will safeguard the Holy Places of all religions; and it will be faithful to the principles of the Charter of the United Nations.

THE STATE OF ISRAEL is prepared to cooperate with the agencies and representatives of the United Nations in implementing the resolution of the General Assembly of the 29th November, 1947, and will take steps to bring about the economic union of the whole of Eretz Israel.

WE APPEAL to the United Nations to assist the Jewish People in the building of its State and to receive the State of Israel into the comity of nations.

WE APPEAL — in the very midst of the onslaught launched against us now for months — to the Arab inhabitants of the State of Israel to preserve peace and participate in the upbuilding of the State on the basis of full and equal citizenship and due representation in all its provisional and permanent institutions.

WE EXTEND OUR HAND to all neighboring States and their peoples in an offer of peace and good neighborliness, and appeal to them to establish bonds of cooperation and mutual help with the sovereign Jewish People settled in its own land, The State of Israel is prepared to do its share in a common effort for the advancement of the entire Middle East.

WE APPEAL to the Jewish People throughout the Diaspora to rally round the Jews of Eretz Israel in the tasks of immigration and upbuilding and to stand by them in the great struggle for the realization of the age-old dream — the redemption of Israel.

Placing our trust in the Almighty, we affix our signatures to this Proclamation at this session of the Provisional Council of State, on the soil of the homeland, in the city of Tel Aviv, on this Sabbath eve, the 5th day of Iyar, 5708 (14th May, 1948)."

Radio Newscasts are broadcast every hour on the hour around the clock and you know another hour has gone by and the news is about to go on the air, when you hear the beep, beep, beep as the minute hand approaches the hour. There are three Hebrew language stations and news in English is on at 7 am, 2 pm, 6 pm, and 8 pm. Most radios pick up the BBC and Voice of America overseas broadcasts. Everyone loves Abie Nathan and his pirate radio ship, anchored "somewhere in the Mediterranean" (opposite the Tel Aviv Hilton, just outside of Israeli waters). The "Voice of Peace" specializes in anti-war songs, American sounds and disc jockeys and it's in English most of the time.

Reading Material (bibliography)   Few subjects have had so much written about them with such diverse attitudes and conclusions as Jewish history, Zionism and Israel, its people and institutions. The source material available is staggering and one hesitates to suggest what should be read first. A glance at the Hebrew newspapers or even the English *Jerusalem Post* every day or week would be a good way as any other than living here, to get a realistic slice-of-life picture of the contemporary scene. Sometimes even classified ads and back page items about who did what to whom in Tel Aviv or Eilat yesterday, can tell more about local events and what is really happening than any books possibly could. In the same vein, there is nothing like *the* Good Book from "In the Beginning" right down through Chronicles and for the Christian, the New Testament as well. Much depends on the reader — who he is and what facets of Israel he is interested in. What follows is a sample bibliography and everyone should decide for himself what is objective and worthwhile. The author believes this material should be reasonably informative and pleasant reading for the average visitor or settler from the English speaking world. Titles are followed by name of author and publisher.

Jewish History

History of the Jewish   Parkes, J.   Pelican
   People

History of the Jewish People	Sachar, A.	Knopf
Jewish Connection, The	Goldberg, H.	Bantam
Jewish State, The	Herzl, T.	Newman
Jews, God and History	Dimont, M.	New American
Judaism	Epstein, I.	Pelican
My People	Eban, A.	Behrman
Popular History of the Jews	Graetz, H.	Hebrew Publishing

Zionism

Battleground, Fact & Fancy in Palestine	Katz, S.	Bantam
Ben Gurion (biography)	St. John, R.	Doubleday
Israelis, The Founders & Sons	Elon, A.	Sphere
Israel Without Zionists	Avneri, U.	Collier
Jews in Their Land	Ben Gurion, D.	Aldus
Rebirth and Destiny in Israel	Ben Gurion, D.	Philosophical Library
Short History of Zionism	Cohen, I.	London, Muller
Tongue of the Prophets	St. John, R.	Doubleday

Israel Today

Edge of the Sword	Lorch, N.	Masada
Facts About Israel	Louvish and Nurock	Keter
Government Yearbook (annual)	Government Printer	Jerusalem
Guide to Israel, The	Vilnay, Z.	Ahiever, Jerusalem
Israelis, The Founders & Sons	Elon, A.	Sphere

Legal System of Israel	Baker, H.	Street & Maxwell
Source, The	Michener, J.	Crest
Who's Who in Israel	Ben-Grunberg	Bronfman-Cohen
Wild Goats of Ein Gedi	Weiner, H.	Doubleday

Restaurants   Eating out costs a lot if you demand European or American standards. Relatively few Israelis do it on a regular basis, unless eating out includes downing a quick felafel or humus-in-pitta or steak sandwich — and if you *don't* want pork, make sure you order *bakar* (beef) steak and not a *lavan* (white) steak, the euphemistic name for bacon and ham. Leisurely, full course dining in restaurants and dinner dates or business lunches is a luxury only tourists and the affluent indulge in. While there are novel and even exotic foods and dishes, Israel is not considered a gourmet's paradise. Finding a delicious, charming and inexpensive restaurant can be a challenge. Hygienic standards and licensing supervision and inspections tend to be haphazard; there are some health inspectors who have announced they wouldn't eat in any restaurant in the country. If you want to be sure that a restaurant is Kosher, check if it has an up-to-date certificate of Kashrut issued by the Rabbinate. Luxury hotels and restaurants have fancy menus, table-cloths, service and prices go up to $60, or so per couple. The best way to find good and reasonable restaurants — and there are such places — is to swap information with tourists and Israelis who eat out and enjoy it.

Retirement   (Old Age) Homes have not caught on for most Israeli families, where most elderly parents live with their children. Those designed especially for affluent tourists and *Olim* have become popular in recent years. Some require substantial, non-returnable deposits and monthly rentals while others charge large monthly fees. Government licensing and supervision is lax compared to the US and the reputation, management and proposed terms of the different homes should be checked out very carefully.

Rights and Benefits (of Olim) in Israel are subject to intermittent public controversy, debate and revision. They generally include fare and freight loans and grants, admission to Absorption Center, Ulpan and hostels at reduced cost, free or subsidized health fund membership, kindergarten and university schooling, temporary exemption from income, travel and other taxes and customs payments for household and professional goods, low interest loans and mortgages, retraining for lawyers, physicians, dentists, accountants, engineers, etc., deferment of military service and postponement of time limit to bring foreign assets and property to Israel. Final rulings regarding who is an *Oleh* and when and what rights and privileges they and their families are entitled to, are resolved by appeals committees of the Ministry of Absorption and the Jewish Agency.

Sabbath (the) and Jewish holidays begin at sundown the evening before. By noon on Friday, most Israelis are no longer taking their jobs seriously except bus and sherut drivers and traffic policemen. At 1:30 pm the big weekly traffic jam is at its peak, with everyone on the road for the "weekend" exodus. Friday nights are stay at home, visiting time and party nights (except for Sabbath observers) and guests often come with flowers or a box of candy. Saturday towards sunset, Israel reverts to its usual noisy, boisterous self. It is bad form to drive in Orthodox neighborhoods on Shabbat and even risky — some streets are closed off with chain barriers and cars and drivers have been stoned by irate residents.

Sabra is a common nickname for the native born Israeli who is supposed to resemble the prickly pear of the indigenous, originally Mexican cactus of the same name, that grows wild in many parts of the country. They are tough and thorny on the outside and sweet and juicy on the inside. Chilled-on-ice, they are sold by pushcart peddlers during the hot summer for anyone curious enough to want to peel or taste a sabra.

Schools What and how you learn in school in Israel is a lot different from what Anglo-Saxon newcomers are used to, but essentially is as good and sometimes better than anything back home. The first important decision is whether your children will be educated in "religious" (orthodox) or ultra-orthodox, private or secular schools, each of which are supported and supervised by the Ministry of Education. Non-Orthodox families may find religious schools are not suitable or even willing to accept their kids. Nurseries and kindergartens are open from 8 to 12 am or 1 pm with WIZO and working mother creches operating till 4 pm. Fees range from $40 to $130 monthly and new immigrants are entitled to complete or partial exemption. Under a recent school reform, elementary education covers first to sixth grades, with secondary education starting with junior high (seventh to ninth grades) and finishing with twelfth grade. Only a few school districts have actually implemented this system and most still operate under the grade — high school division familiar to Americans. Registration takes place in February-March. Parents must present ID cards, birth certificates, plus — in the case of *Olim* — previous report cards or certificates. The main subjects in elementary school are Hebrew, Bible, Math, Geography, History, English plus Physical Education, Music, Art and Manual Training and special Hebrew language instruction and counselling for new immigrants. In one of the country's many miracles, newly arrived pupils completely and happily adjust in Israel in general and at school in particular after a year or even

269

less. What kids don't learn in school they pick up on the frequent trips, outings and class get togethers. Separate high schools emphasize agriculture, trades and humanities, and those who intend to continue on to higher education must take comprehensive, Regent style exams in the major subjects. Successful examinees receive a *tiudat bagrut* (Matriculation Certificate) that is required by many university level institutions; other high school graduates receive a *tiudat gmar* (Completion Certificate).

Shipping (things over) Just a few years ago, American settlers bought and shipped over everything from matches to the kitchen sink. Today you can buy all household goods, furniture and appliances in Israel. It might cost more, but you save on shipping bills and you can get spare parts and repairs and have someone to sue if something goes wrong. If you buy abroad for Aliya, be careful of the fly by night "Israeli specialists" who advertise their services to *Olim*. Insist on receipts, guarantees, warranties and names and addresses of Israeli agents and bring along extra parts in case of breakage. Shipping also requires diligence and every item and box should be carefully itemized, inventoried, crated and fully insured. To avoid unnecessary disappointment, proceed on the assumption that your lift will be shipped to Israel, clear customs and arrive at your home at least three months after the promised delivery date.

Smoking American and local tobacco brands are available though very expensive but despite this everyone seems to be puffing away furiously. With all their problems, it is no wonder Israelis are among the heaviest smokers in the world with anti-smoking campaigns almost non-existent. When peace comes maybe Israelis will switch over to hash; in the meantime, that is just pipe dreaming, and for travellers, hip and straight, Israel is definitely a bad trip if you're busted for marijuana or other drugs.

Social Security has a representative in the US Consulates and monthly checks and other benefits are paid directly to the thousands of pensioners, veterans, widows and others who have moved to Israel. The local counterpart of Social Security is *Bituah Leumi* (National Insurance). Its social security payments are very small compared to America but they also pay birth and children's allowances, unemployment and unpaid alimony judgments as well as death benefits, in an Israeli version of Womb to Tomb social welfarism.

Souvenirs (and presents) Best buys include handmade Yemenite and Arab jewelry, leather coats and knitwear, commemorative coins and medals and if you have any money left — diamonds. For original, inexpensive souvenirs for the folks back home, try bubble gum with Hebrew cartoons and horoscope, Israeli coins and postage stamps, *hamsa* (hand) symbols to ward off the evil eye, coke bottles printed in Hebrew, miniature Israeli dolls, posters, *Mezuzot*, *Magen Davids*, *kova tembel*, the "national" Israeli hat (only nursery kiddies and construction workers — and they're mostly Arabs now — still wear them) and a copy of this book. Israeli purchases that qualify for exemption from US import duties include leather wear, furs, gold and silver jewelry, precious or semi-precious stones, sterling and plated silver, religious medals, original art and antiques, as well as ordinary souvenirs and presents, but double check with the store before buying. Oversized flight baggage is expensive, so whenever possible, have the shop mail it insured and registered.

Students from abroad can enroll in many different study programs in Israel. If they speak Hebrew and are *Olim*, the possibilities are even greater. Special training programs prepare American students for the changeover to the Israeli campus. If you are considering studying in Israel, bring photostasts of diplomas and school records. A valid student ID card and birth certificate are helpful. Partial or full higher education in Israel can prove interesting; for those planning to settle in the country it certainly could be advantageous. Details at Aliya centers and Consulates.

Summer Camps Numerous day camps are run by municipalities and private and other groups. A few kibbutzim have sleep-in camps with three week seasons, but which Israeli mommy is willing to part with her treasure for longer than that (and who would want to put up with them?). English speaking families are particularly welcome at some camps and Club Mediteranee runs "adult" vacation camps in Eilat and Ashkelon.

Sunshine Israel is a sub-tropical country situated in the continent of Asia and the sun is very strong. It is *not* advisable to be exposed to the midday sun for too long, especially in the hot summer or during *hamsin* (desert wind scorchers). Sunburns happen fast at the beach and in the desert and sun stroke and heat stroke may quickly follow. If you do venture into the desert, take along a friend, make sure you have a hat, compass and plenty of drinking water and that someone in town knows where you are and when you are supposed to be coming back.

Swimming is popular in public, country club and municipal pools and some are heated and open all year round. Crowds of swimmers frequent the beaches on the Mediterranean, Lake Tiberias, the Dead and Red Seas. Lifeguards and other facilities function on a seasonal basis, usually from May to October and some beaches charge a nominal entrance and locker fee. The Mediterranean can be surprisingly turbulent, and powerful undertows, even in calm summer weather have been known to take their toll. Black flags are posted when the sea is too rough and bathing is forbidden. Even experienced swimmers should never go in alone or when the black flag is up, especially if there is no lifeguard on duty. Nudists have to go south to Nueba beach in Sinai or around Eilat. The "Beautiful People" hang out at luxury hotel pools and beaches in north Tel Aviv and Herzlia, especially Friday afternoons and Saturday mornings. There is a small fenced beach front for religious men and women with separate bathing, near Independence Park in Tel Aviv. Eilat, Sinai and the coastal areas have some of the best warm water skin diving in the world.

Synagogues The word is derived from the Greek for building. As the site of prayer to an invisible God, it was the prototype for the later Church and Mosque. There are several thousand Synagogues all over the country and almost all are Orthodox. Israeli synagogues are small and modest by American standards and often are located in converted apartments, huts, barracks and pre-prefabricated buildings. A few like the Yeshurun Synagogue in Jerusalem or Shivat Zion and the Great (*Gadol*) Synagogue in Tel Aviv are modern and impressive. The Israeli Synagogues are Houses of Worship or in literal Hebrew *Batei Knesset* (Houses of Assembly). They do not serve as Jewish Community Centers with brotherhoods and sisterhoods and Israelis go there to pray, mourn and study Torah. Only a few have facilities for Bar Mitzva and wedding ceremonies. Friday night services start at sunset and on the Sabbath and holidays, about two hours later. Visitors are welcome and a special guided walking tour of Jerusalem Synagogues on Friday evenings takes in *Batei Knesset* of different communities. Modest dress is the rule (no shorts, bathing suits, or similar attire). Men should wear a hat or skull cap; women should bring a shawl or hat.

Taxes are ridiculous and it seems as if there are endless categories. They are higher than anywhere in the world with 70% of the national income and budget funded by taxes, compared to only 45% in runner-up Sweden where they earn double and triple the salaries of Israelis, so they can afford it. Besides, Sweden hasn't had a war in 500 years, whereas Israel has one every five or ten years and someone has to pay for it. Americans living and working in Israel are supposed to file an annual report to the IRS by June 15th, but may request further extensions. They may also qualify for substantial or complete exemptions if they pay local income tax. Contact IRS representatives at the US Consulates for all forms, publications and advice. People who live and work in Israel soon learn that everything starts and ends with *bruto* (gross) and *neto* (net) and the big difference is what Israelis pay to the Treasury. It usually runs from 25% to 60% on income tax (*not* a typographical error) and additional taxes unheard of in America (on radio, television set, car, refrigerator, movies, plus municipal, state, apartment, house committee, etc.).

Telephones The Israeli system is automatic and you can dial directly from any telephone to anywhere in the country, but be careful to check first if an area code is needed. The lines operate without problems most of the time which is very commendable. No solution has yet been found for the shocking vandalism that ravages so many of the public phones in street booths. If you dial long distance, put four or five tokens in so your conversation won't get cut off automatically before you're finished talking. Another problem is trying to find some *asimonim* (telephone tokens). The Post Office has sold millions, but most are bought out and hoarded by speculators. After the price goes up they begin to drift into circulation again. The phone company people are trying to remedy the situation by reconverting pay phones so they can operate with a one pound coin. Many stores and shops with private phones are equipped with a phone meter and permit visitors to use them, at about twice the cost of phone tokens. Hotels add a "service" charge to local, trunk and overseas calls that can double or triple the actual price of the call. As for installing a phone at home or in your place of business, here is where you start to miss old Bell Telephone. In Israel you have to fill out a detailed application form setting forth a good part of your life history and explaining *why* you need the phone, so you can try for one of the priorities set aside for Knesset members, army generals or little old ladies with heart conditions, living alone, etc. If you don't rate special preference, you pay a $250 installation fee and join the 200,000 others waiting. About 50,000 installations are carried out each year, what more need be said. Some local calls are unlimited, while others are charged at multiple rate units depending on the length of the call. Trunk calls are cheaper between 7 pm and 7 am and on weekends (1 pm Friday to 7 am Sunday). If you have access to a working phone you can use it to send a telegram (dial 171), hear a recorded time announcement or order a wake-up service (15), call a policeman (100), ambulance (101) or fireman (102) or even personal direct dial someone back home (001 plus area code and number in the US).

Temporary Housing Most people can't afford to stay indefinitely at a decent hotel and some won't want to put up with their Israeli cousins (they don't let you bring girls, their English drives you mad, etc.). There is little rental housing and it can cost up to $600 a month in the better neighborhoods of Jerusalem, Tel Aviv and Haifa. Many landlords limit their leases to one year and demand and get paid in advance for the entire period. This may be the time to move into one of the *maonot* (hostels) or *maonot klita* (Absorption Centers), operated by the Ministry of Absorption and Jewish Agency. It's a little like a college fraternity-sorority house, except your housemates are all sizes, ages

275

and types and they may have just flown in from Brooklyn, Buenos Aires or Tiflis — it's only the capital of Soviet Georgia where many "Russian" immigrants are from these days. You can find a room or share an apartment with some Israeli strangers if you prefer. Place an ad in the Hebrew newspapers, but have replies sent to a POB, since you might get a few answers from eccentrics or worse. After all, not that many nice, normal Israelis may be interested in the pleasure of your company until they really get to know you. If you do find an apartment, get expert advice *before* signing any agreements with real estate brokers or landlords.

Terrorism   Terrorist acts inside the country do not happen often even in times of war. Israel's security services are as proficient as the best and attempts to commit some outrage are usually, but not always foiled before they happen, in spite of reports to the contrary by terrorist organizations press releases. Tourists should expect to be frisked at movie theaters and public institutions and subjected to a comprehensive body and baggage search at the airport. When bloodshed follows a bomb or grenade explosion, all Israel mourns as one family. Anyone suffering property damages — Israeli or tourist — is eligible for government compensation. Injured victims receive annuities and all medical and hospital bills are paid by the National Insurance Institute. Statistics prove it is probably safer walking around in Israel than downtown in a large European or American city.

Time   Israel follows the lunar moon calendar with an extra month necessary every few years to catch up with the solar calendar of the Christian world. Moslems use the Jewish calendar without the leap month. The *Jerusalem Post* masthead carries all three dates for anyone who wants to be in time with all three religions. Israel Standard Time is two hours ahead of Greenwich and most of Europe and seven hours ahead of Eastern Standard Time. You feel a marked difference on flights *to* Israel when you lose almost a whole day; flying to the US saves you seven hours. If a direct flight leaves on schedule, you could arrive at about the same time you left. One more point on the subject of time. It's what Israelis believe they never have enough of and so much of their conversation is sprinkled with impatient *"nu's"* (untranslatable) and *"allo's"* said with the accent on the first syllable, meaning "get going", "get on with it". With a mini-weekend, overtime and moonlighting plus annual reserve army duty being par for the course, maybe it's no wonder they are always in a hurry.

Tipping was once frowned upon or rare in egalitarian, socialist, Zionist Palestine. (Yes, "Palestine" used to mean where *Jewish* pioneers were building the Jewish National Home). Today a service charge is added to every hotel and restaurant bill in honor of the good, old days but you are encouraged to leave something in the better hotels and restaurants, very much so if you are a tourist. Never tip or give a present to any government employee including customs officials or cops — this can be considered bribery even if your intentions were innocent, or nearly innocent. If you're not sure who or when to tip, ask an Israeli friend; you'll probably be able to save some money.

Transportation (Public) If you can't drive or are afraid to in Israel, you ride the Egged and Dan co-op buses or sherut taxis. Bus service is crowded and hold on to someone or something tight. If the bus keeps going without letting you on or off yell *"rega"* (rhymes with "mega") a few times, the louder the better. Major lines travel everywhere and provide the fastest and cheapest form of mass transportation (except on Shabbat and Holidays). They generally run from sunrise to midnight, irregular routes by schedule. The bright red minibuses and sherut taxis ply main urban and inter-urban routes competing for passengers. Ordinary taxi service is expensive, but it is unnecessary to tip. Local cabbies have as much chutzpa as anyone in the country and don't be surprised if one stops enroute to pick up a friend or relative, buys a newspaper or eats a sandwich while the meter is running. An official price list covers all out of town trips and drivers pay stiff fines. for overcharging or being too ornery. Keep them in line by insisting on a receipt if you are not certain the price is right. The railway system owned and operated by the government, was built during the Turkish rule, and looks it. There are connections between the major cities and it even reaches Dimona in the south. The Tel Aviv-Jerusalem ride follows a breathtaking, beautifully scenic route and is an exciting experience.

Tree (Planting)   A biblical commandment says, "When you come into the Land you shall plant all manner of trees" (Leviticus XIX (23). Touring Israel's woods and forests or actually planting a tree with your own hands may seem silly to some, but there are tourists and friends of Israel for whom it is a must. Planting costs a few dollars and IGTO or the Keren Kayemet (JNF) people will be happy to show you where and how. After the mission is accomplished you receive a certificate and a map showing where *your* tree is so you can look it up when you come back. It is not true that as you go away, they put someone else's name on it.

TV ("Televisia")   Israel has a single, BBC style government supervised station with educational TV and kiddie programs during the day and adult (Arabic and Hebrew) programs in the evenings. Special antennas pick up Jordan TV, which screens a lot of canned stuff from the US and England. Israeli TV also runs some popular American series plus local imitations of successful programs and a few originals. The best that can be said about Israeli TV, is that there are no commercials and it's all over by midnight.

Ulpan (Ulpanim in the plural) is the unique Hebrew study center in Israel where students of every age, background and status learn the language that is the bridge to the history, faith and society of their new country. It is also an important — for some a key — factor in making a happy and complete adjustment to life in Israel. Residential *Ulpanim* at Absorption Centers offer room and board and others have morning, afternoon or evening classes on a daily, twice or three times a week basis. *Ulpan* is the first and one of the most important steps on the road of the Oleh and the principle is *Rak Ivrit* (Hebrew only), a real challenge for those with real or imagined fears about learning a new language. Actually, it is no more difficult than say, Swahili, Hungarian or Swedish and people speaking all of these languages *have* learned Hebrew in Ulpan. Daily routine includes a mere five hours of Hebrew instruction starting at 8 am, with three different levels of advancement. The emphasis is on simple, practical, spoken Hebrew with an introduction to reading and writing. Only intermediate and advanced courses get into speech patterns, grammar and literature. Ulpan also develops a camaraderie and fellowship based on the common desire to learn the new language. The most comprehensive and convenient arrangement is the 20 week, full time, beginners programs at one of the internationally famous live-in Ulpanim. They cost between $2,000 to $3,500, including full room and board (two or three to a room with air conditioning) and cultural activities plus use of hotel facilities. Three month live-in courses cost about half and external students only pay modest tuition fees. There are also privately run, audio-visual, booklet-cassette and correspondence school courses, but they are not as successful as the intensive Ulpan. Israeli TV shows a television series *"Ivrit be Siman Tov"* in easy Hebrew with accompanying study books and cassettes.

New immigrants are entitled to special reductions for all courses, or can enroll in free, live-in "working" Ulpanim at kibbutzim throughout the country. All that is expected of participants is part-time help in the settlement and not to be a nuisance. *"Be hatzlacha"* ("Good Luck").

Upheaval, the ("Mahapach") refers to the upset victory of the Begin-run Likud coalition in the 1977 elections and the defeat of the Labor Parties after 30 years of running nearly everything. It also symbolizes the controversial social-financial-economic-political changes in policies and practices that the Likud-run government have been carrying out. The aforementioned are to be distinguished from the "Earthquake" (*Reidat Ha'adama*), which is what happened in the Middle East and Israel with the outbreak of the Yom Kippur War and the surprising events and revelations that have continued to take place in its wake.

VAT is only short for Value Added Tax (*Mas Erech Musaf*) and is Israel's latest, but certainly not greatest or last tax. It is somewhat like the sales tax imposed on purchases in some American states, but in Israel is added to almost everything, even services like rent and dentist bills. Like the other levies, charges and taxes imposed on nearly every bill, it is an unavoidable part of life in Israel and there is nothing you can do but grin and pay it.

Visas to Israel are granted upon arrival to holders of valid American passports and citizens of countries which permit reciprocal arrangements. A tourist visa is good for three months and can be renewed. Those intending to work, study or settle should first visit AACI offices or Israeli Consulates abroad. If someone arrives at Ben Gurion airport without a visa, acts strange or doesn't have sufficient funds, he can be denied entry. Those intending to visit Arab countries as well, should request their visa stamps on a separate page or in the entry permit card. Once here keep an eye on your passport; there is a good market for them in the underworld and terrorist organizations. If the police or US Embassy suspect a "lost" passport is being used in connection with any criminal activity, you have problems.

Water is one of Israel's many miracles. For thousands of years the inhabitants of this country had to develop storage and conduit systems to maintain their limited water resources and to bring water from the relatively abundant north to the drier center of Israel and desert south. This is the task of the National Water Carrier and desalination projects. Consumer rates vary for home, industrial and agricultural consumption, but ordinary bathroom and kitchen use is not rationed. Drinking water is safe in hotels and homes, except for the administered areas or from open taps in fields and isolated places. Due to the water shortage, some irrigation and agricultural needs are supplied with chemically treated sewage water. Fruits and vegetables while healthy and delicious, should be washed in soap and water or with special detergents sold in pharmacies, just to make sure.

Weather is generally very pleasant and summery and is measured in centigrade. Three types of climate prevail — the coastal plain including Tel Aviv, Haifa and the heavily populated area stretching along the sea, has mild winters with some rain and sunny, humid summers. The mountainous, hilly regions of the Galilee and Jerusalem have longer, colder, windier and wetter winters with occasional snow and warm summers. The Negev and Jordan Valleys have mild winters with rare rainfall and extremely hot and humid summers. Spring and fall are hardly felt anywhere in the country, especially during the day time. Warm and sunny days are frequent in winter and summer days can be hot and muggy especially during the infamous Middle Eastern *hamsin* heat waves. Unusual for Americans are the sharp extremes and changes in temperature and weather conditions on the very same day, with middays apt to be sunny and warm, even though it can be cool, cold or windy at night.

Yad Vashem in Jerusalem is Israel's official and largest monument to the six million Jewish victims of the Holocaust. The name means "Hand and Name" or less literally, the "Monument and Memorial". The large, stark building houses an eternal flame and a comprehensive, heartrending exhibition hall. Its scholars and historians have developed archives containing records and documents including the name of every known Jewish victim of Nazism. There are similar memorials, museums and monuments all over the country dedicated to the ideal that the dead shall live. School children, visitors and just plain Israelis of every ethnic origin and social level have not forgotten — and will not allow others to forget — the Holocaust and its meaning for Jews and all mankind.

Yeshiva Talmud is what it's all about in these Rabbinical Seminaries and it is continuously read, taught, argued (*Pilpul*) and discoursed in the Orthodox Yeshivot throughout Israel. Traditionally limited to males only, the *Yeshiva Bocher* or young man is sometimes a child three, four or five years old or a grown or aged adult. For devout Orthodox males, it is considered a noble — perhaps the most noble of callings — and many pursue a lifetime of *Talmud Torah* (Talmud study), supported by wives and families. A few of the *Yeshivot* in Israel have special courses in English and are designed to attract the *Chozer Be Tshuva* (born again or "returned" Jew) from the Diaspora who has come back to the ancient land and faith. A visit to such a Yeshiva can be a stimulating event for any tourist.

Youth Movements Keep nearly a quarter million, hyperenergetic Israeli kids from boredom and from driving their parents crazy. They run educational and civic activities as well as social-athletic doings and are an extremely popular institution. The government assists with funds and training of young leaders, but there is no official, national youth movement as in some countries. The Working and Studying Youth (*Noar Oved*) is the largest organization, with about 100,000 participants and is affiliated with the Histadrut. The Scouts (*Tsofim*) with a single organization for boys and girls, are part of the International Scouting Association and participate in Israeli and foreign jamborees. Religious youth make up the membership of *Bnei Akiva* (the sons and daughters of Akiva) the famous Talmudic sage.

Zionism means different things to different people. It is the most important in the frequently confusing lexicon of words and slogans connected with Israel and the national rebirth of the Jewish people in their ancient homeland. It started with the hill in Jerusalem called *Zion* meaning way or sign in Hebrew, which always symbolized the Jewish presence in the Holy Land. Since the last century Zionism has meant the political-social-religious movement for the national liberation of the Jewish people and their return from the Diaspora to Zion.

If justice triumphs –
file an appeal...
(heard at the Tel Aviv courthouse)

Chapter Nine

UNDERSTANDING
THE BEWILDERING

THE ISRAELI LEGAL SYSTEM

Misunderstandings between tourists and Israelis as well as adjustment pains of newcomers are often exaggerated and even caused by a lack of knowledge of the laws and customs of the country. This chapter provides general information and guidance on those important subjects. What follows may be relevant to actual situations some readers find themselves in. Whether visitor, new resident or old timer, it can provide another dimension for those who want to know about the practical Israel, as well as the usual topics of interest that are available for visitors.

The Israeli legal system is not only unusual for foreigners, even its own citizens find it confusing, mainly because it is a composite of so many different sources of jurisprudence. Biblical injunctions and ancient mores, for instance, are still valid in the Rabbinical tribunals, which have sole jurisdiction in matters of marriage and divorce, and usually in alimony and child custody as well. Even foreign nationals living here sue and are sued in these matters in the Rabbinical Court if they are Jewish. At the request of a spouse-adversary, one may even be prevented from leaving the country temporarily or until the completion of the case, as the court may decide.

A few of the statutes invoked during the long period of Ottoman Turkish rule are still in effect, though most have been abandoned. Some of the enactments of the British mandatory government and English Common Law which it brought to Palestine are still applicable, although they are gradually being replaced and supplanted by Knesset made law. Legal philosophies and principles imposed by different rulers in the Land of Israel have become part of its heritage. Some are as valid and important as laws passed since Independence. In a sense, even Sabra legislation represents attitudes and values of the Tribes in the Diaspora which were brought with them or with the founding fathers.

In addition to the religious tribunals of Jewish, Moslem, Druze and traditional Christian denominations, Israel has Labor, Municipal and quasi-judicial courts of the kind common in the USA. The Magistrate's, District and Supreme Courts are where the average person is likely to end up if he becomes involved as a party or witness in some civil or criminal case.

Magistrate's Courts are located in every city and large town and have jurisdiction in civil cases involving up to $15,000 and criminal trials involving misdemeanors, which are crimes punishable by up to three years imprisonment. The five District Courts hear all other civil actions and felony cases. They also serve as Appeal Courts against judgments of Magistrates and other judicial and administrative tribunals. In appeals and criminal trials involving felonies punishable by ten years imprisonment or more, District Courts sit in a three Judge Bench. Otherwise like the Magistrate's Court, a single Judge tries each case. There is no jury system in Israel.

The Supreme Court in Jerusalem is the highest judicial institution in the country. It is the final Appellate Court in civil and criminal cases and has a function similar to an Equity Court. In the latter capacity it considers direct applications from aggrieved persons in matters like Habeas Corpus (for release of persons unlawfully detained or imprisoned) or Mandamus (to restrain local or state authorities who have superseded their legal authority). It is composed of 11 Justices including one woman who ordinarily sit in a Bench of three Justices.

Criminal law and procedure are based on the Common Law and similar to the American system which originates from the same source. For instance, one has the right to remain silent when arrested and if placed on trial. Prior to interrogation by the police as a possible criminal suspect, one must be advised he is so regarded and that anything he says or signs may be used as evidence against him. Unlike most American States there is no right to have a lawyer present while being interrogated, but one may insist on this or remain silent.

Following arrest one has the right to call and retain an attorney or notify his Embassy if he is a foreign national. The law says that the Police must permit arrestees to meet with counsel of their choice at "the first opportunity" but in practice, suspects are often requested and sometimes pressured into making a written statement or confession before they are actually allowed to speak to a lawyer who can advise them.

The US Embassy is not ordinarily informed by the police of the arrest of an American citizen if he is a permanent resident or citizen of Israel. Notice regarding tourists and temporary residents is for the most part made automatically within several days, or as a result of inquiries by consular personnel. If a relative or friend is assumed to be in police custody, a lawyer or the consular officers can find out where and why he is being held.

Every detainee and defendant is bailable unless charged with capital or certain security offenses or crimes punishable by life imprisonment. Capital punishment has been abolished except for genocide, Nazi war crimes or for aggravated treasons. In serious charges involving known and dangerous criminals or foreigners without a permanent local address, bail can be denied or very high but these decisions are appealable.

There are no professional bail bondmen but arrestees are often released on self-recognizance bonds in misdemeanor cases. When foreign nationals are involved or the charges are heavy, release from detention usually requires a guarantor to the bail undertaking or deposit of a cash bond with the Court Clerk's office, or both. A "stop order" is also likely and a tourist's passport may be temporarily confiscated by the police, with Court approval.

The drug scene in Israel reflects official attitudes that are in distinct contradiction to more permissive societies and laws elsewhere. The local statute was first enacted during the British Mandate and considerable changes and additions have been made by the Israeli legislature to modernize and put its law and order stamp on such cases. The "Dangerous Drugs Ordinance" makes it a punishable crime to possess, import, export, transport, sell or use any substance specified including opium, morphine, heroin, cocaine, LSD, mescaline, amphetamine ("speed"), cannabis sativa (marijuana) and the more potent Middle Eastern variety of grass — hashish.

It is not a defense to show one did not act for profit or even know that the substance involved was prohibited, unless the defendant can prove same. Unlike other criminal charges in Israel and all criminal cases in America, the burden of proving lack of knowledge is on the defendant, if it is established that drugs were found in his actual possession or custody. Israeli citizens and residents even though they may also be US citizens, may be arrested and prosecuted if they commit any of the forbidden acts in a foreign country.

The penalties imposed are tough and these offenses can be felonies punishable by up to 20 years imprisonment plus heavy fines for serious violations. Tourists and newcomers can expect expulsion or deportation orders following completion of the sentence imposed, as well as an order preventing future reentry to Israel. This is in addition to possible trouble in the USA if it becomes known that one has been convicted of a narcotics violation. The Embassy is usually informed by the police about drug and other important cases and in turn may be requested to notify the authorities in America. Some jurisdictions in the States can deny such persons the right to become licensed in certain professions or accepted to public office or sensitive government positions.

First offenders and those convicted of possession or use of small quantities of hashish may receive suspended sentences, probation or a fine, with chances for leniency better when defendants are students or relatively "straight" in appearance. Promising to leave the country immediately and showing a Judge a valid airplane ticket home might help in borderline cases. The District Attorney who prosecutes felonies and the police representative who appears in other criminal cases are usually under instruction from higher-ups to request prison sentences in serious cases.

Trials are held fairly soon for persons in jail, but many months and longer pass for those out on bail, unless they make a special application for a speedy trial. Israeli jails are very crowded and have relatively primitive facilities. Except for lawyers and Consular representatives, visitors are not permitted and they are very unpleasant places even to visit except for extraordinarily adventurous types. Young detainees and foreigners have been victims of violent and sexual assaults and should insist on separate cells for self-protection. Time spent in jail awaiting trial can upon request, be credited against the sentence that may be later imposed. Sometimes it is possible to receive a transfer to one of the prisons where conditions are relatively better.

Young people and especially those regarded as hippies by local standards, should expect to be stopped, questioned and even searched now and then by the police. Local policemen do not require a search or arrest warrant if they claim there are reasonable grounds to suspect possession of drugs or that one has committed a felony. A person can also be arrested for refusing to accompany an officer to the nearest Police Station, if found in suspicious circumstances and attempting to evade arrest, or if he has no visible means of support.

The police release some suspects following arrest or within 48 hours. Otherwise they are required to bring arrestees before a Magistrate within two days to receive Court authorization for further detention. Police representatives in Court can ask for and receive up to 15 days remand orders, the usual grounds being "for completion of the investigation". No one can be held in jail for more than 60 days without a special order signed by the Attorney General unless formal charges are filed, or a Judge authorizes detention until completion of the case but such orders and arbitrary bail terms are appealable.

If the police claim a detainee is mentally disturbed and he is a suspect in a criminal case, he can be remanded to a mental hospital for psychiatric observation that will decide his legal competence. Even if he has not been arrested or formally charged, the District Psychiatrist in the Health Ministry can authorize hospitalization of anyone whose physical or mental condition allegedly constitutes a danger to the public health or welfare. If such allegations are confirmed after observation or one makes his presence in Israel undesirable, he may be deported. He, or a friend or relative on his behalf, may oppose either such hospitalization or deportation order and a Court will decide the issue.

Trial procedure is somewhat different than in America. There is no Grand Jury and no indictments are issued. Defendants are summoned to court by the DA or Police Prosecutor through a Charge Sheet or Information which details the criminal acts committed, law transgressed and names and addresses of witnesses for the prosecution. Defendants are entitled to examine and copy statements of such witnesses, as well as any confession given to the police. If there are no preliminary or technical arguments regarding the Charge Sheet, defendants must plead guilty or not guilty at the first hearing.

Trials are conducted in Hebrew but litigants not fluent in this language can insist the proceedings be interpreted into English as the law provides. Rules of evidence are somewhat like those in most American Courts, one major exception to defendant's disadvantage being that "dirty" evidence acquired by illegal police methods may nevertheless be heard. However, a confession obtained by force, coercion, threats or trickery can be objected to and declared inadmissible.

If there is a guilty verdict, the defendant is entitled to submit character testimony and request a presentence probation investigation, but this is not mandatory for defendants over 21 or non-residents. Males under 16 and females under 18 are tried in Juvenile Courts where procedures and punishment are more lenient. Prior to any conviction, the defendant can file an application with the Attorney General to quash the charges if there are legal or personal reasons for so doing, or alternatively, to take into account (and close) all other open criminal charges against him. One may appeal a conviction and/or unduly severe sentence, but under Israeli law the DA is also allowed to appeal an acquittal and/or what he considers an unduly lenient sentence.

Following an unsuccessful appeal, one may petition the President of the State for a Pardon or a Commutation of Sentence. If sentenced to less than three months imprisonment, the prisoner may be able to arrange "outside work" at a local Police Station, (gardening or manual labor) in lieu of actual confinement in a prison. Every prisoner is entitled to receive one third off his sentence for good behavior and after the initial period of incarceration, can ask for occasional "home leave" of up to three days. Short termers are confined to the Massiahu Prison Camp near Tel Aviv where the conditions are easier; long term Anglo-Saxons are usually sent to Damon Prison near Haifa.

The right to counsel principle is not well developed yet and there is no Legal Aid Society or Public Defender to look after every indigent defendant. In certain cases the law does require representation by an attorney. If unable to arrange this due to financial distress, Courts assign counsel from a list of volunteers which, unfortunately, does not include the most experienced and successful criminal attorneys. Foreigners may have difficulty convincing a Judge that they and their families have no funds available to retain a lawyer. Appointment of counsel at the expense of the State also occurs when the defendant is under 16, mentally unbalanced, deaf, dumb or mute, or charged with a serious felony. In other cases, the fact that the defendant was not represented by a lawyer will not impede or invalidate criminal convictions even though this may result in unpleasant consequences.

Only persons with consular diplomatic status are immune from criminal or civil proceedings. American nationals who do not have diplomatic passports are subject to local laws and procedures regardless of whether they are known and understood and no matter how strange and unfair they may seem. The American Embassy can not and will not interfere in any legal proceedings.

Considering how different and complicated these matters can be, it is worthwhile using good old common sense when abroad. If a visitor or newcomer is confronted by a situation which may be unclear, illegal, delicate or serious, he should talk to a knowledgable friend or lawyer. People and things may seem to be the same everywhere, but in reality it is not quite that simple. One is not always successful in living in Rome as the Romans do, particularly here, where Romans are remembered for all the trouble they brought on the people of Israel. Perhaps one should keep in mind the old English adage which cautions people to follow their instincts with due regard for the policeman on the corner.

*Protektzia – what everyone else always
has when things don't work out...
(anonymous)*

Chapter Ten

FINE'S RULE

When in doubt, remember "Fine's Rule." Actually it consists of several principles for facing uniquely Israeli problems and situations. Most newcomers learn them sooner or later on their own, in the Israeli branch of the universal school of hard knocks. They are not a registered patent of the author, who sometimes forgets his own advice. As the adage says: "A lawyer who represents himself may have a fool for a client." When facing some new or different Israeli custom or character and things are getting messy, despite the fact that you have been perfectly rational and reasonable, it is time to pause a moment and consider Fine's Rule. Broken up into a few guidelines, it emerges like this:

1. *Easy (Does it)* Moving to any new country, Israel included, means making constant adjustments and running into surprises, large and small, pleasant and otherwise. It makes sense to do and decide things more carefully than you did in your home town. If you go too fast, you may wind up right back where you started and it will be too late to figure out where and why it went sour or wrong.

2. *Absorption (Klita)* This much heard, somewhat awkward expression is, in a sense, a contradiction. It is contrary to the "separate togetherness" which has characterized the return of the Tribes to the old new homeland and the relationship between them. It is an affront to the need of the average Anglo-Saxon for privacy, a quality most rare in a country which resembles a large kibbutz or non-stop bar-mitzva. At the same time, it is a must for the new settler who wishes to become an Israeli with the inner fulfillment that brings, as well as the burdens imposed merely by living here. The only alternative to Israelizing is withdrawing into the English speaking colony of transient or indifferent residents who live on the fringes of Israeli society. Absorption means talking in Hebrew, making friends with sabras and veteran settlers and getting involved in the issues and affairs that involve all of your neighbors. If you don't make successful klita, it is difficult to get through that tough *oleh hadash* (new immigrant) period that can last as long as you live in Israel. Successful Absorption will help realize more expectations and instill the confidence to cope, adjust and ultimately succeed in what may be the grandest adventure of your life.

3. *Adaptation* A major cause of discontent and frustration among Olim is the natural, but usually self-defeating tendency to compare things and people with the way

they were back home. Israel and Israelis will not change, at least not as a result of the griping, accusations and complaints of newcomers. Much grumbling is a product of undue optimism, misinformation or misunderstandings. At times it is justified, though there might be reasons why things are the way they are. If one is unable to adapt to new realities and conditions and accept the shortcomings along with some tolerance and hope, the process of becoming an Israeli will be grim and problematic. Real changes for the better in the quality of life and unpleasant aspects of the Israeli scene could come about if a few hundred thousand Anglo-Saxons came to settle and made their presence felt, or if one of them (Ahem!) became Prime Minister with a free hand to let some heads roll. Insist on your rights, complain when you should, educate Israelis when they need it, but come to terms with what cannot be changed, at least overnight. After thousands of years some traditions and ways will not be altered without patience. The people who lived here before us are more forgiving. The Arabs say: *"Insh'allah"* (If Allah wills it). Israelis smile and console you with *"yihiye tov"* or *"yihiye be'seder"* (everything will be all right) — although they never say when. The pessimists shrug ... *"K'she yavo ha Mashiach..."* (when the Messiah comes, then...)

4. *Streamlining* Time and energy become dissipated quickly in Israel's hot, mercurial and very red taped and bureaucratic society. If it really isn't necessary, try to avoid the fruitless running around that is encouraged by institutions, bureaucrats and creatures of habit. If something needs doing and isn't fun, maybe you can settle it on the phone; you can send telegrams or cables without getting out of bed or leaving the office. With a little persistence and some sweet talk, it is possible to take care of

many things by telephone or mail, even with Israelis who automatically invite everyone to "come to my office/store/ministry, etc." If you learn how, you can cut down on drudgery and get in more tennis, playing with the kids or whatever it is you do for pleasure. When you *have* to go, like to a dentist or a friendly talk with your bank manager about a small, temporary overdraft, first make an appointment and go there on a slack day and hour. Don't take chances sabra style and drop by during office hours, only to find out *he* is out for a little after-noon delight or shopping and you have to wait an hour or two till he is available. And take along a book/newspaper/radio/knitting or whatever. If you are going to the *Tabu* — what a great name! — otherwise known as the Land Registry Office, take a thermos and a few sandwiches.

5. *Hebrew* It is embarrassing, difficult, tiring and silly to talk *Ivrit* (Hebrew) with EVERYONE (family and Anglo-Saxon friends alike), but for the average person this is the best and possibly only way to learn. After a few months of exasperating whoever is within hearing range, and with madness rapidly approaching, Eureka! — you suddenly make the breakthrough. You have suddenly dreamt or talked back to a bus driver in Hebrew. Living in Israel without being able to speak, read and write the national language is a lot like kissing through a screen door. You lose out on the excitement, flavor, meaning and sense of accomplishment even if you can get along at home or on the job without it. Unless it is absolutely impossible, spend your first half year on a kibbutz or distant ulpan where others will not be trying to learn English with you the teacher.

6. *English* The exception to the "Hebrew only" rule is when it's legal, important or delicate. Then, make sure

you (and others) say, write, explain and — over and above all — *sign* only in English. Otherwise there will be a legal presumption that you understood what was transpiring and misunderstandings or mistakes can prove costly and painful.

7. *Tact* is another hard to find commodity in an uncut diamond rough tough society, but it is what keeps relationships with Israelis in good shape. Since everyone knows and/or is related to nearly everyone else, Israel is like a big fish pond. As a result, one is drawn into contact with different types and individuals you would not have to run into in your country of origin. With privacy and anonymity so hard to preserve in Shikun or on the job, one must somehow learn to get along even with those who may not be your kind of people. Instead of letting this "absorption" and "merger" wear you down and spoil your day or Aliya, put on a little more charm and tact than you thought you had in you. Often it is not enough to be fair and pleasant. When necessary count to ten very slowly or be Levantine and say the most superlative things and make the silliest gestures with the worst neighbors or acquaintances. Never get involved in ethnic or religious remarks, even jokingly, or politics or anything not absolutely required. Save the real you for those with whom you feel comfortable and who won't misunderstand or misinterpret innocuous things you say or do.

Well, there it is, one for every day of the week — *Easy, Absorption, Adaptation, Streamlining, Hebrew, English and Tact,* or if you prefer, *EAASHET.* Now admit it, that sounds like what you need to out-cheek the cheeky Israeli if you run into him. That's all there is to the Fine Rule for surviving the Israeli culture shock with a proven Israeli remedy. All you have to do now is come over and try it. If anyone gives you a hard time, you EAASHET him/her/them/it till *you* become a real Israeli and find some smart-aleck newcomer EAASHETing *you*!

ALPHABETICAL INDEX

The Practical Israel

ACKNOWLEDGMENT

This book started with my parents, who taught me that being Jewish and knowing about what happens in Israel were somehow connected.

I want to thank friends, acquaintances and neighbors, too numerous to mention, who provided me knowingly and unknowingly with ideas and helpful criticism of what was to become a good part of this book.

Finally, a note of appreciation to my beautiful wife Dvora, who had to put up with me whenever I had the urge to write and was always there with Turkish coffee, Hungarian energy food and encouragement.

Leon Fine